The Integration of Behavior

VOLUME II

The Integrative Process in Dreams

The Integration of Behavior

(IN FIVE VOLUMES)

I

Basic Postulates

1952

II

The Integrative Process in Dreams

1953

III

Recurring Sequences and Therapeutic Process

IV

Factor Analysis of Behavior

V

Biological Foundations of Behavior

The Integration of Behavior

VOLUME II

The Integrative Process in Dreams

By

THOMAS M. FRENCH, M.D.

THE UNIVERSITY OF CHICAGO PRESS

THE UNIVERSITY OF CHICAGO PRESS, CHICAGO 37
Cambridge University Press, London, N.W. 1, England

Foreword

At the beginning of these studies we set ourselves the task of analyzing behavior into more elementary reaction patterns and of studying how these elementary reactions are combined and co-ordinated. In our first volume, starting with the working hypothesis that rational behavior, neuroses, and dreams can be analyzed into component factors that are in part common to all three, we sketched out somewhat schematically a picture of the basic pattern of the integrative process in terms of which all kinds of behavior, irrational as well as rational, should be understandable as variations.

In this, our second volume, we shall turn our attention to a more intensive study of dreams. As in Volume I, we start with the common-sense notions of motivation and insight. In the past, psychoanalysis has been chiefly interested in the motivation of dreams, in the thesis that every dream serves the function of fulfilling a wish—or many wishes. In this volume we shall try to show that every dream has also a logical structure and that the logical structures of different dreams of the same person are interrelated, that they are all parts of a single intercommunicating system. Under the activating influence of different situations, we postulate, sometimes one and sometimes another part of this system is brought into focus, while other parts fade into the background.

When we have mapped out some of the main features of this system of interrelated cognitive structures, we shall be ready for the task reserved for our third volume: to trace the emergence of different parts of this system in the course of a patient's treatment. Then, as we compare the recurring, but ever varying, sequences in our patient's dreams, we shall be led back, in Volumes IV and V, to the task which is our fundamental interest in these studies: to analyze our patient's behavior into some of its component patterns and to study how these component patterns are combined and co-ordinated.

Acknowledgment

I continue to be indebted to Dr. Helen McLean for permission to use her case history and her clinical notes in the preparation of this second volume.

Dr. Norman Cameron again helped me with many detailed criticisms of the manuscript, and Drs. Franz Alexander and John Benjamin both made comments which were of great value for the final revision of the manuscript.

In addition to those mentioned in Volume I as having contributed to the thought of these volumes, I am also indebted to the writings of Professor George Mead, whose ideas concerning the cognitive structure of socially oriented behavior I have tried to apply in the study of dreams.

Table of Contents

ix

SECTION V. PHYSIOLOGICAL PATTERN AND INTERPERSONAL FIELD

SECTION VI. THE SPAN OF THE INTERPERSONAL FIELD

SECTION VII. PATTERN OF THE WATER DREAMS

SECTION VIII. ATTEMPTS AT INTERNAL MASTERY

SECTION IX. SURVEY OF RELATIONS BETWEEN DREAM PATTERNS

APPENDIX

BIBLIOGRAPHY

INDEXES

SECTION I
Cognitive Structure

CHAPTER I

Cognitive Structure in Dreams

Opinions differ about the value of studying dreams. Since ancient times they have been regarded with superstitious awe, as inspirations from supernatural powers or as prophecies of the future. Yet others think that they are nonsense, not worthy of serious study.

By detailed analysis of many examples, Freud showed that dreams are not nonsense, that they serve the function of protecting sleep from disturbing wishes by creating the illusion that these wishes are fulfilled. The wishes that disturb sleep today are sometimes acted upon tomorrow. Therefore, it is no wonder that dreams often seem prophetic!

Dreams also give us a key to the dreamer's personality structure. Freud called them the "royal road to the Unconscious." They reveal not only the dreamer's unconscious motives but also his characteristic ways of reacting to his unconscious conflicts.

The Interpretation of Dreams.—Some people are skeptical about the interpretation of dreams. We interpret a dream by finding out how it fits into the context of the dreamer's waking thoughts and waking behavior. But how do we know that our interpretations are correct? Every dream has many meanings. This fact makes it difficult to maintain a properly critical attitude toward dream interpretation.[1] If two people interpret the same dream in two different ways, both interpretations may be correct. Must we conclude that every interpretation offered is one of the over-determined meanings of the dream?

In order really to understand a dream, it is not enough merely to formulate some of its meanings; we must also study how its different meanings are related one to another. *The "overdetermined" meanings of a dream* seem often to have only accidental

1. We touched on this problem briefly in I, 83–84.

3

relations to one another; but when we study them carefully, we find that they *fit together into a close-knit logical structure*. We shall call this logical structure the "cognitive structure" of the dream.

Although every dream has many meanings, it has only one cognitive structure, of which all its meanings are parts. If we have reconstructed the cognitive structure of a dream correctly, it should fit precisely into the cognitive structure of the dreamer's waking thoughts and waking behavior.

The Cognitive Structure of Behavior.—The phrase "logical structure" suggests the syllogistic structure of rational thought: e.g., All A are B; C is an A; therefore, C is a B. Yet Freud (1900) has shown that the logical structure of rational thinking is destroyed in the process of dream formation. In the dream work the latent dream thoughts are treated with the utmost disregard for logic; and emphasis seems to be shifted along any available associative pathway, without regard for reality or logical relations. If dreams do have a logical structure, it is certainly not the structure of rational thought formulated in words.

The logical structure of a dream resembles more closely the cognitive patterns that guide behavior.[2]

The cognitive structure of a dream is a pattern of interrelated meanings. To what in our waking behavior does the meaning of a dream correspond?

The normal behavior that most closely resembles a dream is the imaginative play of a child. For example, a child is piling stone blocks carefully, one upon another. What is the meaning of this play? When I ask him, he tells me that he is building a castle.

Even more obviously, rational purposive behavior has meaning. A man is sawing boards and nailing them together. When I ask what he is doing, he shows me the plan of a bookcase that he is building.

In each of these examples the meaning of behavior has two components: a goal (real or fantastic) and a fantasy or plan directed toward the achievement of that goal.

Some of the Gestalt psychologists have been particularly interested in understanding behavior in these terms. Köhler (1931)

2. See Vol. I, chap. xvi,

emphasized the importance of "insight" for the learning process. For example, in one of his experiments, an ape, baffled at first in its desire to get fruit just beyond its reach, suddenly discovers how to make a longer stick by fitting two shorter sticks together. Kurt Lewin (1935) helps us understand the meaning of an experimental subject's behavior by making diagrams of his "psychological field"; he tries to map out what the experimental situation looks like to the subject. For example, Lewin may picture a child separated from a piece of candy, which is his goal, by a negatively charged barrier of parental prohibition. Similarly, E. C. Tolman (1948) speaks of "cognitive maps" by which behavior is guided. (Following our usage in Vol. I, we shall use the terms, "cognitive field" and "integrative field"[3] to correspond to the "psychological field" of Kurt Lewin and to Tolman's "cognitive map.")

However, only the simplest behavior is guided by a single integrative field.[4] In rational purposive behavior a plan for achieving an end-goal must usually be supplemented by plans for achieving one or more subsidiary goals. Such a hierarchy of plans for achieving an end-goal constitutes the "cognitive structure"[5] of purposive behavior. For example, if I am in Chicago and wish to drive to Cleveland, Ohio, I consult first a map of the Midwestern states that tells me that the most direct route to Cleveland is Route 20; and then I consult a street map of Chicago that tells me how to get to Route 20. Guided by the street map, I drive to the nearest point on Route 20. Then, following the street map, I turn

3. An integrative field is a cognitive field that is exerting a guiding influence on behavior.

4. The following discussion is in part a recapitulation of Vol. I, chap. xliv.

5. In I, 44, we described the "pattern of motivation" of rational purposive behavior as "a hierarchy of goal-directed strivings, in which subordinate goals are related to superordinated ones as means to an end." Now we are describing the "cognitive structure" of purposive behavior as "a hierarchy of plans for achieving an end-goal." Since every plan in such a hierarchy has its goal, the notion of the cognitive structure of purposive behavior obviously includes that of its motivational pattern. We speak of "motivational pattern" when we are primarily interested in relations between the goals of behavior instead of in the total cognitive structure, of which this motivational pattern is a part.

Our concept of the "motivational pattern" of a dream (See Vol. I, chap. xx) is similarly included in our concept of the dream's "cognitive structure."

right on Route 20. Later I can check my conclusion that this is the right direction, for I soon find Lake Michigan on my left, as both maps tell me it should be if I am driving away from the center of Chicago and toward Cleveland.

This example illustrates the notion that *"meaning"* is a relation involving some kind of *equivalence between two cognitive fields.* From the map of the Midwestern states (which we shall call field *MW*) Route 20 gets the meaning of a road leading from Chicago to Cleveland, which I expect to find on the actual landscape (field *EL*, "expected landscape"). The meaning of Route 20 (as a way to get from Chicago to Cleveland) is then transferred to Route 20 on the street map of Chicago (field *St*); and later the route that I trace out on the street map gives meaning to the actual streets designated (field *OL*, "observed landscape") as a way of getting to Route 20 and ultimately to Cleveland.

These equivalences between the two maps (fields *MW* and *St*) and the expected and observed landscapes (fields *EL* and *OL*) have obvious implications for the guidance of my behavior. Since we are trying to reconstruct the logical structure of behavior, I shall try to spell out these implications in a pedantically precise technical language. The fact that I want to drive from Chicago to Cleveland causes the interstate map to be "polarized" for me along Route 20 in the direction from Chicago to Cleveland. This "polarization" along Route 20 on the interstate map is then transmitted to Route 20 on the street map, causing the street map next to be "polarized" by my desire to get from where I am to the nearest point on Route 20. In other words, in the integrative process that guides me in driving from Chicago to Cleveland the essential steps are transmissions of polarization from one integrative field to another; first, from the interstate map (*MW*) to the street map of Chicago (*St*), then from the street map (*St*) to the actual roads as perceived (*OL*), and, finally, by means of the musculature, to the steering wheel and engine of the automobile.

In the orderly execution of a plan such transmission of polarization from one integrative field[6] to another is dependent on a

6. We use the term "integrative field" to designate a cognitive field that is exerting a guiding influence on behavior (see n. 3, p. 5).

certain equivalence of pattern between them. In our example the street map corresponds in pattern to a part of the interstate map; and the actual landscape, as perceived, is equivalent to a part of the street map. If there were no such equivalence between the two maps, we would not transmit polarization from one to the other. For example, if we did not find the lake where the maps show it or if the two maps showed the lake in different relations to Route 20, we should probably be unwilling to proceed until we had decided how to reconcile our conflicting guides. A discrepancy between two of our guiding integrative fields would make us want to bring them into harmony with each other, to correct one of the two maps to make it agree with the other, or to correct both to bring them into harmony with the perceived landscape. In our discussion in Volume I[7] we gave the name of "mutual induction" to this tendency to establish and maintain equivalence of pattern between two integrative fields. When equivalence of pattern has been achieved with resulting transmission of polarization from one to the other, we speak of the two integrative fields as "in resonance with" each other.

We can now use this notion of resonance between integrative fields to round out our concept of "meaning." In our example the "meaning" of a map is the actual landscape or lay of the land designated by it; and the parts of two maps that represent the same area may be said to have the same "meaning." And now we recognize that the meaningful relationships between the two maps and the actual landscape have caused me first to transmit to the maps my desire to drive to the actual city of Cleveland and then to transmit back to the actual streets of Chicago my desire to get to the nearest point on Route 20. Generalizing from this example, we now round out our concept of meaning as follows: When we say that one thing "means" another, we mean[8] not

---

7. See p. 218.
8. To make clear the concept of "meaning" that we are proposing, we should discuss briefly the "meaning" of a phrase or of a sentence. To do so, we introduce the notion of a "syntactical field." To understand a sentence, we must obviously do more than add together the meanings of the words in it. A sentence consists of words fitted each into its proper place in a grammatical form. Such a pattern of words fitted into a grammatical form is a

only that two cognitive patterns are in some way equivalent to each other but also that each of the two patterns tends to elicit some of the reactions appropriate to the other.

Meanings and Cognitive Structure of a Dream.—This same concept of meaning is also applicable to the meanings of a dream. For example, in the anvil dream (12), which we discussed in Volume I,[9] the mother's beating an iron bar in the manifest dream is equivalent in pattern to the fantasy of being beaten by the mother, which is one of its meanings, and also to the fantasy of being beaten by the father, which is another one of its meanings; and the beating of the iron bar in the dream text also tends to satisfy the need to be "beaten into shape" that would have been satisfied by his dreaming of being beaten.

This dream becomes still more meaningful when we consider the two fantasies of being beaten, not as separate meanings of the dream, but as parts of a single cognitive structure. "My analyst, even though she is a woman, is treating me skilfully, just as father used to beat an iron bar into shape upon the anvil." This is the way that we can best translate into words the meaning of these two fantasies when we understand them in relation to each other, to the dream text, and to the fact that the dreamer is being treated by a woman.

However, there is no reason to believe that this thought was ever formulated in words, even unconsciously, in the dreamer's mind. On the contrary, the evidence suggests that the relationships that we have tried to translate into words were present in the dreamer's mind (at the moment of dreaming) in the form of a constellation of fantasies, memory images, perceived relations, etc., in resonance one with another. In our example of the two maps, my desire to get to the actual city of Cleveland was transmitted first to the interstate map, then to the street map,

---

"syntactical field." In the process of learning a language, syntactical patterns acquire relations of equivalence to nonverbal cognitive patterns. When we say that one phrase or sentence means (the same thing as) another, we mean that the two sentences are linguistically equivalent to the same nonverbal pattern of relationships. For example, the two sentences "A man beats a boy" and "A boy is beaten by a man" may refer to the same event.

9. See I, 80–81 and 88–91, reprinted in the Appendix to this volume (pp. 336 and 346–47).

and finally back to the actual streets of Chicago as a desire to drive to Route 20. Similarly, we think of the patient's vague and groping concept of his treatment as in resonance with a fantasy (or memory) of being beaten by his father, and this fantasy of being beaten as in resonance with a fantasy (or memory) of admiring the father's skill in shaping an iron bar upon the anvil; the patient's doubt about a woman doing a man's work has taken form in the picture in the dream text of the mother actually playing the father's role at the anvil (i.e., in resonance with the fantasy of the father's beating a bar upon the anvil), but this picture is also in resonance with the patient's reassuring sense of the analyst's skill in treating him.

Such a constellation of "cognitive fields" in resonance with one another is what we call a "cognitive structure." In our example of the two maps we illustrated how rational behavior is patterned and guided by such a cognitive structure. Our thesis in this volume is that dreams, too, are patterned by cognitive structures and that, in order to understand a dream thoroughly, we must reconstruct this underlying constellation of cognitive fields and map out the relations of resonance between them.

Our purposes in this volume are: (1) to illustrate how we reconstruct and how we check our reconstruction of the cognitive structure of a dream; (2) to consider how the cognitive structures of different dreams of the same person are related to one another. These two topics are closely interwoven. Our best check on the reconstruction of any one dream is to compare it with many different dreams, to determine how each dream fits into the pattern of the personality as a whole.

CHAPTER II

The Pattern of Dream Organization

Even after we have succeeded in grasping some of the meanings of a dream, the language in which these meanings are expressed often seems very strange. Freud was the first to demonstrate that dreams have sense and meaning. Yet Freud,[1] too, distinguishes sharply between logical thinking, which he calls "the secondary process," and the kind of thinking that characterizes the dream work, which he calls "the primary process." How, then, can we reconcile our notion of the logical structure of a dream with Freud's concept of the primary process?

Freud has already suggested an answer to this question. "Whenever one psychic element is connected with another by an illogical and superficial association," he says, "there exists also a correct and more profound connection between the two, which succumbs to the resistance of the censorship."[2]

As I have already indicated,[3] I believe that the dream work can be best understood by comparing it not with rational thought but with the practical "sizing-up" of situations that guides our waking behavior. In his formal presentation of dream psychology Freud reconstructed the dream work by tracing the chains of association that lead from the latent dream thoughts to the manifest dream. When we study the dream work in this way, we cannot escape the impression, which Freud formulated, that energy is displaced along any available associative pathway,

1. Readers who are not already familiar with Freud's *The Interpretation of Dreams* may refer to Vol. I, chap. xvi, for a brief summary of Freud's theory of the wish-fulfilling and sleep-preserving function of dreams and of his concepts of manifest and latent dream contents, of the dream work, and of primary and secondary processes.

2. S. Freud, 1900, p. 489 (I have modified Brill's translation slightly at one point).

3. See I, 72–73 and also p. 4 of this volume.

without regard to reality or logic, guided only by the pleasure principle. However, when we study Freud's own more fully reported dream analyses, we get the impression that at least the most significant part of the dream work is a better-organized process than it at first appears to be.

There is another possible way of studying the dream work. In our usual intuitive approach to the practice of dream interpretation we do not reconstruct chains of associations. We listen to the dreamer's reported associations until the wish that has motivated the dream finally dawns on us, and then we try to understand both the dream and the dreamer's associations as reactions to this dream wish and to the conflict stirred up by it. In other words, we study the dream work not as a tangled network of chains of association but as a reaction to the total situation created by the dreamer's conflict.

In these studies we are trying to make explicit this intuitive approach to the dream work. We start not with the whole body of latent dream thoughts but more specifically with the dreamer's conflict situation; and then, instead of tracing chains of association, we reconstruct a part of the cognitive structure of the dream, which we shall call the *pattern of dream organization*.[4] We interpolate a series of pictures or fantasy patterns that starts with the dreamer's (unconscious) practical understanding of his conflict situation and leads directly, by one or more intelligibly motivated substitutions, to the manifest dream content. We attribute our better-organized picture of the dream work to the fact that, instead of tracing chains of associations, we attempt to follow the modifications in the dreamer's practical grasp of his conflict.[5] We suspect that the seeming chaos of the primary process is in part an artifact, resulting from the study of associations rather than total situations in the dream work.

Dora's Dream.—In order to examine how our interpretive ap-

4. The "pattern of dream organization" is only one part of the dream work or of the total cognitive structure of a dream. For further discussion of this distinction see chaps. iii and iv of this volume. See also p. 27, n. 6, and chap. xxxv for distinction between "pattern" and "process" of dream organization.

5. See Vol. I, chap. xvi, for a more extended theoretical discussion of this way of studying the dream work (which is to be illustrated in the present chapter).

proach is related to Freud's, we shall first study a dream that Freud has already reconstructed. For this purpose we select Freud's synthesis[6] of the first dream reported[7] in his "Fragment of an Analysis of a Case of Hysteria." The text of this dream was as follows:

A house was on fire. My father was standing beside my bed and woke me up. I dressed myself quickly. Mother wanted to stop and save her jewel-case; but Father said: "I refuse to let myself and my two children be burnt for the sake of your jewel-case." We hurried downstairs, and as soon as I was outside I woke up.

This dream was dreamed three times, on the second, third, and fourth nights after Mr. K, whom Dora and her father were visiting, had made a sexual proposal to her, which she had energetically rejected. By questioning, Freud was able to elicit from her an account of the circumstances that served as the immediate precipitating stimulus: On the afternoon after the attempted seduction Dora had awakened from her afternoon nap to find Mr. K standing by her bed (just as her father stood by her bed in the dream text). The next afternoon, when she wanted to lock the door of her bedroom, she found that the key had been removed. She thereupon resolved not to prolong her visit at Mr. K's house after her father left. The next morning she dressed quickly, just as she did in the dream. The dream occurred on the three successive nights after she failed to find the key; and on the day after the last repetition of the dream she left with her father.

Interpretation of Dora's Dream.—Freud interprets this dream as a reaction to Dora's temptation to yield sexually to Mr. K. To protect her against this temptation, she has "summoned up" her infantile love for her father. She hopes that her father will rescue her from Mr. K.

This interpretation is evidently suggested by the striking similarity of the scene of the father standing by her bed in the dream text with the disturbing episode in which she awoke

6. For understandable reasons, Freud left many of his reports of dream analyses very fragmentary; but he has published a few more extended reports, which he calls "dream syntheses."

7. See S. Freud, 1905*b*, pp. 78–113.

to find Mr. K standing by her bed in real life. In the dream text she has substituted her father, in the role of rescuing her, for Mr. K, who in real life was tempting her; for her own sexual excitement the dream text has substituted a house on fire. The fact that Dora has resolved to leave the house with her father is further evidence in support of this interpretation.

Freud believes that the scene of Dora's father standing by her bed is based on a childhood memory: For the temptation scene, in which Mr. K stood by her bed, the dream text has substituted a reassuring memory from her childhood when her father stood by her bed to wake her up and prevent her wetting the bed.

It is evident that this interpretation of Freud involves not free displacement of energy along any available associative pathway but the substitution of one total situation for another. The dream work has substituted a memory of her father's waking her up to protect her from a sexual temptation (bed-wetting) in childhood, as a fantasied solution for her present conflict about Mr. K's sexual advances. In other words, Freud has reconstructed this part of the dream work in the way that we propose. This illustrates the statement that we made earlier,[8] that our method of studying the dreamer's practical grasp of his conflict is no innovation but only an explicit formulation of a method that all psychoanalysts use intuitively.

Pattern of Organization of Dora's Dream.—Finding an interpretation is an imaginative or intuitive act, which cannot be reduced to rules; but, once an interpretation has been found, checking it should be a careful deductive procedure. By "interpreting a dream," we mean discovering how the dream fits into the context of the dreamer's real life-situation; we try to find out to what (in the dreamer's present situation) the dream is a reaction and to understand the nature of this reaction. We check a suggested interpretation, first, by inquiring whether it really does account for the details of the manifest dream and whether it is also consistent with the dreamer's other behavior and thoughts at the time. *When we reconstruct the pattern of organization of a dream, we make this first check on our interpretation system-*

8. See I, 72.

atically. *To reconstruct the pattern of dream organization* we first compare the dreamer's conflict situation with the situation portrayed in the manifest dream; then *we interpolate the steps by which the dreamer's picture of the conflict situation must have been transformed in order to account for the manifest dream. If our interpretation is correct, each of these steps must have been intelligibly motivated.*

To illustrate this procedure, we shall next reconstruct the pattern of organization of the jewel-case episode in Dora's dream. Actually, Dora is in conflict between her waking resolution to leave the house with her father and her temptation to stay behind and accept Mr. K's sexual advances. Instead of this internal conflict, the dream text has portrayed a conflict between her father and her mother. Her mother wants to save her jewel case, but her father insists on getting her out of the burning house. To make this substitution intelligible, we resolve it into two steps:

1. Making use of the fire and jewel-case symbols, the dream work has first substituted for her sexual conflict a conflict between escaping from a fire and saving a jewel case.

2. Then, projecting both her conflicting motives, this dream has ascribed to her mother her own reluctance to leave the temptation situation, and to her father her decision to do so.

We examine next how each of these steps is motivated:

1. The jewel case is one that Dora received as a gift from Mr. K. It is an acceptable symbol that refers most obviously[9] to her tender attachment to him. The fire is an acceptable symbol, too—even though it symbolizes directly the underlying sexual excitement—because it is an impersonal danger whose sexual implications need not be recognized. By substituting the fire and the jewel case as contrasting symbols, the dream work has transformed the dreamer's picture of her conflict into the more

9. We seem here to be ignoring the significance of jewel case as a symbol of the female genitals. The reason is that we are now interested not in the "deeper" meaning of the dream symbolism but in the dynamic balance between conflicting motives that determines what is suitable for representation in the dream text. *The jewel-case symbol can be permitted to appear in the dream text because it refers more obviously to Dora's tender attachment to Mr. K than to the wholly unacceptable underlying sexual fantasies.*

acceptable one of a conflict between her reluctance to give up a symbol of her tender relationship to Mr. K, on the one hand, and her desire to escape from an impersonally conceived danger (fire), on the other hand.

2. Then, by ascribing to her mother her own reluctance to leave the temptation situation, the dreamer not only relieves herself of responsibility for her reluctance but also puts her rival, the mother, in conflict with her father. Actually, as Freud points out, her father has had some responsibility for exposing her to temptation from Mr. K; but in the dream text his energetic insistence on getting her out of the house is part of the wish-fulfilling solution of Dora's conflict that this dream as a whole is attempting: to turn away from Mr. K as tempter to her father as rescuer.

We have postulated[10] that the dream work, like the thought-processes directing our ordinary waking activity, is dominated by the need to find a solution for a problem. Is this true of Dora's dream? And, if so, what has the dream work accomplished in relation to her problem?

It is evident that this dream has not found a solution for Dora's conflict. As Freud points out, her decision to leave the house with her father was arrived at in the afternoon before the dream, when she discovered that the key had been removed from the door of her bedroom. Evidently this decision was not a result of the dream work.

Freud insists that this decision, like any other material from the preceding day, was merely utilized by the dream work in its attempt to find fulfilment for the patient's infantile sexual wish for her father. However, according to Freud's own interpretation, the dream seems to be centered about Dora's conflict about yielding sexually to Mr. K. As Freud puts it,[11] Dora "summoned up an infantile affection for her father so that it might protect her against her present affection for a stranger." According to my interpretation, which is based on this statement of Freud, Dora's dream is organized about her conflict about yield-

10. See I, 72–73.
11. S. Freud, 1905b, p. 104.

ing to Mr. K; the dream work has utilized, first, the memory of being waked up by her father, and then her recent resolution to leave with her father, in an unsuccessful search for a solution of her present problem. Then the jewel-case episode gives evidence that her decision to leave with her father is itself in conflict with her desire to cling to her former tender relationship to Mr. K in spite of his sexual advances.

If our reconstruction is correct, what has been accomplished by the two steps in the process of dream organization that we have postulated?

The first step can be characterized as an attempt to solve Dora's problem, but it was an attempt that failed. The jewel case is a symbol of the dreamer's longing to cling to her former tender relationship to Mr. K in spite of his sexual advances; but the threatening fire is a sign that her own sexual wishes, to say nothing of Mr. K's importunities, make such a compromise impossible.

The second step in the organizational process is not an attempt at solution of the problem; it is rather an attempt to withdraw from the conflict, to gain distance from it. The dream must still give recognition to Dora's conflict but portrays it in a projected form that is less disturbing to her. The dream pictures her as only passively involved in a quarrel between her father and her mother.

I agree with Freud that dreams only exceptionally[12] achieve real solutions for a dreamer's conflict. In most cases, as in Dora's dream, we find that particular steps in the process of dream organization are either unsuccessful attempts at conflict solution or attempts to reformulate or fragment the problem in such a way as to bring it within the span of the dreamer's integrative capacity.[13]

Needs and Hopes in Dora's Dream.—In our next chapter we shall compare this reconstruction of the pattern of organization of Dora's dream with Freud's analysis of the jewel-case sym-

---

12. Freud maintains that, even in these exceptional cases, solution of the dreamer's problem is only incidental to the dream work (see I, 74, n. 9).

13. See I, 74; and, for more detailed elaboration of this concept, see Sec. VI of this volume.

bolism; but before concluding this chapter we shall use this dream to illustrate two more of our hypotheses about dreams.

Our first thesis[14] is that, in order to understand the cognitive structure of behavior, we must distinguish between what it is trying to get away from, which we call its "negative goal," and what it is seeking, which we call its "positive goal." The "negative goals" of behavior we call "needs"; its "positive goals" arise out of "hopes," which may be based either on present opportunities for satisfaction or on memories of previous satisfaction, or both.

We postulate,[15] further, that dreams, like waking behavior, are polarized between negative and positive goals, between needs and hopes, or between the pressure of a conflict and hopes of a solution. As we reconstruct it, Dora's dream illustrates this thesis: Her conflict about yielding to Mr. K's sexual advances is the negative pole of the pattern of dream organization; her hope of turning to her father for protection is its positive pole. And this hope has its roots, as we postulated, both in a reassuring memory (the memory of her father's waking her up) and in a present opportunity (the possibility of leaving the house with her father).

The Process of Awakening in Dora's Dream.—In an earlier chapter[16] we proposed also the hypothesis that the chronological succession of manifest dream episodes reflects, first, (*a*) an attempt to deny the dreamer's conflict by means of a reassuring dream hallucination; then (*b*) progressive emergence of the pressure of the conflict; and, finally, (*c*) a reality-based solution, equivalent to the turning of interest back to external reality in the act of awakening.

When the jewel-case episode is interpreted as we have proposed, the chronological sequence in Dora's manifest dream corresponds to this formulation: (*a*) By substituting the reassuring childhood memory image of her father standing by her bed, the dream work tries at first to deny the reality of the dreamer's

14. See Vol. I, chap. xi.
15. See I, 58 and again 96.
16. For more extended discussion of this hypothesis see Vol. I, chaps. xlii and xliii.

present conflict; but (*b*) the fire symbolism indicates that this reassurance is failing as the dream begins.[17] Then the pressure of the disturbing conflict emerges progressively, beginning with the patient's dressing quickly and culminating in the father's refusing to let his two children burn for the sake of the mother's jewel case; (*c*) leaving the house as the dream ends corresponds to the dreamer's waking decision to leave the house with her father.

17. In the dream text, fire is mentioned first, but the statement that the father "was standing" beside her bed implies that awareness of the fire and of the father are simultaneous. When we speak of the "chronological sequence" of manifest dream episodes, we mean order of dreaming, not order of telling.

CHAPTER III
Historical Analysis

Freud's Synthesis of the Jewel-Case Episode.—Our reconstruction of the pattern of organization of Dora's dream is really only a further elaboration of Freud's interpretation. However, Freud approaches the synthesis of this dream by a different method; he attempts to reconstruct the complexly interwoven chains of association that meet and find condensed expression in the dream text in the word[1] "jewel case." We shall now summarize briefly Freud's synthesis[2] of this part of the dream work.

Freud finds that the contrasting ideas "wet" and "fire" form a nodal point in Dora's associations. The notion "wet" is intimately associated not only with Dora's wetting the bed in childhood but also with the fact that a woman becomes wet in the sexual act, that she receives something fluid from the man in the form of "drops." The notion "wet" is also associated with her mother's and her own leukorrhea, which in her own case is associated with masturbation. Her mother also has been sexually wet by the father and, Dora believes, has received her leukorrhea from him. Thus being "made wet" is closely related to the notion of being "dirtied."

The notions of being "wet" and "dirtied" are too offensive to be permitted direct representation in the dream text and are replaced by more acceptable references to jewelry. The "pearl drops" that the mother desired[3] as a gift from the father are associatively linked with the "drops" that she received from the father in the sexual act; and ornaments and jewelry are related as something clean to the unclean sexual wetness. Finally, the

1. In German "jewel case" is only one word.
2. See S. Freud, 1905*b*, pp. 106–13.
3. In the associations to this dream Dora tells of the mother's refusing a gift of jewelry that the father had given her and wanting "pearl drops" instead.

word "jewel case," which is the one that actually appears in the dream text, brings this whole complex of sexual thoughts into relation with the gift received from Mr. K and with the notion of Dora's returning his gift by yielding to his sexual wishes (giving[4] him her "jewel case").

Historical Analysis of Dora's Dream.—We should now like to know how these complexly interwoven chains of associations centering on the word "jewel case" are related to our reconstruction of the dreamer's attempts at practical grasp of her conflict. Comparing our reconstruction with Freud's, we find that the two reconstructions relate to different parts of the dream work. Our reconstruction, starting with Freud's interpretation of the dynamic structure of this dream, is concerned with the dreamer's integrative task of finding a solution for the conflict arising out of Mr. K's sexual proposal. This part of the dream work we call the "pattern of dream organization." Freud's reconstruction of the thoughts associated with the word "jewel case" leads us away from the dreamer's immediate present problem to the conflicts in the dreamer's past that constitute the historical background of her present problem.

The pattern of dream organization, which is the dreamer's reaction to his present conflict situation, is only part of the dream's cognitive structure. Like other behavior, dreams react to present situations according to patterns acquired in the past. Another part of the dream work leads back to the historical background of the dreamer's precipitating conflict and to memories that served as precedents in past experience for each step in the pattern of dream organization.

Since Freud has analyzed so thoroughly the historical background of Dora's dream, it is possible for us to apply our own method to his data. In this chapter we shall try to reformulate

---

4. In the dream text, Dora's mother wants to *save* her jewel case—but Freud has frequently pointed out that a wish (or other mental content) may be represented in the manifest dream by its opposite. In our own reconstruction we have postulated a similar reversal—substitution of a tender attachment to Mr. K (keeping his gift of a jewel case) for her physical sexual wishes. In our attempt at historical analysis (see p. 21) we postulate that this substitution is based on a reaction formation in which Dora substituted a desire to be pretty for the sexual impulses that wet and soiled her.

or translate Freud's analysis in terms of practical grasp of total situations instead of displacement of energy along associative pathways. We shall try to reconstruct the cognitive structure of this dream's historical background.

Although the associative chains in the latent thoughts of this dream seem complex, the kinds of situations referred to are only few in number, and each one of these few situations can be recognized as background or historical precedent for some part of the pattern of dream organization as we have reconstructed it.

Background of the Precipitating Conflict.—The question of whether or not to yield to Mr. K's sexual advances is the precipitating conflict of this dream. The associations show that this conflict has its roots in earlier conflicts about sex, in conflicts between sexual wishes and disgust at the thought of being wet sexually. The associations referring to this conflict include memories of bed-wetting and of masturbation with resulting leukorrhea, and fantasies of being wet and soiled sexually by Dora's father.

Sources of the Jewel and Fire Symbolism.—In the first step of the process of dream organization, the dreamer, to avoid being dirtied, struggles to repress her desire for physical sexual gratification and to substitute fond memories of the tender attachment between her and Mr. K. The jewel case that Dora received as a gift from Mr. K serves as a token of these fond memories; and the wish to receive from the father the gift of jewelry that the mother refused is an earlier historical precedent for this substitution of a tender attachment for physical sexual wishes.

The contrast, which Freud points out, between sexual wetness (which is dirty) and jewels (which are clean and pretty) suggests that this substitution is reminiscent also of still earlier memories, of a reaction formation in response to her early training in cleanliness, in which she substituted a desire to be pretty and attractive for the infantile sexual impulses that wet and soiled her.

Our next task is to account for the fire symbolism. When Dora and her father first came to Mr. K's house, there was a thunderstorm, and the father had expressed fear of the house burning down, since it had no lightning rods. However, Freud is not satisfied that this accidental occurrence is an adequate explanation of the central role played by fire in this dream. He also calls attention to the association of the ideas "fire" and "wet," as opposites, and reminds Dora of the widespread superstition that a child's playing with matches may lead to bed-wetting.

Following out this suggestion of Freud, I believe that we can best account for the substitution of fire for sexual wetness in this dream by reference to the principle of complementary substitutes, which we discussed in Volume I:[5] Every substitute gratification, we postulate, is less satisfactory than direct gratification. When compared with the gratification originally desired, the substitute always lacks something and tends to be supplemented by a craving for another substitute to supply what is lacking in the first one. In the case of Dora's dream, jewels are an incomplete and inadequate substitute for sexual gratification. When Dora's reaction formation substitutes holding onto her jewels for sexual gratification, much of her sexual excitement continues unsatisfied. In the next version of the dream text, fire appears to represent her unsatisfied sexual excitement. In other words, jewels and fire are a contrasting pair of complementary substitutes[6] for sexual wetness.

Precedents for the Projection Mechanism.—The second step in the process of dream organization projects both of the dreamer's conflicting wishes. The dream text ascribes to her mother what is really her own reluctance to leave the temptation situation, and to her father a determination to rescue her. In the associations to the dream, memories of her mother's receiving jewelry from the father and also thoughts about the mother's being wet sexually by the father serve as background for the dream's projection of her own sexual wishes; and the memory of the father's waking her up to keep her from wetting the bed is a precedent for her present hope that he will rescue her from temptation.

Cognitive Structure of Dora's Dream.—What we have just done is comparable to rewriting the equation of a curve in terms of a new set of co-ordinates. If the new co-ordinates are well chosen,

5. See chap. xlvi.
6. *Ibid.*

the equation may show essential relationships more simply and clearly. The equation of a circle is simplest, for example, when the co-ordinate axes are so chosen that they run through its center at right angles to each other. We have just attempted something similar. We have used the two steps in the process of organization of Dora's dream as a new set of co-ordinate axes; and we have re-examined the latent dream thoughts in relation to these new axes. When we do so, we find that what seemed to be a tangled web of chains of association resolves itself into a small number of recurring situations from the past, each one of which has served as a pattern for one of the steps in the dream's organized attempts to deal with the precipitating conflict.

In Figures 1 and 2 we have represented diagrammatically the two parts of the cognitive structure of Dora's dream that we have reconstructed. In Figure 1 we have diagrammed the pattern of organization of this dream; and in Figure 2 we have arranged the corresponding groups of memory and fantasy patterns so as to indicate how they are related to each other. This system of relations between the memory and fantasy patterns that have served as a dream's historical background constitutes the "pattern of the dream's historical background."

Unfortunately, it is impossible to communicate to the reader our concept of the cognitive structure of a dream except by describing in words conflict situations which the dreamer must have grasped without words (i.e., in nonverbal cognitive fields). In our diagrams, in order better to convey this notion of a constellation of nonverbal cognitive fields, we have boxed in separately the words describing each cognitive field and have designated by connecting lines the relations of resonance between them, with arrowheads pointing always in the direction from precipitating situation to dream text.

To appreciate the significance of the "background pattern" of a dream, we must consider the problem with which the integrative mechanism is faced in trying to utilize past experience as a guide for present behavior. When a student makes use of a library, he may need only a few books out of the many thousands that are available. His task of selection would be hopeless, were it not for the fact that the library provides him with a carefully systematized catalogue. Similarly, in searching for a solution to a present problem, the integrative mechanism must select a small number of patterns out of a vast number that are potentially available. To account for its selection of appropriate patterns from the past, we must assume that the integrative mechanism, too, has some kind of catalogue at its disposal. We are reconstructing a small part of this cataloguing system when we study the background pattern of a dream.

Often it is helpful to plot the background pattern of a dream as a kind of map—in which different kinds of relations between fantasy (and memory) patterns are represented by different directions or as different dimensions. For example (see Fig. 3), we can map out the cognitive structure of Dora's dream in two dimensions: (*I*) (plotted horizontally) corresponding to Dora's reaction formation against sexual wetness, resulting in the substitution of jewels and fire as contrasting symbols; and (*II*) (plotted vertically) corresponding to the projection of Dora's conflict, substituting father and mother, respectively, for the two sides of Dora's conflict.

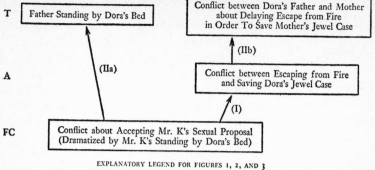

EXPLANATORY LEGEND FOR FIGURES 1, 2, AND 3

T = Manifest dream (dream text)

FC = Focal conflict (see chap. iv of this volume)

A = Intermediate version of dream text

X = In conflict with

→ = Activating and in resonance with

I = Reaction formation resulting in substitution of jewels (Ib) and fire (Ia) symbolism

II = Projection of Dora's conflict, substituting conflict between father (IIa) and mother (IIb)

FIG. 1.—Pattern of organization of Dora's dream

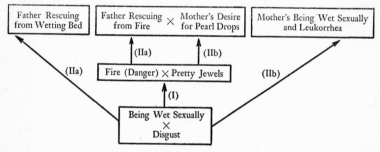

FIG. 2.—Historical background of Dora's dream

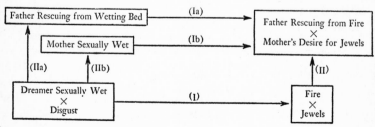

FIG. 3.—Historical background of Dora's dream (in map form)

CHAPTER IV

Reconstructing a Dream's Cognitive Structure

We Recapitulate.[1]–Every dream has many meanings. To reconstruct the cognitive structure of a dream, we map out how these many meanings are related to one another; we study the relations between present situations, past events, and fantasies that have helped shape the dream.

One aspect of a dream's cognitive structure is its *motivational pattern*, which we reconstruct by studying how the dream's motivating wishes are related to one another.

Reconstructing the cognitive structure of a dream involves a number of steps:

1. First, *we interpret the dream.* By "interpreting"[2] a dream we mean discovering how it fits into its context in the dreamer's life. When we interpret, we are not content merely to enumerate the dream's "overdetermined" meanings. We wish also to know how the dreamer's interest is distributed quantitatively between these meanings. We try, first, to find the most intensely cathected meaning, i.e., the meaning on which the dreamer's interest centers. There is usually a problem from which all the dream wishes radiate. This we call the *focal problem or focal conflict (FC)*[3] of the dream. For example, in Dora's dream the focal problem was whether to yield to Mr. K or to leave the house with her father. *The focal problem,* since it is the problem with which the dreamer is unconsciously preoccupied at the moment of dreaming, *is always anchored in the present.*

1. See chap. i of this volume.
2. See Vol. I, chap. vi, for more extended discussion of interpretation.
3. Summary of symbols in this chapter, and of their meanings:

$$FC = \text{focal problem or focal conflict}$$
$$T = \text{manifest dream (dream text)}$$
$$R = \text{present opportunity (reality)}$$
$$H_R = \text{hope based on present opportunity}$$
$$H_M = \text{hope based on reassuring memory}$$

Interpretation is an art that requires scientific imagination and cannot usually be reduced to rules; but reconstructing the cognitive structure of a dream can be a systematic deductive procedure, when once the dreamer's focal problem has been found; and this deductive elaboration of the dream's cognitive structure should serve as a multiple check on the correctness of our initial interpretation. If our initial interpretation was incorrect, we expect it to lead us into ever increasing inconsistencies as we try to fit it into the details of the dream text and associated thoughts and then into the larger context of the same patient's other dreams and behavior.

Occasionally, more than one interpretation seems focal. If so, we assume that the focal problems are intimately and intelligibly related; we try to discover how they are linked together in a single motivational pattern.[4]

2. Our next task is to *reconstruct the pattern of dream organization*, the process by which the dreamer's picture of his conflict situation has been transformed into the manifest dream content. We reconstruct the steps in this process by *interpolating between the focal problem (FC) and the manifest content (T) of the dream.*

However, we must not forget that dreams,[5] like waking behavior, are polarized between needs and hopes. The focal conflict corresponds to our concept of need; to round out our picture of the pattern of dream organization, we must also include the hopes about which the dream has been organized. *A complete reconstruction of the pattern of dream organization should show how the manifest dream content (T) is itself interpolated between the focal conflict (FC), on the one hand, and the present opportunities (R or H_R) and reassuring memories (H_M) on which the dream's hopes are based, on the other hand.*[6]

4. We have already illustrated this procedure in discussing the bridge dream (10a) and the anvil dream (12) (Vol. I, chaps. xx and xxiii). As another example, see our analysis of the pig dream (43) in chaps. vi and xviii of this volume.

5. See Vol. I, chaps. xiii, xix, and xxi, and also pp. 16–17 of this volume.

6. We have spoken of the dream's "pattern of organization" rather than of its "process of organization." Our reason for this distinction is that the actual "process" of dream organization probably does not begin with the

3. Finding reassuring memories belongs strictly to our next step, which is *reconstruction of the historical pattern of the dream*. Our reconstruction of the pattern of dream organization is our starting point for this task; we try to trace back both the focal conflict and the several steps in the pattern of dream organization to their sources in past experience.

4. Theoretically, our final task should be to trace back the wishes motivating a dream to the underlying biological drives and other inherited reaction patterns. This task cannot be attacked directly. As one approach to it we study the dream's *physiological pattern:* We try to reconstruct the pattern of physiological activity implied by each successive step in the pattern of dream organization and by each pattern from the past that has contributed to the dream's historical background. We shall illustrate this kind of physiological analysis in Section V of this volume.

5 and 6. From a dream and its immediate context alone, we cannot hope to make a reconstruction that approximates in completeness the outline that we have just sketched out. We supplement what we can learn from the immediate context by two methods: (5) by analysis of the dream symbolism and (6) by comparison with other dreams.

In the third and fourth sections of this volume we shall discuss systematic methods of symbol interpretation and how they can be checked by comparison with later dreams. In later chapters we shall explore briefly but systematically how the symbolisms and cognitive structures of all this patient's dreams are interrelated.

---

focal conflict and end with the manifest dream, as our method of reconstructing the "pattern" of dream organization would suggest. On the contrary, *the actual "process" of dream organization probably begins at both ends:* It starts *with a need to bridge the gap* between focal conflict and reassuring hopes, and it continues by a process of interpolation or mutual induction between them. Thus Dora's dream succeeds in bridging the gap between her conflict about Mr. K and her hope of turning to her father for protection, just as in our example of the automobile trip my choice of the two maps was determined by the gap between my being in Chicago and my hope of driving to Cleveland.

In Sec. VI of this volume we shall consider other complications in the actual "process" of dream organization.

SECTION II
Pattern of Dream Organization

CHAPTER V

Our Case Report Continued

As data for our study of dreams in this volume we shall, from time to time, supplement the dreams that we studied in Volume I[1] with reports of later periods of our patient's treatment. In this chapter, as a first instalment, we shall continue our review of his psychoanalytic sessions, beginning where we left off at the end of his twenty-fifth hour.

As previously, we shall postpone interpretive comment until our next chapter.

After discussing the pencil-stealing dream (25),[2] the patient missed the next hour and reported six days later (26th hour) that he got mixed up on the dates. He wonders whether he has a mental defect, then reports the following dream:

Dream 26.—Bunch of men, 4 or 5; don't know who they were;—on country dirt road, brush on both sides of road. All had golf sticks, all I had was a broom. They were to hit ball, and I was going to hit squirrel partly covered in dead leaves. I was annoyed at that. Now make something out of that. More to it I don't remember.

In association to the road he recalls that he once before dreamed of a street and another time of an alley. On both sides there was growing brush, young oak trees. He inquires if he is on the road.

The squirrel in the dream was alive, was wriggling her tail. He was told to hit it with a broom, and they were hitting balls. He leaves the interpretation up to the analyst. . . .

The analyst comments that the patient wants her to do the associating. The patient protests that he is unable to compare the dream with anything. The analyst hints that a broom is a woman's

1. For the convenience of the reader we have reprinted as Appendix to this volume our reports of the first twenty-five sessions of our patient's treatment (Vol. I, chaps. xvii and xxxiii) and also our interpretive comments (Vol. I, chaps. xviii and xxxiv).

2. See Appendix to this volume (p. 342).

weapon, and the patient states that he uses it lots of times around the basement at home. After putting coal in the furnace, he sweeps up. He swept snow off the steps twice.

The analyst suggests that the squirrel in the leaves is like a baby. The patient protests that he was supposed to play golf with the broom. Why didn't he have a golf stick like the rest? He never played golf. He had no business being there. He agrees readily to the analyst's interpretation of his feelings of inferiority in relation to women. He laughs as he replies, "I am a failure all right. . . ."

In the twelve days following the report of the broom dream (26), the patient missed two hours and came to his appointment at the wrong hour three times. In the 27th hour he says he was quite distressed about this. Then he reports a dream:

Dream 27.—I was supposed to lend a book to a woman. She returned it. She came in the house with her sister and gave me the book. She told me that there were two shares of stock in the book; the stocks were called Pitman that she was giving me. She said she paid $3.50 and now down to nothing practically and if I wanted it I could have it.— The certificate was all crumpled up, mistreated by someone. [*He laughs.*]

Associations.—The girl is one who used to live across the street. She is married now and her sister too. "We knew her for a long time, since 1919 or 1920 when she was a little tot going to school. She and her sister came over often." The patient hasn't seen her for two or three years. The book was Sinclair's *Brass Check* about how publishers and newspapers work together. The patient feels that this is a fact. The press is controlled by wealthy men. There is nothing against capital in the newspaper, always against labor. The patient tells how hard it is for him to get his articles published.

Yes, the girl was giving him something worthless. At least she said so. The patient wonders why he took it. The girl's sister is a child just out of school. The older girl worked in a bank. The patient looked up the name of the stock in the paper, and there is no such stock. He once worked with a man by the name of Pitman. They worked together two years as partners, got along fine, played cards together— . . . made dates to go to a gambling house. He was younger and single. The patient had just gotten married. The patient has only seen him once since then.

He interrupts to protest against his late hours at work. The analyst interprets the dream as a guilt reaction on account of the patient's resentment of the gap between her and himself (capital and labor). She says that the patient is protesting that she gives him only what she receives from him and that what she gives him is worthless.

The patient replies that someone was going to throw away the stock in the wastebasket. He didn't know what to say when it was offered to him, but didn't think much of it. In fact, when he first came to analysis he didn't think much of it. . . .

In the five weeks that followed the borrowed book dream (27) the patient stayed away from his treatment frequently for a number of days at a time. In the first part of this period he complained a great deal about feelings of inferiority, particularly about his fear of talking freely, especially to women. He says he gets asthma when he gets rid of his inferiority feelings. While dwelling on this theme in the 32d hour, he recalls a childhood memory. At the age of seven or eight he stole a nickel from his father's cashbox and bought a knife with it; but he felt guilty, and that night he confessed. Another time he took a knife from a neighbor's house and told a girl he had found it, but later he felt so guilty that he had to give it back. . . . Toward the end of this hour, he tells of his envy of his father and of his next younger brother. Some weeks later he mentioned the fact that during the analyst's ten days' vacation, which immediately followed this hour (32), his right arm felt dead.

In the 37th hour the patient is disturbed because his younger child is doing poorly in school. He begins to wheeze when the analyst suggests that he might help the child with his lessons.

In the 39th hour he reports a dream:

Dream 39.—Remember bunch of men, outdoors. Woman cooking in big kettle and stirring it with a ladle, dipping it up and letting it flow back. Big iron kettle with fire under it. One side bunch of men.

Associations.—In answer to the analyst's question, the patient says there were six men perhaps. He did not recognize them or the woman. The place was "outdoors somewhere. . . . These women!" In the kettle was some kind of milk, he supposes. She lifted it up and then poured it back. There was a big log fire with smoke all around. The woman, he thinks, represents the analyst "stirring around in my empty head." The analyst inquires why there are so many men. "Maybe the woman was cooking for them," the patient says. "There was plenty of food for a regiment, like gypsy life." When the analyst inquires about ladling the liquid, the patient asks if it has any meaning. . . . "It is just a dream to me. I did not like the looks of the food. It was full of smoke—there might be dust around—the woman was stirring with a stick or spoon." The analyst suggests that the other men are her patients. The patient protests he does not know her other patients. The analyst suggests that the food that he does not like is the analysis. "Food sickened me when I looked at it," he replies. "Don't know what I was doing there. I was on the side just looking at it. I had no connection with woman or men."

The analyst interprets the dream as indicating that the patient is bound to a woman and does not like it. . . . The patient continues that when he left home there were only three brothers—not six—the others were not born. He could not recognize the woman—"My mind is weak, I cannot remember things." Outdoors always appealed to him. "We used to go out for a day and night in the wilderness." The patient liked it but still missed the mother's care, the cooking and comfort of home. "During the day was all right as long as we had enough to eat, but when sleeping on hard ground under the stars, I missed home then. Then at home I wanted to get away." The analyst suggests that the patient's asthma came from this conflict. The patient reacts to the analyst's interpretations with a peculiar helplessness—"how overcome this—where will we look for the rest?" He wonders what is stirring up his emotions. Last time he was here he was upset; he has forgotten what it was about. The analyst reminds him that he talked about his son. "Oh, yes, he is not so bad as I thought. I saw his teacher. She said to force him—he is lazy. He knows his lessons better than he wants to. He is jolly at times, that is a good sign, eh? Why is it I always get dry and hoarse in the throat when I come here?"

After this dirty food dream (39) the patient canceled two appointments and did not come back for a week. Then (after the 40th hour) he was not seen again for two weeks more.

In the 41st hour the patient reports that his asthma has not bothered him much but that he has been nervous and jumpy. He got a bill from the Institute but will not be able to pay it this month. Then he reports the following dream:

Dream 41.—Digging basement for a home, full of dirty water—location at 107th and Torrence Avenue. There housing project is going on. Looking at hole and dirty water.

Associations.—He goes by this place every day. The dream was dreamed night before last. He says they were pumping the dirty water out with a gasoline pump. It was running through a hose. "Just some more dirt." The analyst suggests that the dream refers to the analysis. The patient agrees, "It's not very pleasant —I think a lot about the analysis all right." He considers analysis like going to confession—confessing "sin or wrongdoing like immorality." "Dirt of my life. You pumping it out of me. You are the pump; hole is my empty head. Don't know what purpose I was there for. More to dream, I cannot remember. Is that a sign of weak mind?" The analyst suggests that the patient perhaps feels guilty about sexual feelings toward her. "You get all the dirt," the patient says. "Keeping everything secret hurts me more than revealing. Yes, that had an awful effect on me" (i.e., keeping that secret). . . .

In the 42d hour, two days after reporting the pump dream (41), the patient is much troubled by the fact that the Home Loan is demanding more payments on his house. The next day he says he has been awake all night wheezing. Then he reports the following dream:

Dream 43.—Dream about pigs. Lady living in next block supposed to buy two carloads of pigs. She was cheated—one car empty and other had only ten pigs in it.

Associations.—"Pigs are something dirty. The dream means the lady was cheated. The lady is a friend of ours. Her husband worked in the railroad yards. He has been sick for the last six or seven years. During his sickness they borrowed one hundred dollars from me. They have not paid it back. I have wondered how I could get it. He does not work. He depends on his children. I lent it to the old man and woman. I suppose his boys know about it. They will never be able to pay. I wonder if the boys might pay." He has no idea what the two carloads might mean. "You tell a dirty child that it is like a pig." The analyst adds that pigs are also greedy. "Maybe I want a lot, eh?" the patient replies. Carload half-full and half-empty? (The patient is silent). He saw the pigs fenced in, and the woman told everyone she got cheated. "Maybe she was trying to tell me she would not be able to pay me back." The patient is waiting to hear what the analyst has to say. The analyst suggests that perhaps the patient wants some money from her and that that makes the patient feel like a pig. Perhaps the patient wants to be taken care of as the woman's husband is. The patient denies this energetically. The analyst suggests that the patient feels he is cheating her. The patient continues that one car was only half-full. He laughs as he says that the empty car means that he is empty-headed. The analyst says that the patient feels that he has nothing to give a woman except to be a dirty pig in relation to her—that he feels guilty toward women.

During the whole hour the patient asked many times "What does it represent?" and refused to give spontaneous associations. He seemed to want the analyst to do all the work.

The patient opens the 44th hour (after an intervening week end) by inquiring after the analyst's child. Then he reports another dream:

Dream 44.—Scene in woods or forest, in a shack. Woman again with little boy. Woman like Mexican woman, dirty. Awful shack, half-buried in ground. Boy outside, naked, covered with scars. Woman pouring some solution and patient rubbing it with rough scrubbing brush on boy. The patient held his left arm and scrubbed with a brush.

Associations.—He wonders if the Mexican woman is his wife. The boy is eight or nine years old—all dirty and covered with scars. The woman is pouring acid to take them off—the patient holds his arm and scrubs it with a brush. It is the left arm, and the boy does not resist at all. The scar suggests disease or dirt. Is the boy the patient's son? The boy in the dream is younger, looks like a Mexican boy. [*Silence.*] What are the woods all around? The surroundings are nice. There is a green lawn around. The patient has seen places like it back home and here. He has told his wife that she looks like a Mexican. There are places like that in Texas; Mexicans are there, too. The skin disease reminds him that he had something as a child on his face at the same age. The analyst asks why the patient makes her a dirty Mexican. The patient laughs as he says that she told him, "This is going to take this off." The woman knew what the medicine was. She said it was like acid. The Mexican woman didn't look like the analyst—she was short and fat. No, his mother was slim and tall. The Mexican woman was more like the patient's wife, who is short and fat. She might represent the analyst. "You give the solution. I am a dirty helpless child full of scars. . . ." The patient often tells his wife that she is dirty. He will be the same because of his association with her. He insists that the analyst is not dirtying him but is cleaning him and that his mother was a clean woman. He thought a lot of his mother, loved and respected her. When the analyst reminds him of the sexual thought associated with her in the last hour, he protests that at the age of twelve or thirteen a child does not have such thoughts. . . .

At the beginning of the next hour (45) the patient says he is still wheezing; then tells of going to a picnic with a bunch of men from work. Most of the party came with their wives, but the patient came without his wife and didn't even tell her. He wheezed there considerably, felt guilty and embarrassed, tried to drown it with two drinks, and gave asthma as an excuse for going home earlier. He was attracted to a woman there and was afraid someone might talk about it. His wife might find out, and then there would be hell! He wonders if that gave him asthma. He was afraid of a scandal.

After this introduction he tells a dream of the night before:

Dream 45a.—In Strand Hotel. The patient came in and alongside of registry desk was a square stove. Lady asked him to fix the fire. The patient looked in, and fire was going out. Ashpit full of ashes, mixed with coal. Dirty place. Stove wasn't taken care of right. Lady asked him to clean out ashes and separate them from coal and get fire to burning.

In association he says that he has been in the Strand Hotel two times for Legion meetings. . . . Again the lady is giving him orders. The lady must be the analyst. What is the stove? Fire, heat or feeling. It was like a cabinet, square, narrow, and tall, great big ashcan under it, full of ashes and good coal. . . . Ashes is refuse, useless. With coal you feed the fire. The lady must be analyst. He goes by the Strand Hotel on the way to meetings, which are now held in another hotel. Fire is passion. Coal, material for fire. Ashes, waste, goes in ashcan. Also it is dirt. Is the stove a woman? He wonders if that has any connection with the parties he attended in the hotel. Men and prostitutes. He didn't like it, was ashamed of it. It gave the organization a bad reputation. . . . He wasn't pleased and told them about it, too.

Immediately after discussing the fire-tending dream (45a) the patient reports another dream.

Dream 45b.—About home here [his wife and another lady were housecleaning at the time]. This lady dumped a bucket of sand into a tub, told him to turn water on, to wash sand down into sewer. The patient asked her why she did that. He wanted to raise hell with her but she just said, "Oh turn the water on, it washes it down."

Associations were meager to this dream, as it was near the end of the hour. Sand is like ashes. "She told me to wash the dirt down the sewer because I was angry at her dumping the sand in. It was dirty. In every dream there is a woman and dirt all right."

The next day the patient sees the analyst's baby in the hall and remarks, "We were all sweet at that age." Then he says he has wheezed all night and reports a dream:

Dream 46a.—Alongside of railroad yard out on the prairie, burning up ties and logs. Great big bonfire in three, four piles. Myself and older boy went there to get ashes for fertilizer. Someone warned us not to go close, lot of snakes there. The patient turned around; a big cliff with two snakes hanging down looking at them. Half of snake was coiled up and half hanging down. Hot fire. Ashes still hot. Boy wanted to pick it up. The patient told him to leave it alone until it burned out, then they could use it as fertilizer in the garden.

In association the patient says he couldn't figure it out about the ashes. Lot of hot fire and charcoal, that a lot of boys had just started to burn. Flame is passion; hot charcoal is passion; ashes, waste of passion. There was a lot more to be burned. . . . A snake is unpleasant. He hates even to talk about a snake. A snake is an enemy. "Snake in the grass." "We were warned that there are snakes under fire and ashes."

In association to his son he says that he is past fourteen this month. He is in the age where passion will attack him. Maybe he better warn him, better tell him something about sex. The family doctor said he would talk to him. . . . When the analyst interprets the patient's fear of her and her husband, the patient reports another dream:

Dream 46b.—I was getting up, sitting on edge of bed in pajamas. Penis outlined. Older boy walked in and said "How big it is."

In association he says he has always been careful around the house. "Why is the boy implicated in it? Maybe because I gave some thoughts to him on how to instruct and approach him. He is getting to the age where he will be bothered by it."

In answer to the analyst's question the patient says that he did once see his father's penis when he was in swimming. He was surprised, it was of good size. The patient was twelve years old. The analyst remarks that his fear of the snake is fear of his father or of a sexual rival. The patient continues: He was always afraid of snakes. The men played a trick on him at work. They put a grass snake in his pocket. He never wore the coat again because the snake was in it. It was an awful fear. When the analyst suggests that he was afraid of being attacked by his father, he replied, "Not sex, do you mean? Hell no, his morals were high, he was too respectable! He was passionate too." The patient then proceeds to tell how he learned of his father's being accused of an extra-marital affair with a teacher when the patient was nineteen or twenty. The patient was surprised. The girl was a

family friend. He never heard any complaint from his mother
or grandmother. . . .

At the beginning of the next hour (47), after a week-end interruption, the patient put out his cigarette, remarking, "Didn't
kill that, eh?" and then, "I'll *smother* you." "The storm is over,"
he then reports. His wheezing continued for two more days but
was better "yesterday," and there is almost no wheezing today.
In answer to the analyst's question, he says he has no idea as to
what the cause of the "storm" was, except that he was really
worked up about the Home Loan office. The chances are it
was the analysis—about sex affairs. After a silence he remarks,
"I'll fall asleep if I don't say something." . . . Then, after another
silence, "Never get anywhere this way doctor. . . . have to stir
up something." [*Silence.*] "You will have to take the lead, that
is all; without your help I am lost. What a man! Without a
woman's help I am lost." After accepting the analyst's interpretation of his dependence, he adds, "There is where the trouble
comes at home . . . that woman [the patient's wife] doesn't in-
spire me to anything. Same rut. There is where I miss a lot. I
look up to a woman too much. I think more of a woman than
she is worth." [*Silence.*] At this point the patient starts to wheeze,
and the analyst associates this with his depreciatory thoughts
about women. The patient continues, "I don't say all women;
some women or one woman at least. I might be a crank to desire
more than I'm worth . . . yes, I don't expect too much. I want a
woman to be respectful and clean [coughs] and it starts in again"
(i.e., his asthma). . . .

In the next hour (48), three days later, he reports wheezing
again. . . . Later he remarks that the analyst wants to know more
about his childhood. "Up to seven years I was not unhappy"
(except for his eczema, which had been mentioned in connection
with the woman in the Mexican woman dream). "I was easy to
stir up and cry. If I was scolded I cried, had fear of spooks
and all that." Then he recalls that he had a dream about horses
but could not remember it. He says that he used to like horses;
had a horse as a child to ride. The first picture he could draw
was a horse. Horses' power, pride, and beauty too; dumb animal,

"I am like a horse. Once I was injured by a horse. The horse in the dream was chestnut color. The horse I had as a child had chestnut and white hair mixed." In answer to the analyst's suggestion that the horse represents a person, the patient replies, "Some people have grace and charm but are dumb; they don't know how to use it." He thinks that way about women.

The next hour (49), four days later, he reports that he has not been wheezing much. He asks how he is getting along with his treatment. . . . "I came close to being killed on Sunday. Me and partner looking over some cars; practically under car; felt safe. Just the minute I walked away from car it moved about four car lengths. . . . "I could have been a dead man today. Guess my time had come. Forgot about all the rest of my troubles." The analyst suggests that his real danger has relieved his need for self-punishment. "Maybe I need to be scared more," the patient replies. He recalls his fear of his father, and then that he had asthma attacks on two occasions when he was home at Christmas and again once after the married woman with whom he was having an affair became pregnant. Then once more after getting married, he was dissatisfied and got more and more asthma. He often thinks fifteen years of his manhood were wasted. Perhaps that is choking him. He wheezes.

CHAPTER VI

Interpretive Comment

We shall now illustrate again our initial approach to dream interpretation by interpretive comment on the dreams reported in chapter v.

Repudiation of the Analyst's Encouragement.—In the dream sequence that ended with the pencil-stealing dream (25) the analyst's tolerance for forbidden impulses had a paradoxical effect. By diminishing the patient's fear, the analyst's encouragement first permitted the forbidden wishes to be activated; then these disturbing wishes activated the associated fears. The net effect was not to diminish but to intensify the patient's fears.[1]

This mobilization of the patient's conflict gives us the key to an understanding of the dreams that follow.

In the broom dream (26), which is reported next, he disavows his intention to hit the squirrel. At first he says he "was going to" hit it, but in the second telling he "was supposed to" play golf with a broom, thus attributing responsibility for his impulse to someone else. This makes good sense in the context of the therapeutic situation. Repudiating his disturbing impulses, he attributes them to the analyst, interpreting her encouragement to become aware of them as though she were suggesting to him the act that he finds so repugnant.

His attitude toward analysis of the dream corresponds to this disavowal. He wants the analyst to take all the responsibility, to do all the work. This attitude is well expressed in the remark with which he concludes the dream: "Now make something out of that."

However, this interpretation is evidently incomplete, since we do not yet know the significance of his wanting to play golf with the other men.

1. See Vol. I, chap. xxxvii.

The next dream (27), which we shall call the "borrowed book dream," continues the theme of repudiating the analyst's encouragement by insisting that the gift that a woman is giving him is worthless. As the analyst points out, the worthless gift that he is receiving from a woman represents the analysis. This interpretation is based not only on the dream but also on the patient's other behavior. In the eighteen-day period since the pencil-stealing dream (25) he has missed six appointments; and his reaction to the interpretation brings further confirmation. He not only admits that at first he "didn't think much of" the analysis but also adds the dream detail that someone threw the worthless stocks into the waste basket.

As the analyst points out, this repudiation of the therapy as a worthless gift is part of a self-justifying argument. The dreamer would like to prove that he is not under obligation to the analyst. In support of this argument the first part of the dream text pictures her not as giving him a gift but as returning a book that he has loaned to her. This need to prove that the analyst is not really giving him anything can best be accounted for on the assumption that he already feels guilty toward her. It is particularly disturbing to receive help from someone toward whom one feels guilty, since receiving a gift makes the debt still greater.

We do not know yet why he feels guilty. A possible clue is the dream detail that the stocks are "crumpled up"; later he laughs when he says they were "mistreated." The significance of his laughing can be guessed when we recall that he "was supposed to" hit a squirrel in the broom dream (26). In the last hour the analyst had suggested that the squirrel was "like a baby."

The patient's continued rejection of the analyst's help and encouragement accounts both for the relatively infrequent analytic interviews during the next six weeks and also for the fact that he complained repeatedly of feelings of inferiority, especially about talking to women. He is so dependent on encouragement from a mother that when he rejects such help, his attitude becomes one of "giving up," of resignation to feelings of inferiority and of inadequacy as a man. Although he does tell of stealing money and a knife, these are memories relegated far into the past, and they are followed by feelings of "deadness" in his right arm.

Flight Interrupted by Longing for Mother.—In the dirty food dream (39), which is the first after a long dearth of dreams, he is sickened by the food that a woman is offering. He himself identifies this woman with the analyst. His associations give us a vivid picture of his conflict between wanting to get away from home and longing for his mother's care when he was away from her. He would "go out for a day and night in the wilderness" but would miss the "cooking and comfort of home" when he had to "sleep on the hard ground under the stars." The dream (39) fills in the additional detail that the food was full of smoke and dust; it was not like mother's food at home.

It is easy to see how this description fits the patient's present emotional situation in the therapy. He has been on a long flight from the analyst's help and encouragement. Now he is longing again for a mother's love and care. Yet the "food" that she offers is still distasteful. In the dream text (39) he is only "on the side looking at it." His behavior during the interview is consistent with this picture. He thinks of the analyst as "stirring around in my empty head." Taking no active part in attempting to understand the dream, he reacts with helpless bewilderment to the analyst's interpretations.

What is so distasteful to him is still not clear. Many men receiving "some kind of milk" from one woman suggests the many children in his mother's home. If he should return to his mother, he would be one of six to share her love, just as there are "six men perhaps" in the dream. The patient's emotional upset while discussing his conflict about leaving home leads him back to his being upset in the immediately preceding session, when the analyst suggested that he help his son with his lessons. Apparently this suggestion involved him in a conflict about sharing the analyst's interest with a child. The fact that in the dream (39) there is "food enough for a regiment" is another indication that he is struggling with the problem of sharing.

But why is the food "dirty" and "sickening"?

Relief by Confession.—The patient himself interprets the reference to dirt in the pump dream (41), which he reports next. The analysis is like going to confession, he says, like confessing "sin or wrongdoing like immorality." "Dirt of my life. You pumping it out of me. You are the pump; hole is my empty head." He is relieved when the analyst takes this as a hint that he has a confession to make. The analyst's guess that he has sexual feelings toward her elicits not denial but much relief. "You get all the dirt," he replies, and then adds, "Keeping everything secret hurts me more than revealing." "Keeping that secret," he repeats, "had an awful effect on me."

This relief from accepting an interpretation marks a sharp change in the patient's orientation toward the analysis. Instead of repudiating her encouragement, he now welcomes reconciliation with her by confession. His readiness to confess continues in his discussion of the next dream (43). This pig dream is probably a reaction to the interpretation just mentioned, which was the analyst's first direct interpretation of the patient's sexual wishes toward her. The dirty pigs in the pig dream again have reference to his "dirty thoughts." In association to this dream he first identifies a pig with a dirty child. When the analyst adds that pigs are also greedy, he is quick to take the suggestion as a reference to himself. He seems eager to identify himself with a dirty, greedy pig. He is eager to continue his newly won sense of reconciliation with the analyst by condemning himself as a dirty pig.

Since it is the patient who is being characterized as a dirty pig, the "lady" in the dream text (43) must be the analyst. Interpreting the dream in this sense, the analyst suggested that the patient feels guilty toward her for his dirty, greedy wishes. The fact that the "lady" of the dream text owes the patient money supports this interpretation, since it shows that the patient is under pressure to deny guilt or obligation toward her. By choosing just this lady to represent the analyst, the dream work is denying that he owes her anything; he is protesting, on the contrary, that she is under obligation to him.

Physiological Disintegration of a Confession.—Yet, although this interpretation fits the dream (43) into the context of the therapeutic situation, it does not account for a number of significant details. Why are there so many dirty pigs? If a pig is a dirty child, many pigs must be many children. This suggests that the "dirty children" whom the pigs represent are the patient's many brothers and sisters. If so, it is the patient who feels cheated. He wanted his mother's exclusive love, but his mother presents him instead with dirty little pigs. These feelings find projected expression in the dream text in the lady's repeated protests that she has been cheated.

Yet this interpretation does not quite fit either. If the patient is protesting that there are too many dirty children, how do we account for the fact that in the dream text (43) the lady is protesting because she does not receive more? The one who feels cheated because there are not enough children must be not the patient but the mother. Taking account of this discrepancy, we can probably best express the sense of this dream by putting the lady's protest back into the patient's mouth with a sarcastic twist. In the dream text the notion of two carloads of pigs, one empty and the other only half-full, condenses most paradoxically the concepts of "too many" and "not enough." This patient's mother had six children. "This woman can never get enough dirty pigs," the dreamer is protesting.

Evidently we are confronted again with the problem of overdetermination. According to one interpretation, the lady is the analyst (mother) who is protesting that the patient is a dirty pig on account of his sexual wishes toward her. Another interpretation argues that the lady is the patient, who feels cheated because his mother presented him with too many brothers and sisters. Are both these interpretations correct? If so, according to our working hypothesis, they must be understandably and intimately related to each other.

We shall postpone attempting to find this relationship until we study[2] the dream symbolism; but it is already significant that our two interpretations, when put together, sound like an angry argument between the patient and the analyst or mother. This suggestion brings these interpretations back into relation to his confession in the 41st hour. He has experienced much relief from

2. See chap. xviii of this volume.

confessing his sexual wishes and from realizing that the analyst has not been estranged by this confession. He longs to continue this sense of reconciliation with her. But in the meantime something has stirred up his conflict about having more babies with whom he must share a mother's love. This conflict again threatens his sense of reconciliation with the analyst. Not only does he feel cheated, but he pictures her as feeling cheated by his rejection of her babies. The dream work apparently started out with the hope of again achieving reconciliation with this mother-figure by confession and mutual understanding. He understands how she feels cheated, but he feels cheated too. Then his feelings become too intense, and he expects hers to be equally intense. The attempt at confession and mutual understanding degenerates into an angry quarrel. The woman calls him a dirty pig. Thinking of his mother, he retorts with the angry question, "Can't you be satisfied with half a carload of dirty pigs?" In the end his conflicting feelings become too violent even to be expressed in words. What started out as a confession becomes an angry cry. The dream ends with a physiological disintegration[3] of his attempt to talk: In order not to be further estranged from the analyst, he must even struggle to suppress the angry cry and must wheeze all night as a consequence.

Renewed Attempts To Co-operate in the Analysis.—In the Mexican woman dream (44), which comes next, both sides of this argument continue. The boy who is being scrubbed represents both the patient himself and his younger son.

The patient's memory of his own rash when he was the same age indicates that the eight-year-old boy, "all dirty and covered with scars," represents himself. According to our first interpretation of the pig dream (43), the patient himself is a dirty pig. After condemnation comes punishment. In the Mexican woman dream (44) the dirty little boy is getting a scrubbing.

According to our other interpretation of the pig dream (43), the dirty pigs are the patient's brothers and sisters. Similarly in

3. See Vol. I, chap. xxvi, for further discussion of this concept of physiological disintegration. For further discussion and examples of the relation between confession, crying, and asthma see T. M. French, F. Alexander, *et al.*, 1941, *Psychogenic Factors in Bronchial Asthma*, esp. Part I, chap. iv.

the Mexican woman dream (44) the patient identifies the dirty little boy with his son (a brother-figure) and pictures himself as helping the analyst (Mexican woman) administer the punitive treatment.

In the fire-tending dream (45*a*) the therapeutic situation receives another interpretation. From the associations it is evident that this dream is a reaction both to the sexual temptation at the picnic and to the analyst's interpretation of the patient's sexual wishes in the preceding (44th) hour. The dream text says nothing about sexual temptation but substitutes the lady's request that he stir up the fire.

His reaction to this temptation is ambivalent. In the dream text he calls the analyst a "lady," but in the associations he equates her with prostitutes hired for sexual purposes at stag parties he has attended. He does not approve of such parties, is ashamed of them. His ambivalence is expressed also in the dream symbolism. The fire is going out, and the ashpit is full of ashes mixed with coal. The lady is asking him to clean out the ashes and to get the fire burning. This is probably a projection of his own conflict. He is accusing the "lady" of trying to stir up his "passion." The fire clogged with ashes is his own reluctance to respond to sexual temptation.

In view of this resistance, it is not surprising that in the dreams (46*a* and *b*) reported in the next hour he is once more turning away from the analyst, whose interpretations and encouragement are proving so seductive. In the burning-logs dream (46*a*) the burning logs correspond to the fire in the stove in the preceding dream (45*a*). As in the fire-tending dream (45*a*), the patient is projecting his own sexual excitement (fire), which he attributes to the logs or to the woman whom the logs represent. "Do not touch her," he is advising his son, "but wait until she has cooled off. Let passion burn itself out. Then perhaps we can use the ashes for reproductive purposes (fertilizer)." In the context it is evident that this sexual instruction is intended not so much for his son as for himself. It is more acceptable to his pride to dream of giving instruction to his son than to admit to himself his own longing to be instructed by a father. In the penis envy dream (46*b*), too, instead of remembering his own envy of the father's penis, he dreams rather of being admired by his son.

CHAPTER VII

The Pattern of Dream Organization
More Examples

As we have already stated,[1] interpreting a dream means finding out how it fits into its psychological context. In particular,
we try to discover the focal conflict, the problem with which
the dreamer is preoccupied at the moment of dreaming. This
procedure we illustrated in Volume I[2] and again in our last
chapter.

Our next step in mapping out the cognitive structure of a
dream is to reconstruct its pattern of organization. This we do
by interpolating between the focal conflict and the manifest
content of the dream. In this chapter we shall illustrate this second step by further examples.

The focal conflict (FC)[3] in the bridge dream $(10a)$[4] is one
between sexual impulses toward the analyst and the dependent
need for her love and approval. To reconstruct the pattern of
organization of this dream, we interpolate two steps between this
focal conflict and the manifest dream content (see Fig. 4).

1. See chap. iv, p. 26.
2. See pp. 84–93 and 171–73, reprinted in the Appendix to this volume
(pp. 342–52).
3. Summary of symbols and their meanings (for this chapter and Figs.
4–10):

FC = focal conflict
T = manifest dream (dream text)
A = first interpolated version of dream text
B = second interpolated version of dream text
R = present opportunity (facilitating reality)
H_R = hope based on present reality
H_M = hope based on reassuring memory
X = in conflict with
↑ = activating
‖ = facilitating influence of hope

4. See I, 79–80, 84–88, reprinted in the Appendix (pp. 335, 343–46, and 349).

1. First, a conflict between sexual wishes toward a younger woman and fear of offending her mother (version A) has been substituted for the focal conflict (FC), in which the analyst is both the object of his sexual wishes and the mother-figure whom he is afraid of offending.

2. Then, in the manifest dream (T) we find two successive reactions to the conflict about sexual wishes toward the younger woman. ($2a$) First he gives harmless outlet to his sexual wishes by giving the girl a playful pinch. ($2b$) Then, returning the girl to her mother, he wins the mother's thanks and a glass of milk.

($2c$) The final episode in the dream text also achieves a direct solution of the deeper (focal) conflict by giving the dreamer "cool refreshing milk" as an oral substitute for sexual gratification, as well as thanks and approval from the same mother-figure.

As we have already pointed out,[5] the pattern of organization of a dream is determined not only by its focal conflict but also by the hopes about which it is organized. The focal conflict is only one pole of the organization process; the dream's organizing hopes are the other pole. In the bridge dream the organizing hopes are: (H_M) the hope of pleasing a mother by returning her daughter to her (based presumably on reassuring adolescent memories); and (H_R) the hope of pleasing the analyst by bringing her a dream (based on present reality).

We have represented these relations diagrammatically in Figure 4.

The anvil dream (12)[6] is again a reaction to the patient's sexual[7] wishes toward the analyst. He is again in conflict between his sexual wishes and his need to be loved by her as a mother.

We reconstruct the pattern of organization of this dream (12) by interpolating three steps between this focal conflict (FC) and the manifest dream content (T) (see Fig. 6):

5. See chap. iv, p. 27.

6. See I, 80–81, 88–90, reprinted in the Appendix (pp. 336 and 346–47).

7. We are deliberately postponing discussing the underlying hostility toward a brother-figure (see Vol. I, chap. xxiii) until later chapters (see Secs. IV and V of this volume).

1. The conflict between his sexual wishes and his need to be loved is intolerable. Therefore, he turns away from the mother, who tempts him, to the father, who used to beat him severely. Better be punished by father (version *A*) than totally estranged from mother!

2. This solution is too painful. The next step in the dream work tries to protect him from submitting to so much pain. Retiring into the role of observer, he substitutes an iron bar to be beaten in his stead. For the memory of being beaten by his father, he substitutes a scene in the blacksmith shop, where he used to admire and perhaps envy his father's strength and skill (version *B*).

3. The third step is a direct reaction to the analytic situation. The patient has had doubts about the ability of a woman to beat him into shape; but the analyst's interpretations of his first dreams have reassured him. He admires her skill as he used to admire his father's skill in the blacksmith shop. Perhaps, after all, a woman can do a man's work! In the manifest dream he has given expression to this reassuring thought (H_R) by picturing his mother as skilfully playing the father's role in the blacksmith shop.

We summarize these relations diagrammatically in Figure 6.

The focal conflict *in the fireplug dream* $(19a)$[8] is again one between sexual wishes toward the analyst and fear of offending her. In the pattern of dream organization (see Fig. 5), the intermediate version (A) that we must interpolate differs slightly for the two episodes, (a) and (b), of the dream text:

($1a$). The first step in the process of organization of episode (a) is to substitute a child for the analyst in both roles; he fears to offend a child by his erotic wishes toward her. ($2a$) The second step finds a solution for this conflict: In the dream text he wins erotic response from the girl by helping her carry a water can.

($1b$) In the intermediate version (Ab) of episode (b), fear of offending the girl's mother emerges; the conflict has become one between erotic impulses toward the girl and fear of offending

8. See I, 167–68 and 173, reprinted in the Appendix (pp. 340–41 and 352).

her mother. (2*b*) The second step in the pattern of dream organization protects the dreamer from this conflict by having the mother call the girl and thus interrupt their embrace.

The focal conflict in *the pencil-stealing dream* (25)[9] is between the patient's temptation to respond to the analyst's apparent permissiveness for forbidden (sexual) impulses and his fear of offending her as a mother-figure.
The pattern of dream organization can be resolved into two steps (see Fig. 9):
1. The first step has substituted the trivial symbolic act of stealing the analyst's pencils and pad for the forbidden sexual impulses that threaten to estrange him from her.
2. In the second step the analyst's office has been replaced by the freight yard, where the patient works, as the place of temptation; and the analyst's two conflicting roles have been divided between two men, a permissive switchman and a forbidding watchman.

The focal conflict in *the borrowed book dream* (27)[10] is one of guilt on account of hostile wishes toward a person[11] from whom he is receiving help. In this dream we can understand the pattern of organization without interpolating intermediate versions between the focal conflict (*FC*) and the dream text (*T*). The dream text has two parts, each of which is a denial that the patient has any guilt or obligation toward the analyst (see Fig. 10):
1. First, he pictures a woman as (merely) returning something that she has borrowed.
2. Then she tells him that what she gives him is worthless.

In *the Mexican woman dream* (44)[12] the focal conflict (*FC₂*) is again one between sexual wishes toward the analyst and his

---

9. See I, 169–70 and 173, reprinted in the Appendix (pp. 342 and 352).
10. See pp. 32–33 and 43 of this volume.
11. The patient is receiving help from the analyst. Impulses to "mistreat" her child are felt as hostile impulses toward the analyst herself.
12. See pp. 36–37 and 47–48 of this volume.

need to be loved by her as a mother. Yet behind this sexual conflict we sense a conflict (FC_1) between hostility toward a brother-figure (the patient's son) and need for a mother's love. As in the bridge dream (10a), we suspect that the sexual conflict has arisen by mitigation[13] of a hostile impulse into an erotic one.

We reconstruct the process of organization of this dream (44) by interpolating two steps between the sexual conflict (FC_2) and the manifest dream (T) (see Fig. 7):

1. In the first step the patient finds his way back to acceptance by the analyst-mother by fantasying himself being scrubbed by her.

2. The next step is to relieve himself of the pain of being scrubbed by substituting a child to be scrubbed in his stead.

By this second step he also finds a well-rationalized outlet for the underlying hostility to his son as a rival for a mother's love.

We have represented these relations diagrammatically in Figure 7.

In *the fire-tending dream* (45a)[14] again sexual wishes toward the analyst are in conflict with fear of offending her as a mother.

To reconstruct the pattern of organization of this dream, we must again interpolate two steps between this focal conflict (FC) and the dream text (T) (see Fig. 8).

1. First, he turns away from the seductive analyst, whom he now condemns as a prostitute, to the company of men at a stag party.

2. However, in the second step he turns back to the analyst, having found a way of making her respectable again by substituting for her sexual interpretation the "lady's" harmless request that he stir up the fire.

13. See Vol. I, chaps. xx and xxi.
14. See pp. 37-38 and 48 of this volume.

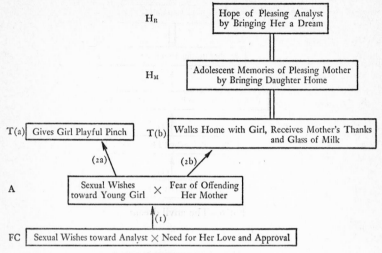

FIG. 4.—The bridge dream

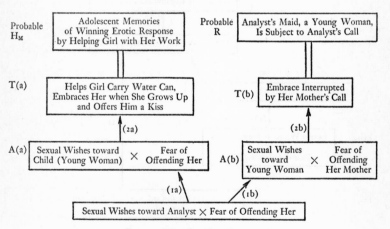

FIG. 5.—The fireplug dream

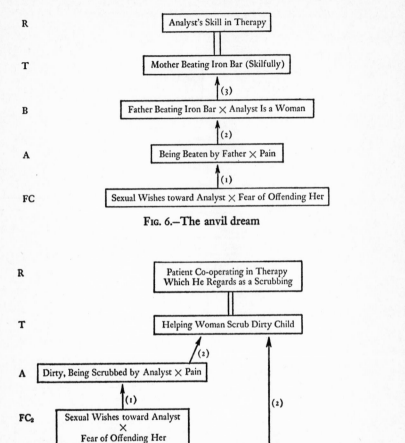

R   Analyst's Skill in Therapy

T   Mother Beating Iron Bar (Skilfully)

(3)

B   Father Beating Iron Bar × Analyst Is a Woman

(2)

A   Being Beaten by Father × Pain

(1)

FC   Sexual Wishes toward Analyst × Fear of Offending Her

FIG. 6.—The anvil dream

R   Patient Co-operating in Therapy Which He Regards as a Scrubbing

T   Helping Woman Scrub Dirty Child

(2)

A   Dirty, Being Scrubbed by Analyst × Pain

(1)

FC₂   Sexual Wishes toward Analyst × Fear of Offending Her

(2)

FC₁   Hostile Wishes toward Son × Fear of Offending Analyst (Analyst's Child)

FIG. 7.—The Mexican woman dream

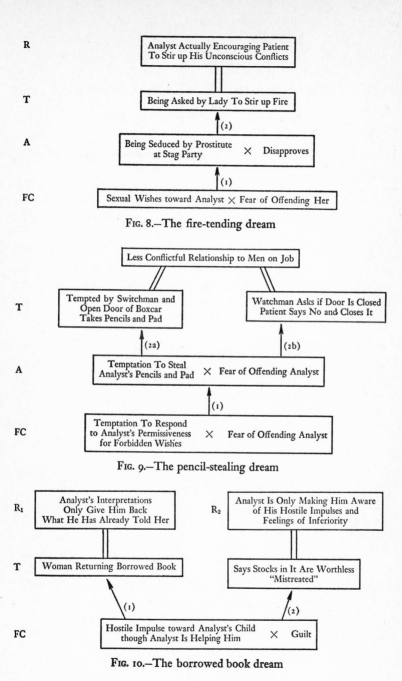

R   Analyst Actually Encouraging Patient
To Stir up His Unconscious Conflicts

T   Being Asked by Lady To Stir up Fire

(2)

A   Being Seduced by Prostitute
at Stag Party   ×   Disapproves

(1)

FC   Sexual Wishes toward Analyst × Fear of Offending Her

FIG. 8.—The fire-tending dream

Less Conflictful Relationship to Men on Job

T   Tempted by Switchman and
Open Door of Boxcar
Takes Pencils and Pad   Watchman Asks if Door Is Closed
Patient Says No and Closes It

(2a)   (2b)

A   Temptation To Steal
Analyst's Pencils and Pad   ×   Fear of Offending Analyst

(1)

FC   Temptation To Respond
to Analyst's Permissiveness   ×   Fear of Offending Analyst
for Forbidden Wishes

FIG. 9.—The pencil-stealing dream

R₁   Analyst's Interpretations
Only Give Him Back
What He Has Already Told Her   R₂   Analyst Is Only Making Him Aware
of His Hostile Impulses and
Feelings of Inferiority

T   Woman Returning Borrowed Book   Says Stocks in It Are Worthless
"Mistreated"

(1)   (2)

FC   Hostile Impulse toward Analyst's Child
though Analyst Is Helping Him   ×   Guilt

FIG. 10.—The borrowed book dream

CHAPTER VIII

Checks on Our Reconstructions

We can check our reconstruction of the pattern of organization of one dream by comparing it with later similar dreams.

Bridge Dream and Fireplug Dream.—For example, in the bridge dream (10a), we interpreted the patient's pinching the girl as a playful erotic gesture; and the fact that her mother thanked him for walking home with her daughter in the dusk suggested an underlying conflict between sexual wishes toward the daughter and fear of offending the mother. This conflict, which we reconstructed as *version A* in the pattern of organization *of the bridge dream* (10a), *appears almost without disguise in the text of the fireplug dream* (19a), when the patient's embrace of the girl is interrupted by her mother's calling her (cf. Figs. 4 and 5).

We also suspected that in the bridge dream (10a) the glass of milk which the patient received from the girl's mother served as a substitute for sexual gratification. A closely parallel detail in the fireplug dream (19a) tends to confirm this interpretation. Just as he wins the mother's thanks and a glass of milk from the mother by returning her daughter to her in the bridge dream, so he wins the girl's thanks and a kiss by helping her carry a water can in the fireplug dream (19a).

We can test our reconstruction still more rigorously by trying to account for the differences between the two dreams in terms of events that have occurred in the interval between them. In Volume I[1] we have already attempted such an analysis: In the interval between the two dreams (10a and 19a) the analyst's interpretations had destroyed the patient's hopes that he might win her by renouncing his erotic impulses, but had awakened a new hope that she might even approve of his erotic impulses. The differences between the two dreams (10a and 19a) are a direct effect of this modification of the pattern of the patient's hopes and fears. At the time of the fireplug dream (19a) he has no longer any

1. See chap. xxxvi.

incentive to try to win the analyst by renouncing his erotic wishes; but her apparent tolerance does encourage him to act on them, and this mobilizes his underlying conflict between these erotic wishes and his fear of offending the mother.[2]

An Obscure Detail in the Anvil Dream.—We use later dreams not only to check our reconstructions but also to throw light on obscure details of earlier dreams. When the significance of a dream detail cannot be guessed from the psychological context alone, we wait for a similar detail in a later dream to reveal its meaning more clearly.

Such an obscure detail is the iron bar that is being beaten in the anvil dream (12). We have recognized that this dream is protecting the patient from his need for punishment by substituting an iron bar to be beaten in his place; but we do not yet know why it must be an iron bar that is to be beaten upon the anvil.

Behind this question is hidden a more important problem. In the anvil dream (12) neither dream text nor associations reveal the exact content of the impulses for which the patient must be punished. Perhaps the iron bar symbolizes the content of these disturbing wishes.

Checks on the Use of Symbol Interpretation.—We have deliberately avoided making use of the dream symbolism in interpreting this patient's dreams. To analysts with sure intuitions, symbol interpretation is a valuable tool; but this method of interpretation is also easy to abuse. When fascinated by translating symbols, we can easily lose ourselves in a maze of "interpretations" that have no relation to real life. We should, therefore, carefully check interpretations that are suggested only by the dream symbolism.

The most important test of any interpretation is to find out whether it makes good sense in the psychological context of the

2. This comparison illustrates one way in which psychoanalytic therapy can modify a patient's reaction patterns. The analyst's understanding and interpretations of the patient's disturbing impulses tend to destroy his hopes of hiding them from her; but her tolerant and encouraging attitude tends to induce new hopes of her indulgence. Consequently, impulses that previously had to be repressed or renounced tend to become manifest; and an impulse or problem that was activated as an intermediate phase in the pattern of organization of an earlier dream often appears much less disguised or even undisguised in the text of a later dream.

dream and associated dream thoughts. To test the correctness of a symbol interpretation, we must first insist that it be consistent with the interpretation arrived at, without the aid of symbols, by fitting the dream into its emotional context. Then, as a further check on our symbol interpretations, we should wait for later material. The next time that the patient alludes to the same topics or uses the same symbols, his associations may permit us to fill in more completely the psychological context.

Anvil Dream and Fire-tending Dream.—A rigid bar usually symbolizes an erect penis. This interpretation meets our first test: it fits well into our interpretation made from the psychological context of the anvil dream (12). The iron bar, symbolizing an erect penis, represents directly the sexual wishes for which the dreamer needs to be beaten.

The associations give us the additional clue that this iron bar is used to remove clinkers from the furnace of a locomotive; but the psychological context tells us nothing more about the significance of this detail.

Can we now check our interpretation of the iron-bar symbol by reference to a later dream? The symbolic act of removing ashes from a stove occurs again in the fire-tending dream (45a), in a psychological context that reveals its significance more clearly. From the associations we learn that this fire-tending dream (45a) is a reaction both to the sexual temptation at the picnic and to interpretations in the last analytic session which the patient evidently felt to be seductive. The dream text says nothing about sexual temptation but has substituted the lady's request that the patient stir up the fire. In this context it is evident that the stove symbolizes a woman; that fire is symbolic of sexual excitement; and stirring up the fire, of coitus.

This interpretation of the stove and fire symbolism in the fire-tending dream (45a) corresponds to and confirms our interpretation of the iron bar in the anvil dream (12) as a phallic symbol; but the significance of removing ashes from a stove is not yet indicated by the psychological context of either dream (12 and 45a). We shall inquire later[3] into the meaning of this symbolism.

3. See chap. xviii of this volume.

Patterns of Organization of the Two Dreams.—We shall now compare the patterns of organization of these two dreams (12 and 45*a*) and then check our reconstructions by trying to account for the differences between them in terms of the events that have occurred in the interval between them.

In reconstructing the pattern of organization of the anvil dream (12), we have not yet taken account of the fact that the iron bar was substituted not only to receive a beating but also as symbol of the patient's sexual wishes toward the mother. According to our first reconstruction, the iron bar was substituted for the patient in the fantasy of his being beaten by the father. The motive for this substitution was to make the beating fantasy less painful. But our study of the dream symbolism has led us to the conclusion that the substitution of the iron bar occurred earlier, that another step must be interpolated in which the iron bar was substituted for the patient's sexual wishes toward the mother. In Figure 11*a* we have made this interpolation.

Let us now compare the pattern of organization of the anvil dream (12) with that of the fire-tending dream (45*a*) (cf. Figs. 11*a* and 11*b*). In both dreams the symbol of stirring up the fire in a stove has been substituted for the patient's sexual impulses toward the mother; but at this point the two patterns of organization begin to diverge. In the anvil dream (12) the patient reacts to his sexual impulses toward the mother with a need for punishment, which activates, first, the memory of being beaten by the father and then the fantasy of the iron bar being beaten by the father; in the fire-tending dream (45*a*), instead of being punished, he is being encouraged to remove the ashes and stir up the fire.

However, on closer scrutiny we find a motive in the fire-tending dream (45*a*) that parallels the need for punishment in the anvil dream (12). In the fire-tending dream (45*a*), instead of himself needing punishment, he condemns the "lady" as a prostitute.

When we take account of this parallel, the patterns of organization of the two dreams (12 and 45*a*) become closely analogous. In the pattern of organization of each dream the patient first turns away from the woman who is tempting him to a father-figure; but he is then able to find his way back to the analyst: In the anvil dream (12) he turns to the father for punishment (mechanism *1a* in the diagram); but then, reassuring himself that the analyst, too, is a good clean workman, he turns back to her (mechanism *3a*). In the fire-tending dream (45*a*), condemning his "seductive" analyst as a prostitute, he turns from her to the company of men (mechanism *1b*); but then he turns back to her (mechanism *3b*) as a "lady" who is making the harmless request that he stir up the fire.

Effects of Intervening Events.—Thus these two dreams (12 and 45*a*) agree in condemning sexual impulses. Even in the fire-tending dream (45*a*) his identifying the analyst with a prostitute shows that he is still much influenced by his mother's condemnation of sexual impulses. However, the fire-tending dream (45*a*) is able to discriminate between the analyst's encouraging or "seductive" attitude (in the dream text) and the mother's condemning attitude toward sexual impulses (implicit in his condemnation of the analyst); whereas the anvil dream (12), which identified the analyst with a punitive mother, was unable to make this distinction. In order to account for the difference between the two dreams (12, 45*a*), we must assume that in the interval between them the patient has made progress in distinguishing between his analyst's tolerant attitude and his mother's condemning attitude toward his sexual wishes.

Review of the course of the analysis during this interval confirms this assumption and accounts rather fully for the new features in the later dream (45*a*). After the anvil dream (12) he began to realize that the analyst's attitude was therapeutic rather than punitive (see kindly policeman dream, 17); and soon afterward (in the fireplug dream, 19*a*) he responded to his sense of the analyst's encouragement by kissing and embracing the young girl. His increased boldness was short lived and promptly mobilized his fear of the mother; after the pencil-stealing dream (25), in deference to this fear, he repudiated the analyst's encouragement. However, after a long period of resistance his repudiation of her again yielded to her encouragement. After the confession elicited by the analyst's interpretation of his sexual wishes in the 41st hour, he responded with a much better sense of co-operating in what the analyst was really encouraging him to do. He tried to continue his confession (dream 43), then pictured himself as helping scrub a boy who represented his own dirty impulses (dream 44). Evidently he was not only recovering from the preceding period of resistance but also discriminating much more realistically between his mother and his analyst than he had previously been able to do.

The fire-tending dream (45a) belongs to this dream sequence (41, 43, 44, 45a, 46a) and corresponds closely to what we should expect after the series of events that we have just reviewed. As in the preceding resistance period, there is still a need to project and repudiate his "dirty thoughts" (i.e., the dirty food, 39; the dirty water, 41; the dirty pigs, 43; the dirty little boy, 44; and now, finally, the prostitute, 45a); but his capacity to discriminate between analyst and mother has increased, and his fear of the analyst's encouragement has correspondingly diminished. Now he can come much nearer to making a confession (41st hour, dream 43) than he could in the pencil-stealing dream (25); he can conceive of the treatment as a scrubbing (dream 44) instead of a beating (dream 12); he can co-operate in the treatment (dream 44) instead of only watching and admiring the mother (dream 12); and, finally, he can picture the mobilizing of his sexual wishes in the analysis as a harmless stirring-up of a fire (dream 45a) instead of needing to be beaten for them (dream 12).

Thus we have checked our interpretation of the phallic significance of the iron bar in the anvil dream (12) by a method similar to the one we used in checking our reconstruction of the bridge dream: first, by finding a later dream (45a) in which the meaning of the same symbolism is clear directly from the psychological context, and then by showing that the differences between the two dreams (12 and 45a) are adequately accounted for by events that have occurred in the interval between them.

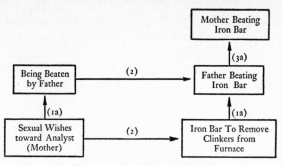

FIG. 11*a*.–Anvil dream (12)

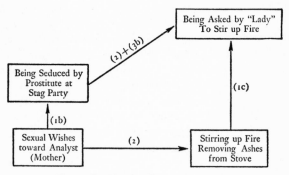

FIG. 11*b*.–Fire-tending dream (45*a*)

KEY* TO MECHANISMS AND MOTIVES (FIGS. 11*a* AND 11*b*)

(1*a*) Turning to father for punishment, in reaction to fear of offending the mother.

(1*b*) Turning to men–projecting guilt by condemning analyst as prostitute.

(1*c*) Projecting responsibility on analyst but without condemnation.

(2) Deanimation of conflict†–motivated by need to make conflict and resultant need for punishment less painful.

(3) Return to admiring relationship to analyst:
  (3*a*) As a punitive figure.
  (3*b*) With continued projection of responsibility.

* In this figure and in a number of later figures, we have changed our form for diagraming the pattern of dream organization. In the earlier diagrams (see Figs. 1–10) we represented each version as a conflict (e.g., sexual wish toward analyst × fear of offending her); we have simplified Fig. 11 and later diagrams somewhat by representing only the disturbing wish (or fantasy) in each version. Then we add a "Key to Mechanisms and Motives" in which we indicate the reactive motive that is responsible for each step in the pattern of dream organization (e.g., 1*a*—turning to father for punishment—in reaction to fear of offending mother).

† See chap. xxvi of this volume for further discussion of the motivation of this step.

SECTION III

Historical Background of the Water Symbolism

CHAPTER IX

Systematic Interpretation of Symbols

In the next few chapters we shall discuss symbol interpretation. The dream symbolism is a highly condensed record of the dreamer's past experience. It records not only his individual past experience but also that of the culture in which he was brought up and probably much of the biological history of his race,[1] as well.

In the course of a psychoanalytic treatment the patient's past gradually unfolds to our understanding. If we can understand the language of his dream symbolism, we can speed up this process very much. The dream symbolism can tell us many things that the patient will be able to remember consciously only after many months, if at all.

Yet symbol interpretation is an intuitive art, whose value depends on the skill of the person who uses it. To develop a more scientific procedure, we should formulate explicitly the premises on which we base our symbol interpretations. Accordingly, even at the risk of seeming pedantic, we shall try in the following chapters to spell out both the reasoning by which we arrive at interpretive hypotheses and the methods by which we check them. As our first example we shall try to reconstruct the historical background of the water symbolism in our patient's dreams.

Symbol Translation.—As starting point, we return to a detail of the bridge dream (10a), for which we have not yet found an explanation. We still do not know why the girl is leaning on a bridge looking at boats on the river. There is nothing in the psychological context to explain this detail. This bridge was a place where the patient used to meet girls, but this does not explain why the dream should have selected just this place of rendezvous or why the girl should be "leaning on the bridge, watching boats."

The most usual approach to dream symbolism might be called

1. See S. Ferenczi, 1924.

67

"symbol translation." Certain objects have well-nigh universal symbolic meanings. Water, bridges, and boats are a few of the best known of these universal symbols. A bridge is often a symbol of coitus. Water and boats suggests the theme of pregnancy. In the bridge dream the patient is returning a daughter to her mother; perhaps the dream symbolism is alluding to an unconscious fantasy of giving the mother a child.

This kind of "symbol translation" might be compared to trying to read a paragraph in a foreign language when we know only a few of the words and have no understanding of the grammatical structure of the language. The symbolism of a dream is an organic part of the dream's cognitive structure; and we can understand a dream's symbolism only by discovering how it fits into the cognitive structure of the whole dream.

A Symbol Interpretation Should Fit into the Psychological Context.—Let us try again. Water, and especially flowing water, has another universal significance—as a symbol of urination. This meaning of the water symbolism fits more directly into the psychological context of the bridge dream (10a). In this dream the patient fears that his sexual wishes will offend his mother; but we do not know much about the content of these sexual wishes. Receiving a glass of milk from the mother implies a craving for oral gratification. However, since this wish is acceptable to the mother, it cannot be the one that he must renounce for fear of offending her; a desire to urinate, symbolized by the river, may be the repressed sexual wish that we are looking for. If so, we can recognize the bridge as a symbol of the patient's mastery of that wish. Renouncing this wish, he treats it as an impersonal force outside himself, as a river which he can walk over on a bridge.

We can elaborate this interpretation further. Back of the erotic gesture—pinching the girl—we have recognized a hostile impulse toward both her and her brother. Perhaps the river is symbolic also of the patient's hostile impulses toward the girl. One can drown in a river. Perhaps the bridge is a symbol of his renunciation of a wish to drown the girl and of his successful defense against it. The bridge protects the girl by lifting her up out of reach of the dangerous river.

In this series of interpretations we have illustrated the first principle of a properly critical approach to symbol interpretation: We start not with the symbol but with our usual attempt to understand the dream from its psychological context. A sound symbol interpretation must fit into and round out the interpretation arrived at directly from the emotional context. As we have already stated, we should try to find out how the dream symbolism fits into the cognitive structure of the dream as a whole.

"Functional" Interpretation of Symbols.—An airplane pilot has his motors checked frequently on the ground, so that he may fly with more assurance while he is in the air. Similarly, when we know that we are going to check our interpretations systematically, we can feel safer in giving free rein to our interpretive imagination.

We shall next discuss what we shall call a "functional"[2] approach to the interpretation of symbols.

In the customary method of symbol interpretation, which Stekel discovered and Freud later accepted, a symbol represents some object or act, usually a person, or a part of the body, or some physiological function. Thus a house may represent a woman; a person within an inclosed space may be a symbol of pregnancy; swimming, a symbol of coitus; being rescued from water, a symbol of birth.

We can supplement this kind of symbol translation by taking account of the ordinary function of the object used as a symbol. Dreams are trying to fulfil wishes and to satisfy the fundamental needs underlying them. We expect them to be concerned with the usual functions of common objects in relation to human needs. Accordingly, when an object is used as a symbol, we ask how its ordinary functional significance fits into the adaptive problem with which the dream is struggling.

We return to the symbol of the girl leaning on a bridge looking at boats on the river. What is the ordinary function of a boat? By keeping us on top of the water, a boat protects us from getting wet or from drowning. Of course, we use it also to get across a

2. Our functional approach is an extension and elaboration of Silberer's "functional" interpretation of symbols (see H. Silberer, 1911*a* and *b* and 1912).

body of water; but a boat can get us across the water only if it can keep us from drowning in it.

The function of a bridge is similar. We use a bridge to get over a stream without falling into the water. A bridge, like a boat, is a symbol well suited to reassure a dreamer against the fear of drowning.

This functional significance of a bridge and of boats fits well into our context interpretation of this dream, in which we have already recognized that the bridge lifts the girl up out of reach of the dangerous river.

We turn next to the functional significance of water. Water is something to drink and something that we excrete;[3] it is also something that we sometimes choke over when we try to drink it. This mishap, though unusual in adult life, is much more common in infancy; and few people escape profound early impressions of the danger of drowning in deep water.

Can these facts help us understand the symbolism of the bridge dream? We suspect that the river symbolizes a sexual impulse to urinate on the girl and also a hostile impulse to drown her. Can drinking be fitted into this context? Perhaps the fantasy is one of urinating into her mouth or of her drinking the dreamer's urine; the connection between drinking and choking may be the one already suggested, of choking over what one is drinking. Actually, this dream (10a) ends with the patient drinking a glass of milk. Still it is not yet clear how all these suggestions might fit together into a single cognitive structure.

Literal Implications of the Dream Symbolism.—Another way of reasoning about symbols is to try to account for the implications of the symbolism literally and as completely as possible. We shall discuss later[4] how this principle can be used to test our interpretations; but we can also use it to help us elaborate our interpretive hypotheses. If the bridge protects the girl from drowning, why is the patient also on top of it? Is he, too, in danger of being

---

3. We do not mention separately the use of water for washing because psychoanalysis has shown so clearly that washing serves as both a sublimation of, and a reaction formation against, pleasure in the excretory functions.

4. See chap. xii of this volume.

drowned? Does he fear that someone will do to him what he is impelled to do to the girl? Perhaps he fantasies that someone will urinate into his mouth and that he will choke over it. If so, drinking milk may have been substituted as a much less alarming alternative for this disturbing fantasy.

Our Deductions Must Next Be Checked.—Evidently we have elaborated our interpretation far beyond anything that our knowledge of the dream context alone could justify. We have done so deliberately, to test our proposed methods of reasoning about symbols. By carefully fitting the common-sense implications of the dream symbolism into the total dream context, we believe that we can safely make deductions far beyond what we can learn directly from the dream and its context alone.

However, our functional approach has so far yielded us only a few suggestive hints. To test these suggestions, we must determine whether they fit together into an intelligible picture of the cognitive structure of the dream as a whole. This we shall be able to do only after we have checked what we have surmised, by careful comparison with later dreams.

CHAPTER X

More Transparent Symbolism in a Later Dream

Another Dream a Year Later.—We skip ahead to a dream reported thirteen months later in the analysis.

In the interim there had been much discussion of the patient's sexual wishes toward mother and analyst and of his hostility to brother-figures. He had gained little insight into his hostility toward brothers and sisters but had acquired considerable tolerance of discussion of the sexual impulses. In the hours immediately preceding the dream next to be reported, he had even confessed some sexual interest in the analyst.

The following dream was reported in the 115th hour:

Dream 115.—Some place in basement of a building; floor flooded. We had to stay there and walk in that dirty water. A girl was fixing up a cot for my little boy to sleep on. We were washing our faces in the dirty water. Lot dirty too, all muddy.

In answer to the analyst's question, the patient adds that the mattress was muddy and that there were no sheets. Anyway, it was all dirty. In association the patient recalls that his own basement had been flooded several times and that he had had to go down and wash it. In the dream he was barefoot. The girl is a neighbor, a pretty, attractive girl of twenty-two or twenty-four years. The boy is the girl's brother. The patient supposes he was attracted by the girl lots of times. The boy is the same age as the patient's younger son. No, a year older. Eleven years. When the patient was that age, he was attracted by "that girl" minding the baby (a few hours before he had admitted having made sexual advances to her). She wasn't so old, only two or three years older than he. He recalls being scolded by his mother.

In association to the dirty water: he thinks sex is dirty . . . perhaps he dirtied the mattress when he had a wet dream. In response to the analyst's suggestion that sex is soiling, he says he was taught that sex was something dirty (he spits as he says this).

"You spoil the girl's body. There is a lot of guilt behind it all
right. ..."

In answer to the analyst's interpretations of sexual impulses
toward the mother and in the transference, he surmises that he
may have been attracted by his mother's legs. He has seen his
mother's legs many times when she scrubbed the floor. There is
no doubt that she was pretty attractive. She always stayed young.
She had a big chest and bosom, small waist. Round hips, and legs
were shapely. He always did admire mother's youth and shape.
Naturally he didn't reveal it to anyone, denies it to himself, because it would be a sin (he becomes hoarse at this point). Yes,
he recalls seeing the mother naked once. She was taking a bath
behind a screen. He was sitting in the opposite corner and could
peek through the folds of the screen. He was about five or six.

Interpretive Comment.—As the patient indicates in his associations, this dream (115) is a reaction to discussion of his sexual
wishes in the preceding hours. To the dirty water he associates
sex. The girl reminds him of one to whom he once made sexual
advances. The wet mattress suggests to him that he might have
soiled the mattress with a wet dream. To us the flood of dirty
water suggests even more plainly the infantile equivalent of a wet
dream—enuresis.

Evidently the patient is struggling again with the problem that
was so central in his earlier dreams. The flood dream (115), like
the bridge dream (10a), is trying to reconcile his sexual impulses
toward the analyst with his need for a mother's love. More specifically, this dream (115) is a reaction to his free discussion of sex
in the preceding hours and particularly to his confession, in the
hour before, of sexual interest in the analyst.

Such sexual wishes stir up anxiety in this patient. In his associations he recalls that his mother reproved him sharply for his sexual advances to a young girl in the home. Now he can reassure
himself that the analyst encourages free discussion of his sexual
impulses; but he also depreciates her for her tolerance. He shares
his mother's feeling that sex is dirty, and he identifies the analyst
not with his mother but with the young girl to whom he dared
make sexual advances. The manifest content of the dream expresses well this mixture of secret satisfaction with conscious de-

preciation of the tolerant attitude of the analyst. The analyst, too, is "walking in that dirty water" and "washing her face in the dirty water."

Water and Room Symbolism.—In this flood dream (115) we can interpret the water symbolism directly from the psychological context. The dream is evidently based on a fantasy of having wet the bed in reaction to an impulse to urinate upon the girl. Yet these fantasies do not appear in the dream text. In place of his impulse to urinate, there appears in the dream text a flood. Instead of representing directly his sexual impulse toward the young woman, the dream tells of a flood that has entered a basement. Just those elements that have been denied direct expression in the dream text have been represented in the dream symbolism.

CHAPTER XI

Historical Analysis of Flood Dream

We are now ready to begin a historical analysis of the flood dream (115).

Every conflict, we assume, has a past history. Since the patient has been struggling with the same conflict for more than a year, he should have learned by this time that the analyst does not disapprove free discussion of his sexual impulses. His confession in the last hour is evidence that he is aware of her tolerant attitude. Yet he still feels that his sexual impulses are dirty. Evidently his depreciation of his sexual wishes must be based on earlier memories.

Not long before this dream (115) the patient reported such a memory: Once his mother rebuked him for making sexual advances to a girl who was taking care of a baby in his mother's home. From his associations we learn that he was eleven years old when this occurred; the eleven-year-old boy in the dream text is an allusion to this memory.

Evidently the dream work has substituted a corrected version of the disturbing memory. Instead of recalling his sexual advances to the girl, the dream (115) implies that the eleven-year-old boy has wet his bed. The implied fantasy is that the patient was not the boy who made sexual advances but the baby whom the girl was taking care of. We reconstruct the motive for this substitution as follows: If a very young infant wets the bed, the mother just makes the bed again. By substituting the infantile impulse to wet the bed for his sexual impulse toward the analyst, the patient now hopes to assure himself of the same kind of tolerant treatment. In spite of his depreciation of the analyst, he is not sure of the tolerance that he condemns her for. To be sure that she will not reprove him as his mother did, he must make himself an infant and substitute urination for genital sexuality.

To account for the way this memory is elaborated in the dream text (115), we interpolate three successive substitutions:

75

1. Wetting the bed has been substituted for the patient's sexual impulses toward the girl. We have just discussed the motivation of this substitution.

2. The patient's eleven-year-old son, whom he also identifies with the girl's eleven-year-old brother, has been substituted for the patient. The motive for this substitution is pride; nearly every child is sooner or later shamed out of wetting the bed. By attributing this impulse to his own son, the patient not only disavows it but soothes his pride further by reminding himself that he is a father.

3. In the third substitution both the impulse to wet the bed and the fantasy of urinating on the young woman have been rejected even more energetically. In the dream text these impulses are recognized not even as the impulses of his son but as an impersonal force, a flood that has entered the basement. To account for this substitution, we postulate that the guilt based on the mother's condemnation of his sexual impulses still attaches to the impulse to wet the bed and to the accompanying fantasy of urinating on the girl.

We assume that this guilt, too, has a history. At some time in the patient's childhood, impulses to urinate must have served as a significant outlet for his sexual cravings and must have incurred the mother's disapproval, just as his adolescent genital impulses later did. Probably the water symbolism of the flood dream (115) is based on dreams and fantasies of the patient's childhood that accompanied his wetting the bed. We assume that these enuretic fantasies, too, were reactions to earlier occurrences in real life, that they reflect some earlier event in which the patient incurred the mother's displeasure, perhaps by urinating upon her or in her presence in reaction to infantile sexual excitement.

Thus in our historical reconstruction we postulate that each step in the process of dream organization is polarized between memories of two kinds: (1) a disturbing or traumatic memory and (2) a reassuring or satisfying memory (see Fig. 12). In this case the associations to the dream (115) led us directly to the disturbing memory about which the dream is organized, and we deduced schematically the other memories necessary to account for the dream work.

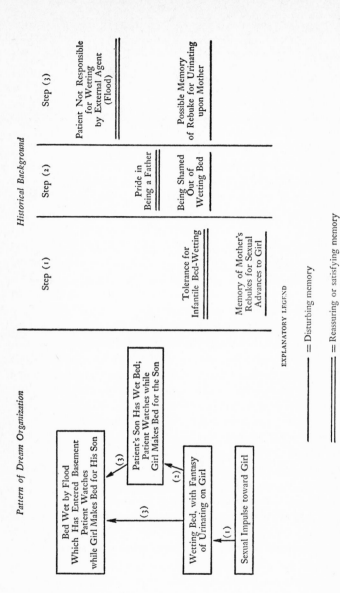

Pattern of Dream Organization

Bed Wet by Flood
Which Has Entered Basement
Patient Watches
while Girl Makes Bed for His Son

(3)

Patient's Son Has Wet Bed;
Patient Watches while
Girl Makes Bed for the Son

(3)

(2)

Wetting Bed, with Fantasy
of Urinating on Girl

(1)

Sexual Impulse toward Girl

Historical Background

	Step (1)	Step (2)	Step (3)

Tolerance for
Infantile Bed-Wetting

Pride in
Being a Father

Patient Not Responsible
for Wetting
by External Agent
(Flood)

Being
Shamed
Out of
Wetting Bed

Memory of Mother's
Rebukes for Sexual
Advances to Girl

Possible Memory
of Rebuke for Urinating
upon Mother

EXPLANATORY LEGEND

——— = Disturbing memory

===== = Reassuring or satisfying memory

FIG. 12.—Historical analysis (partial) of flood dream

CHAPTER XII

Literal Interpretation of Dream Symbolism

Reconstruction of Repressed Memories.—Psychoanalysts used to devote much effort to attempts to reconstruct repressed memories. To check our reconstructions, we waited for the patient to recover conscious memory of the events that we had reconstructed. Usually we had to wait a long time.

Later (1914) Freud pointed out that the patient tends to relive past events that he cannot bring back to consciousness. Such reliving of past events constitutes a more elementary kind of remembering. Freud utilized this principle extensively both to reconstruct the patient's past and also to check his reconstructions.[1] Our reconstructions in the last chapter were based on a systematic application of this same principle. We started with the assumption that in the pattern of organization of a dream each step is based on past experience, on a reaction pattern from the past.

Freud's criterion for an adequate dream interpretation was that it should account for every detail of the dream text. In the next few chapters we hope to show that we can make our systematic reconstruction procedure both more effective and more trustworthy by applying this criterion very strictly: by trying to account in literal detail for the text of the manifest dream, including its symbolism.

Unexplained Details in the Flood Dream.—When judged by this criterion, several details of the symbolism of the flood dream (115) puzzle us. According to our interpretation, the flood entering the basement is a projected representation of the dreamer's fantasy of urinating upon (into) the girl or upon the mother for whom the girl has been substituted. If so, the basement must represent the girl's (or the mother's) body and whatever is inside the basement must be inside the girl's (or the mother's) body. If this inference is correct, then (1) we should not expect either the patient or the girl to be inside the basement, and (2) we should

1. See S. Freud, 1918, for an extended example of his method.

expect that the flood would threaten only the girl and not the patient also. Yet in the dream text (1) the patient and the girl and the child are, all three, inside the basement, and (2) both the patient and the girl are walking in the dirty water and washing their faces in it. How can these discrepancies be explained?

Only two of the implications of this symbolism fit immediately into the interpretation suggested by the dream context. We shall consider these implications first.

We have just concluded that fear of offending the analyst as a mother has compelled the dreamer to substitute urination and wetting the bed for his genital sexual impulse toward the analyst; but that his pride has repudiated the impulse to urinate and has sought reassurance by reminding him that he is really the father of a child. In the dream symbolism we now find both these trends carried further.

The fact that the patient himself is in the basement implies a more deeply regressive fantasy than that of wetting the bed. If the basement is the mother's body, the patient must be fantasying himself inside the mother's body, as an unborn child.

On the other hand, the boast that he is the father of a child is also elaborated further in the dream symbolism. According to our interpretation, the flood entering the basement symbolizes the act of coitus. Inside this basement is the patient's child. Literally interpreted, this must mean that the flood entering the basement has impregnated the young woman. This interpretation gives significance to a dream detail to which we have not yet called attention. In the dream text the "flood" is relegated to the past. The floor is already flooded. A flood has entered the basement, and now a child is there!

Thus the two infantile fantasies that are condensed together in the dream symbolism reflect the same dynamic problem that we have already reconstructed from the psychological context of the present situation. In the present situation the patient cannot rid himself of the fear that his sexual impulses will cost him the dependent relationship to a mother that he so much needs. On the other hand, his pride will not let him recognize frankly the infantile character of his impulses. He compromises by recognizing his infantile need for a mother's love and care only in a projected form as the impulses of his child, while he soothes his masculine pride by reminding himself that he is a father. The infantile fantasies represented in the dream symbolism constitute a similar compromise. On the one hand, he imagines to himself how he was once inside the mother's body, but he also fantasies that he can emulate the father and give the mother a child by urinating upon her. Then, as now, he made use of this fantasy in the effort to convince himself that he could be a man like his father in spite of the infantile form of his sexual impulses.

Early and Late Versions of the Dream "Text."—Yet even after we have made this reconstruction, we have only partly accounted for the literal implications of the dream symbolism. Why is the girl also in the basement? And why is the patient as well as the girl threatened by the flood?

There are two possible ways to apply our criterion of literal interpretation of the dream symbolism. One is the method that we have just illustrated. Starting with our interpretation from the dream context, we have tried to fit into this context further implications suggested by single details of the dream text; yet there are parts of the dream symbolism that are not accounted for by this reconstruction. Another possible approach to symbol interpretation would be to start with the literal implications of the dream symbolism as a whole and then try to reconstruct how they are related to the dream context.

In reconstructing the pattern of a dream's historical background, our basic assumption is that the dream text is like a manuscript, based on successive versions of earlier manuscripts. In accordance with this basic assumption, we shall assume that both the procedures just mentioned are permissible. Since the dream is struggling to solve a present problem, reconstructions that remain close to the interpretation suggested by the dream context will probably be late versions of our "manuscript"; but reconstructions whose relationship to the present situation of the dreamer is less direct may be much closer to some of the historical sources of the dreamer's behavior patterns.

When we apply these principles to the flood dream (115), literal interpretation of the dream symbolism suggests the following fantasies: (1) that the patient has given the girl a child by urinating upon her; (2) that he pictures himself as sharing with the girl a feminine role in relation to the impregnating flood; and (3) that he himself is inside his mother's body, sharing with the girl and the child their intrauterine position as though they were his sister and brother.

We have just examined how these three fantasies are related to our interpretation from the dream context. In the next few chapters we shall check them against later dreams of this patient.

1. We have already pointed out that the impregnation fantasy is an extension of the patient's compensatory boast that he is a father. Another dream detail makes it possible to elaborate further the childhood fantasy on which this boast is based. The child in the dream is not only the patient's son but also the girl's brother. This suggests a childhood fantasy in which the patient and his sister are playing father and mother to their brother.

2. Since the dream context offers no confirmation for our reconstruction of a feminine fantasy in relation to the flood, we shall have to wait for later dreams to check this hypothesis. We shall study such a dream in the next chapter.

3. The intrauterine fantasy suggested by the symbolism is consistent with the dependence on a mother's love and approval which we have already recognized in this dream, but we shall have to wait for later dreams to explain why he is sharing the intrauterine position with a sister and a brother.

CHAPTER XIII

A Feminine Version of the Flood Dream

We shall consider next the rather puzzling implication of the symbolism of the flood dream (115), that the dreamer is picturing himself as sharing with the girl a feminine role in relation to the impregnating flood.

In accordance with our proposed procedure we shall first check this symbolic interpretation against later dreams; then, if we find confirmation for it, we shall ask whether it fits into the pattern of organization of the dream (115) as a whole. With this plan in mind, we turn now to the dreams and associations of the next analytic hour (116).

Two More Dreams.—He starts this hour by reporting a dream:

Dream 116a.—About weeding grass in front of a man's house.

He wheezed on awakening from this dream. In association he recalls that he had had a similar dream[1] before, which was interpreted as pulling something out of the mother. The man, he says, could represent his father. He is big and strong. The weeds can represent a penis. They were like carrots in the roots. The patient next recalls that he went down to get a graft of a plant from this man and saw these weeds. They talked about this grass which makes a lawn like a blanket; and the man promised to give the patient some of this grass in the spring. In the previous dream[1] it was in the patient's yard—now it is in the other fellow's. The analyst interprets the dream as wanting to castrate the father and get the penis or baby out of the mother; and the patient then admits: "I wanted to destroy it, I didn't want mother to have any more babies."

Then he reports a second dream:

Dream 116b.—About barroom and drinking. Four, five of us from work went there. Everyone had drinks. Don't remember clearly. Something like a quarrel. They wanted me to drink whiskey and I

1. See Dream 55 reported in chap. xx of this volume.

didn't want to. Someone swung a leg at me like kicking me in the belly. I stalled off drinking whiskey. Some fellow danging[2] came up and kicked me in genitals.

The man was the one referred to in the first dream (116a), and there were, besides, two or three others with whom the patient works. Whiskey, he says, makes him sick. It has an awful effect on him, smell and sickly feeling. He takes it, now and then, to be sociable. The other men drank it and smacked their lips, and here the patient suffers from it. Whiskey makes him drowsy, funny feeling, rotten taste. It has a burning, choking effect. It is like medicine. He was afraid to take it as a child.

Whiskey had the same effect on his father. Father was sick on it, thought he would die on the night he was so sick after it. He lay on the floor like a dead man. (In answer to the analyst's comment) many times the patient has wished his father dead. . . . Everyone made fun of father because he could not take whiskey and cigarettes. He wasn't a man in drinking and smoking, and father always knew that, particularly on the night that he came home sick. The patient was nine or ten. They brought father home at night in the winter, and he fell on the floor and was out, vomited; whiskey was the cause of it. . . . The patient avoids whiskey—he changes his drink and they crack fun at him. It is embarrassing. He was never in a barroom until he was seventeen or eighteen. Here he sees lots of saloons.

Interpretive Comment.—In the associations to the first of these two dreams (116a) the patient shows an extraordinary willingness to accept symbolic interpretations with a sexual content. This corresponds to the tolerance for discussion of sexual topics that was symbolized by "washing his face in the dirty water" in the flood dream (115). By accepting and repeating unpleasant interpretations, the patient has found a somewhat masochistic way of adapting himself to the analytic situation, getting unrecognized pleasure out of the discussion of sexual topics without thereby seeming to endanger his dependent relationship to the analyst as a mother.

The analyst in this instance elaborates on the patient's symbolic

2. This is probably a typographical error in the case report. I am unable to guess what the patient actually said.

interpretations but fails to call attention to the more immediate sense of the weeding dream (116a) in relation to the present situation. The associations distinguish sharply between weeds and lawn grass. In the dream (116a) the patient is pulling up the weeds. The aggressive meaning of taking something from the father, which he and the analyst agree upon, is correct in a sense that is much closer to present reality. Evidently, the patient feels it to be an aggression against the analyst's husband to be discussing sexual topics so freely with her. In the dream text (116a) the weeds growing in the other man's lawn are his own guilty sexual wishes, which the analyst is tolerating. He is shocked by these "weeds" and in the dream text is tearing them up.

The next dream (116b), which the patient reports immediately after the analyst's interpretation, is a protest that her interpretations are too strong a drink for him. The associations make it clear that this dream is motivated by guilt toward his father. In the past he probably took secret satisfaction that the strong father whom he so envied was "not a man in drinking." Now he must be suffocated and almost killed by strong drink, as his father once was.

In the dream text (116b) the analyst's husband is the father-figure toward whom the patient's guilt feelings are directed. The man who is trying to force a "suffocating drink" upon him is the one in whose garden the weeds were growing (dream 116a). The analyst's interpretation of the patient's incestuous wishes toward her (as mother) is the drink that he "is not man enough" to take. In the dream text (116b) he has turned away from his guilty relationship to the analyst and has substituted a masochistic relationship to a man who represents her husband. Instead of the analyst, the dream pictures her husband as the one who is trying to force a strong drink upon him.

How This Feminine Fantasy Fits into the Flood Dream.—Thus the feminine fantasy suggested by the symbolism of the flood dream (115) has proved premonitory of the patient's turning-away from the analyst in the next hour (116) to dream of having a suffocating drink forced upon him by her husband.

In the light of what we have learned from the two later dreams

(116*a* and *b*), it is now evident how this feminine fantasy fits into the pattern of organization of the flood dream (115). In reaction to the patient's guilt, the impulse to urinate upon the girl (analyst) has been turned back against himself as a fantasy of being urinated upon by her husband. But in the flood dream (115) this turning away to a submissive relationship to the husband has been temporarily interrupted by the seductive influence of the analyst's permissiveness. Regaining courage, he has rejected the masochistic fantasy; and, substituting an impersonal flood for the husband, he and the girl are joining in a symbolic masculine protest. Instead of submitting to the flood, they are, first, "walking in that dirty water"; then the girl's fixing up a cot for his little boy reminds him that he is the father of a child; and, finally, the last dream episode is an even bolder gesture of active mastery of the underlying masochistic fantasy: instead of letting the suffocating drink be forced upon him, he, of his own free will, washes his face in it.

Yet the relief that the analyst's permissiveness gives the patient in the flood dream (115) proves to be only temporary: Although in the flood dream he does wash his face in the dirty water, in the whiskey dream (116*b*) the drink is a suffocating one that will knock him out.

Thus by interpolating a fantasy of being urinated upon by the father (between the fantasy of urinating on the girl and the manifest dream content) (see Fig. 13), we have not only accounted literally for a perplexing detail of the dream symbolism[3] but also rounded out our understanding of a number of other details of the dream text and brought the pattern of organization of this dream (115) into relation with that of the whiskey dream (116*b*) in the next hour.

Historical Implications, Another Rule of Interpretation.—Our identification of the analyst's husband with the patient's father in this interpretation already points to the historical implication of this step in the process of dream organization. In the dream the patient turns away from heterosexual temptation in the analytic situation to symbolism suggestive of a feminine sub-

---

3. I.e., the fact that the patient, like the girl, is threatened by the flood (see p. 81).

missive relationship to her husband. We suspect that this reaction reflects childhood memories of turning away from sexual interest in his mother to feminine submissive wishes toward his father.

If so, what motivated this need to turn away from mother to father? Was it the patient's own conscience, or fear of punishment by the father, or fear of losing the mother's love? The context of the three dreams (115, 116a and b) suggests the following reflections on this question: The fact that the weeding dream (116a) refers to the patient's sexual wishes toward the analyst as weeds growing in another man's garden indicates that the patient's own conscience is reminding him of the analyst's husband's claim on her. But is this self-reproving thought based on identification with his mother's reproofs or on fear of punishment from the father?

To guide us in answering this question, we suggest tentatively the following *principle of interpretation*. When fear of punishment is the inhibiting motive, we expect to find in the dream context some reference to a memory of punishment, threatened or inflicted, upon which this fear is based; but when the forbidden impulse is merely turned back against the patient himself, with nothing new added to its content, we suspect that the original inhibiting motive was fear of loss of love.

Applying this principle: Since we find no reference to punishment or threat of punishment in the text and associations of flood dream (115) and whiskey dream[4] (116b), we conclude that fear of punishment was not the inhibiting motive. The masochistic fantasy in both flood dream (115) and whiskey dream (116b) has arisen by turning back against himself his impulse to urinate. From this fact we infer that the inhibiting motive is not fear of punishment but fear of loss of love. This suggestion is confirmed by the fact that a memory of rebuke from the mother played an important role in the organization of

4. This statement ignores the detail of the patient's being kicked in the whiskey dream (116b). We do not know the origin of this detail, but kicking in the stomach is not usual as a punishment for sexual impulses. It is possible that this detail, too, may have arisen by turning back against the dreamer a hostile impulse of his own; but we cannot yet fit this suggestion into the context of the rest of our interpretation. (It fits better into the fantasies that we shall discuss in the next chapter.)

the flood dream (115). We conclude that the guilt that inhibited the patient in this dream was based not on fear of punishment by the father but on fear of loss of the mother's love.
To escape rebuff from the mother, he transfers his affections
from mother to father. Following the implications of the dream
symbolism (115), we conclude that he is both surrendering
the object of his heterosexual interest to his father (since the
girl, too, is threatened by the flood) and also himself turning
to a feminine submissive relationship to the father.

Two Discrepancies.—Yet, before finally accepting this reconstruction, we must not fail to call attention to two discrepancies:

1. According to our interpretation of the flood dream (115)
from the emotional context, the patient's sexual impulses are
directed toward the girl, not toward a mother-figure.

2. In the whiskey dream (116*b*) the man who represents the
analyst's husband is one of four or five men with the patient
in a barroom. Literal interpretation of this symbolism suggests
that the analyst's husband is a brother-figure rather than a father.

Or are we dealing in both cases with two different versions
of the dream text? Perhaps in a later version of the flood dream,
a sister-figure played a role that was played by the mother in
an earlier fantasy; and in the historical background of the
whiskey dream, his demand for the mother's love may have involved him sometimes in rivalry with the father and at other
times in rivalry with his siblings.

Our next chapter will bring some confirmation of these suggestions.

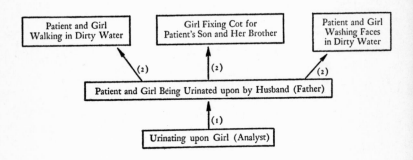

KEY TO MECHANISMS AND THEIR MOTIVATION

(1) Fantasy of urinating turned back against
    patient himself in reaction to guilt

(2) Masculine protest reactions

FIG. 13.—Pattern of organization of enuretic* fantasies underlying flood dream

* We have simplified this diagram by omitting references to wetting the bed which have
already been included in Fig. 12. We have also simplified this diagram further by ignoring the
fact that the girl in the dream is not the analyst but a substitute for her.

CHAPTER XIV

Interpretation of the Intrauterine Sharing Fantasy

We turn next to another implication of the flood dream's (115) symbolism. The patient and the girl and the child are all three together in the basement room. If the basement represents the mother's body, then this symbolism, when literally interpreted, implies a fantasy in which the patient and the girl and his child are brothers and sister, all sharing the position of an unborn child inside the mother's body.

How could such a fantasy have arisen? In our first discussion[1] of the bridge dream (10a) we recognized sharing the mother as a solution for the conflict arising from rivalry for exclusive possession of her love. The glass of milk that the patient received from the mother in the bridge dream (10a) suggested that the rivalry underlying this dream detail was for the mother's breast. The intrauterine symbolism of three people in the same basement suggests another kind of rivalry for the mother: a rivalry, stimulated by the mother's pregnancies, for the unborn child's position inside the mother's body.

A fantasy of sharing the mother may or may not succeed in binding the pressure of the underlying hostile impulses toward rivals. If the sharing fantasy is satisfying enough, it may make rivalry unnecessary. But if hope of the mother's love and approval diminishes, the integrative capacity[2] of the sharing fantasy may become inadequate to absorb the pressure of emerging rivalrous impulses. This is what has occurred in the whiskey dream (116b), in which four or five men in the same barroom are quarreling. In this dream (116b) the fantasy of sharing the same room is no longer able to bind the rivalrous impulses; and these hostile impulses must now be turned back against the patient in a fantasy of being kicked in the belly (another sug-

1. See Vol. I, chaps. xviii and xx.
2. See Vol. I, chaps. xii, xix, and xxi.

89

gestive reference to hostility to the mother's pregnancy) and of having a suffocating drink forced upon him.

Thus the symbolism of the whiskey dream (116b) brings us back directly to the interpretation already suggested by our functional analysis[3] of the water symbolism, that the water in these dreams is a projected symbol of the patient's impulse to urinate on the pregnant mother and drown her unborn child. The sharing fantasy symbolized by the patient and his sister and brother all together in one room is an attempt at solution of this rivalrous conflict; but, when[4] this sharing fantasy is unable to bind the pressure of emerging rivalrous impulses, the hostile "flood" begins to penetrate into the protecting room. In the basic fantasy this "flood" threatens all in the room, not only the brother and sister figures but the patient also. If the patient fantasies sharing the mother's love, he must share the danger, too. We shall discuss the significance of this fact in a later chapter.[5]

To check these formulations we turn now to later dreams that make use of the water symbolism.

More Dreams about Water.—In the few hours preceding the material next to be reported, the question had been raised of why the patient did not leave his wife and have an extramarital affair, since he resented his marriage so much.

In the 154th hour he reports that he has been wheezing since the last (153d) hour, when there had again been a discussion of the possibility of his leaving home. He brings the following two dreams:

Dream 154a.—I was on a hillside; down below in valley was a river. Train going by, as last coach passed, it started to turn over. Last six coaches tipped over. Supposed to be a troop train. I rushed over, guard

3. See chap. ix of this volume.

4. The time relations referred to in this paragraph are time relations in the process of organization of the dream. These should not be confused with time relations which are part of the content of the dream text (i.e., one dreams that something has already occurred, e.g., that the floor is already flooded), or with the chronological order of the episodes of the dream text.

5. See chap. xxxvii of this volume.

wouldn't let me by. Red Cross nurses there. [He sits up, coughs, and spits.]

Dream 154b.—I took out my lower teeth and broke them in two.

The analyst's attempts to get associations irritate him. He adds a few details in telling the dream again. It was like in the country . . . open spaces . . . the train was on the other side of the river in the valley. Rear coach tipped over and then the rest of them. He could see the heads of soldiers sticking out of windows.

He remembers that a car in the past has been a woman; the heads are like the heads of babies sticking out of the woman. There were doctors and nurses. The six cars may be six women or—he breaks off with irritation but denies that he is angry with the analyst. Later he speaks of the soldiers as symbols of youth and manhood.

The analyst interprets the open country as a symbol of sexual freedom and tells the patient he is angry at her for pushing him out into the open when he desires to return to the mother. The number "six" she interprets as a reference to the six children in the parental home. . . .

In the interval between this dream and the ones next to be quoted, there was considerable discussion of the patient's sexual potency. He said he was potent only with prostitutes and then not always. One day he started wheezing when he was attracted to a woman while waiting for a streetcar. Then he recalled his fear some months before when he saw a man nearly run over by a train. In the 160th hour he started to wheeze on seeing the analyst. He spoke of his desire for a "higher type of woman," but he was afraid. In childhood he used to sleep with his mother when he was sick, at other times with his father, until he was five or six years old. In the 161st hour he told of resolving to face the analyst without fear, to be "conscious of her." Then he "smoked a cigarette and spit and forgot about it." He coughed hard, wheezed, and spit as he told this.

In the 162d hour, three days later, he reports a dream of two nights before:

Dream 162a.—I went in barroom and ordered a beer. Saw man who works with me next to me. His beer dark and thick—so I ordered the same. Two women came in and asked me to buy them a drink, so I did. One woman took whiskey and the other woman candy or something sweet.

Associations.—The dark, thick beer that the other man was drinking was supposed to be better than the beer the patient was drinking. The patient envied this fellow. He is successful, happy-go-lucky. He is afraid he is jealous of him. He is a nice man, nice home, shrewd and successful in real estate and stocks. He does not know who the two women are. They wanted him to buy them a drink—the one took whiskey, the other candy. They took him away from the bar and went over to a place with a lot of candy, and he bought some. The patient agrees to the analyst's interpretation that thick, dark beer is potency. That is what he lacks, he says. . . . After further discussion of his envy the patient brings up a second dream.

Dream 162b.—Something like inspection of railroad yards. Two bosses inspecting the buildings. I was in railroad box car, red hot stove in it. As they came toward me, I urinated on top of stove, and it made awful smell. I ran out, and they came in and were gagged by awful smell. One said, "awful smell in this shanty."

The patient interprets the urination as "discharging potency." The red-hot stove is like a woman, gives an awful odor. He objects to the analyst's interpretation that he is showing his two bosses his potency. It was like playing a dirty trick on them. He didn't want to show them anything. He wanted them to walk in and find the strong odor. He had been hiding from them. . . .

The dreams just quoted were discussed only a short time before the second summer interruption of the patient's treatment. When the analyst returned in the fall, the patient was full of complaints about his wife. By this time his sexual fantasies and his hostile wishes toward his wife and children were coming to much franker expression. For example, in the 171st hour he laughed when he told of his wife's tripping and hurting her face and arms and of his jokingly saying it was a pity she didn't break her neck. In the following hours he recalled also death wishes against his two children. In the 175th hour he complained of a burning sensation in the mouth, feared he had cancer, reported going to a physician, who assured him there was no cancer. Then he dreamed that he had a woman's breast in his mouth, which afterward became a man's penis, and of the woman also taking his penis in her mouth. In discussing his fear of cancer, the analyst suggested that the patient received some homosexual gratification from being examined by the physician. "Naturally he took a swab stick," the patient replied.

In the 185th hour he reports a dry feeling and tightness in his chest. He says his wheezing is not so loud but comes on and off. Then he reports the two following dreams:

Dream 185a.—Walking through woods or streets, leaves dry on ground. I had to dodge the limb. A woman with me.

Dream 185b.—About a neighbor. I was dressing in bathroom. A neighbor woman lying in bathtub. I had on only trunks of pajamas. She could see my penis and said, "If it was stiff she could have a lot of pleasure." Then saw her husband standing in corner of bathroom.

"That's enough to remember," he comments after telling the two dreams. To the woods he associates "Nothing"; but he liked walking over dry leaves. The leaves were pretty thick. He had to watch not to get the branches in his eye. They were low and thick. He covered his face so as not to get hurt, but he enjoyed walking on the dry leaves. The leaves remind him only of "something wilted, dead." He becomes irritated as he reiterates that he doesn't know what they represent. He felt no fear, he says. The woman in the dream (185a) was just a shadow, a woman following him. When the analyst reminds him that she is behind him, he agrees, then reverts to the dry leaves, he enjoys tramping on them. It is like the past. He agrees to the analyst's suggestion that the dry leaves are like the feeling in his chest, an achy, burning feeling in nose and throat, "dry and like inflamed in lungs." So dream might have something to do with analysis. "Suppose I'm still trying to dodge something. Some places I had to stoop low to dodge." . . .

He agrees that the second dream (185b) is very clear. "Woman tells me if I were a man I could have pleasure. Husband like a shadow. Woman in bathtub fully dressed. Yes, there was fear of husband all right because I just saw like picture of him." The analyst suggests that her husband is a shadow to him, then reminds him of his memory of seeing his mother naked in the bathtub. "Yes," he says. "One time I saw her through a crack, she was like a shadow more." He was curious. "Yes, maybe sex aroused. Didn't see her naked but partly so. Took bath in big wooden tub in corner of kitchen. I knew she was taking a bath and was naked. Don't remember how much I was aroused." . . . "Yes, still afraid and put blame on women. Still don't want to admit it. I was choking yesterday all right. Think you aroused a little attraction in me yesterday. Perhaps why I wheezed more here than I did all day." . . .

In the next hour he reports a vague dream of two or three nights before (but after the last hour):

Dream 186.—Don't know what I was dreaming. Must have been about sex. Supposed to have wet dream but couldn't discharge. Went back, funny sensation. Was afraid, was there, and then went back.

After suppressing orgasm, he started to "wheeze and cough and choke. Felt like burning and heat. . . ." Yes, it was his first wet dream for a long time, and he has had no sex relations. "No, sir, I'm more dead than I ever was [laughs]. Fear more than ever. Don't know if I had dream about sex pleasure but if I did, fear knocked it out of my memory. I was at point of discharge, had pain when I woke up. Felt like it went back, like stopping in channel and dissolved and went back. Little pain with it and then heat inside. After while it got normal. Felt no pain nor nothing." . . .

Later he recalls that he once had a wet dream about the analyst. When the analyst inquires about enuresis, he can recall only one incident at the age of twenty. He told the landlady about it. He admits he must have been fond of this landlady or he wouldn't have lived in her house, but after her baby appeared he disliked the place, "began to choke right after the baby was born." He was sick for a month until his mother made him quit the job and come home.

In the next hour, two days later, he reports that he has been wheezing all night, then tells the following dream:

Dream 187a.—Some gathering or entertainment. One girl supposed to dance. Before she went on, she kissed me and told me to wish her luck.

In association he states that the girl is the eighteen-year-old daughter of the real estate man who cheated him (referred to in the 17th hour). "She's a little overweight. She's bright. Haven't seen her for a year or more, we used to play cards at his house." Then he reports a second dream:

Dream 187b.—Lady out on a little lake. Boat tipped over, somehow she got on top of boat, she was in danger.

His associations return to the girl in the first dream. He was attracted by her. She wore brassiere and shorts. More people there. He has seen her at entertainments at the Legion. He admires her ambition and personality. In face she is attractive woman, fully developed, nothing wrong with her. He also saw her mother there too. Something like a dressing-room. He can think of no one whom she could "impersonate" unless it were the analyst. He laughs when the analyst suggests that he wishes her to single him out. . . . He insists that he was attracted by the young girl, not by her mother, thinks he dreamed of her because he is less afraid of her than of the analyst.

The analyst's request for associations to the lady in the second dream (187b) brings out little that is new. "Don't know woman, only remember woman tipping over, she was disappearing in water and then climbing up on boat. Woke up excited and fearful. Felt danger and then felt easier when she came up. Woman in danger. She was in bad place in water, could have been you, too. Why always pick on women in dream? Some men, too, but I don't remember—saw fellow I borrowed [i.e., loaned] money to [this is again the father of the girl in the first dream], just recollect he was in picture. Last night talked with man about this debt. He promised to see chief of probate court under whom this man works. Possible the superior could scare him by loss of job. But woman in boat, maybe wife I wish dead. Well, I don't come into contact with other than you and wife. One of you! If there was wish to drown, suppose it was wife. You haven't done anything to me. Drowning means death. Felt sorry for it."

The analyst inquires about the patient's sister. The patient was six or seven when she was born. No, he must have been younger than six. "She dead about six or seven of scarlet fever and *diphtheria with choking*. No, she was older—guess she was ten or eleven at death. Did dream represent sister? Drowning is choking. [He wheezes.] Well, possible, because I felt awful bad about her death, couldn't forget it. Got along bad with brother and better with sister, even expressed myself to brother that I'd rather see him die than sister, guess in reality it existed. Very touched by sister's death, and here I had to be content with brother I couldn't get along with. Didn't like brother and did like sister. Sorrow for long time. Suppose in dream I seen her die and wish her back."

After this hour he missed two appointments, owing to his wife's misinterpretation of a message from the analyst. On his return he reports a dream:

Dream 188a.—Some time about seeing woman practically naked, all she had on was a pair of pants, lot to it but don't remember.

The woman in the dream was the woman down the street who took the analyst's telephone message. He laughs at the suggestion it might be the analyst. It could be any woman—especially strange women.

Then he reports another dream:

Dream 188b.—I was riding in streetcars. Couldn't find my way around, kind of lost. Streetcar wasn't getting me there. I was worried and lost.

In association he thinks the streetcar is a woman. "Couldn't get along with it, anyone the wrong one and not getting me where I was going, had to get off and take another. Lost, I'm in that state now, lost, wandering. . . ."

The next day he reports that he has been wheezing, coughing, and spitting ever since the last hour. Two days later he reports another dream:

Dream 190.—Was up here like a utility room, I was vomiting but only a little stream like water coming out of my mouth. Your husband got big five-gallon can. Water turned out muddy color in can. I pretty near filled up the can. You and your husband and maid there. Your husband mopped up floor. Woke up wheezing.

Afterward he couldn't remember the dream until he was getting off the streetcar on the way to the analytic hour, then he started to wheeze again.

He thinks the dream must have to do with the analyst and her house. There was no force to the vomiting. It was "like thin stream of water coming out of my mouth—continuous. Had no control over it—I was embarrassed—like urinating, but out of mouth. The can was handy." Analyst's husband shoved it over to him. "I wet the floor and your husband mopped it up. Something unclean—but water running out looked clean—then gray color in can." It was like the mucus the patient coughs up. He notes particularly "all of you not angry at me—in particular you being very pleasant. You said it was all right and good fun —maid cheerful—your husband smiling and got busy with mop— I was embarrassed, and this thing running out of me. Stream size of pencil." The analyst says that the patient wishes to soil the whole family. The patient agrees . . . he is soiling the analyst's husband's house and making him clean up.

We shall next report a dream (205) which the patient reported about six weeks after the vomiting dream (190). In the hours just preceding, the analyst had made a number of interpretations about the patient's reactions to her. In the 201st hour she had dwelt on his dependence on her. The next day, when the patient told of quarreling with his wife because he didn't like her food and because she looked sloppy, the analyst told him that this was a displaced reaction of anger to her interpretation of his dependence. In the next two sessions he brought four dreams,[6]

6. In one of these dreams (203*b*) the patient was looking for a nurse who was like his mother and who had once advised him to divorce his wife; in another (203*a*) he was in the bottom of a well inside a mountain, from which someone told him he could see the universe; and in the dream of the 204th hour a one-armed alderman was having his bodyguard frisk the patient for arms. In her interpretations the analyst identified the nurse with herself, and

three of which the analyst interpreted as referring to herself. Then in the 205th hour he immediately reported the following dream:

Dream 205.—About hole in ground. Hole in ground in front of house. I was filling it with water, had garden hose, but water ran slowly, no pressure behind it. Two women mixed up in it, one woman got into hole after it was half-filled with water and dirt. She was standing up and I embraced her, rubbed my cheek against hers, felt her breasts—then saw her husband coming toward us.

After reciting with his usual facility the symbolic interpretation of the hole in the ground as a woman's genitals, the hose as a penis, and the difficulty in getting the water to run fast enough as his "weakness," the patient identifies the woman as a woman he knows, "supposes" he was attracted by her, she is like the analyst. The analyst then elicits the fact that the patient wheezed slightly on awakening from this dream and had a headache across the forehead which lasted a long time. He adds that he felt little joy in holding the woman and then felt fear and embarrassment about her husband. In the past he always picked up courage even toward his wife, but now he is dead. In answer to the analyst's comment, he protests that his wife is not a mother to anyone. A prostitute is more attractive. Last night he was embarrassed when a friend called for him. While the friend was waiting, the patient told his wife to bathe the younger son's infected hand and get him ready for school the next day. His wife jumped all over him to such an extent that the man said, "Another word from you and she'll be on your neck." The rest of the hour was spent discussing the patient's dependent and critical attitudes toward his wife. The analyst closed the hour by an interpretation of the sexual mother-transference.

In the next hour (206) he reported wheezing the night before and feeling like vomiting in the morning. His wheezing had been aggravated by his family's shouting and yelling while he was trying to sleep. His choking up had started at the movies

---

the hole from which he was told he could see the universe she identified as the patient's dependent picture of the analysis. An important detail in the alderman's appearance also seemed to refer to the analyst and to the patient's fears in the therapeutic situation.

the night before. The analyst compared the romantic sex scenes at the movie to his memory of observing parental intercourse and reminded him that he had yelled "murder" at that time. In the next hour (207) (five days later) the patient again reported that he had been wheezing a lot for two days and that he had been sick to his stomach again the night before. Then he reported the following dream:

Dream 207.—Was in corner drugstore and druggist wrapped up two carrots, two parsnips, and spinach—supposed to be my diet. This raw stuff my diet! First I took out two carrots and twisted off green top, did same with parsnips—threw away tops—then added spinach and cabbage and wrapped it up—I was to eat it raw.

Associations.—At home, the patient says, when meat and potatoes sicken him, he "sometimes switches to greens." He grinds them in a grinder and puts on vinegar and oil—until he tires of this, too, and goes back to meat. The day before, he had been "awful hostile" toward home, wanted to vomit. He had been angry at his wife and especially at his younger son, told him that he was dirty, greasy, and sloppy and that his handwriting was scratchy. The analyst suggests that these feelings might have been displaced from the analytic situation and the analyst's child.

Interpretive Comment.—When we review this series of dreams, new aspects of the significance of the water symbolism emerge progressively more clearly into view.

The analyst interpreted the train wreck dream (154*a*) as a reaction to discussion in the preceding hour of the possibility of the patient's leaving home. Just as he resented his brother's remaining with the mother when he was sent away to school in his adolescence, so now he resents the thought of leaving home so much that he wishes the death of the children who still remain with the mother. In the dream façade he compensates for this wish by trying to rush to the scene of the accident. We are left to infer that he was rushing to the rescue, but the fact that the guard stops him and that he breaks his lower teeth in two in the next dream (154*b*) gives additional evidence of the underlying hostile impulses.

In this context we find again the symbol of the river. Is the

train perhaps tipping over into the river? As the analyst points
out, the six coaches that tip over correspond in number to the
children in the home of the patient's parents.

The beer dream (162a) and the hot stove dream (162b)
were preceded by considerable discussion of the patient's impotence and of his reacting to sexual excitement with asthma.
In the first of these two dreams (162a) the patient is competing
with another man. The real object of the competition is apparently the two women. Although the other man's beer is better, the two women come to the patient.

In the second dream (162b) the desire to gag and choke the
two men is evidently a spiteful revenge for his impotence and
envy. Others enjoy sex, but he only chokes up with asthma.
He gets even by choking others.

In the beer dream (162a) one of the two women chooses
whiskey to drink. Whiskey, we recall, is a drink that the patient
chokes over (see associations to whiskey dream, 116b).[7] We
have suspected that the underlying fantasy is one of choking
or drowning someone by urinating into his mouth. In the urination dream (162b) he urinates upon a hot stove instead of directly
on the two men, but the result is the same—to choke them.

In the capsized boat dream (187b) the notion of drowning
appears undisguised in the dream text. Since the dreams (185b
and 186) of the two preceding hours were struggling with
sexual temptation in the therapeutic situation, the patient's sexual
impulses must be the danger that threatens the girl and the
"lady" in the two dreams of the 187th hour. Allowing for the
projection in the capsized boat dream (187b), we reconstruct
the underlying fantasy as one of tipping the "lady" over and
drowning her. Since the preceding hour (186) ended with a
memory of wetting the bed associated with his choking up with
asthma immediately after the landlady's baby was born, it is
easy to guess that the "little lake" in which the "lady" almost
drowns is a projected symbol of the dreamer's own urine.

This unconscious fantasy of drowning the girl (dream 187b)

7. See chap. xiii, p. 83.

is followed in the vomiting dream (190) by one in which the patient himself is vomiting up a lot of dirty water. The thin stream of water is evidently the patient's characterization of his own much inhibited associations in the therapeutic sessions. With a characteristic tendency to project responsibility, the dreamer is picturing the water as becoming dirty only in the analyst's can. When we contrast this dream (190) with the whiskey dream (116b), the analyst's husband's friendliness and cheerfulness about mopping up show how much easier the patient is now finding it to accept the analyst's tolerance and even to assume her husband's tolerance for his "dirty thoughts."

The patient's description of his vomiting as "urinating" "out of the mouth" brings the water symbolism of this dream (190), too, into relation with the enuretic fantasies that we have been discussing. Vomiting nearly five gallons of dirty water probably implies a fantasy of having swallowed it.

Confirmation of Our Hypotheses.—In our first attempt to interpret the water symbolism we suspected that the river in the bridge dream (10a) is a projected symbol of both the erotic and the hostile wishes that threaten to estrange the dreamer from his mother, that the river symbolizes an impulse to urinate on the girl and that this impulse is an erotic impulse, first of all, but also masks a wish to drown her with his urine.

In the psychological context of the flood dream (115) we found direct confirmation for our interpretation of water as a symbol of urination and for the erotic significance of urination. In this dream we found no direct confirmation for our suspicion that water has also a hostile significance, but our attempt to account literally for the dream symbolism later led us back to this hypothesis.

To test this hypothesis further, we have now been reviewing a series of later water dreams; and in these dreams we find the hostile significance of water progressively emerging into clearer view: In the whiskey dream (116b) the patient is having a suffocating drink forced upon him. In the train wreck dream (154a) a train full of soldiers is tipping over, probably into the river. In the hot stove dream (162b) the patient chokes two men by urinating on a hot stove; and in the immediately preceding beer dream (162a) he is treating a girl to the same drink that threatened to suffocate him in the whiskey dream (116b). Finally, a memory of wetting the bed, associated with his choking up with asthma just after his landlady's baby was born, is followed by the capsized boat dream (187b) in which a "lady" is in danger of drowning; and then comes the memory of his sister's "choking" to death with diphtheria.

In discussing the "functional" significance of water, we pointed out that in everybody's experience water is related in three different ways to basic human needs: as something that we drink, as something that we excrete (urine), and as something that we sometimes choke over and may drown in. These three facts, we postulated, should be our best clues for understanding the water symbolism. The dreams that we have just reviewed bring abundant confirmation of this expectation. In this series of water dreams we find the themes of urination, drinking, and choking inextricably interwoven.

Yet our analysis of the symbolism of these water dreams also points repeatedly to a theme, very familiar in the psychoanalytic literature, which our functional analysis has not yet accounted for. In the psychoanalytic literature being in the water or in a boat has long been recognized as a symbol of pregnancy and coming out of the water as a symbol of birth. Is there any "functional" explanation of this association of water with pregnancy and birth?

CHAPTER XV

Further Confirmation of the Literal Implications of the Flood Dream

Whenever the psychological context of a dream confirms the interpretation of water entering a room or boat as a symbol of coitus, then the literal interpretation of this symbolism implies that any person inside the room or boat is an unborn child.

By strict application of this rule to the flood dream (115), we deduce a fantasy in which the patient is sharing the intrauterine position with brother and sister (for convenience we shall call this fantasy an "intrauterine sharing fantasy"). If the method of symbol interpretation that we are now testing is trustworthy, such an intrauterine sharing fantasy must have been a part of the historical background of the flood dream (115).

By applying the same rule in relation to another part of the dream context, we have deduced another fantasy. The immediate psychological context of this dream (115) suggests that the dreamer has an impulse to wet the bed. The flood that has entered the basement is a projected symbol both of this enuretic impulse and of the fantasy that underlies it, of urinating upon the girl. Starting with this infantile sexual fantasy and from the fact that the patient's own son is in the basement, we have deduced an impregnation fantasy as follows: The flood has entered the basement, and now the patient's child is there. Translating the symbolism, we interpret this as a fantasy that the dreamer has urinated upon a woman (either the young woman in the dream text or the mother for whom she is a substitute) and given her a child. If our reasoning is correct, this impregnation fantasy, too, must have been a part of the historical background of the flood dream (115).

Since this patient's treatment was discontinued before either of these fantasies appeared without disguise, we shall not be able to offer direct evidence in support of our two interpretations;

but we can check them against two kinds of indirect evidence. First, we shall discuss a dream in which this symbolism seems transparent. Then in later chapters[1] we shall attempt to reconstruct and compare the organizational patterns of this whole series of water dreams and to check whether they are intelligible as variations resulting from the influence of different situations upon a single underlying pattern.

In the dirty hole dream (205) the patient is evidently reacting to the analyst's repeated interpretations of his emotional reactions toward her. These interpretations the dream work has chosen to interpret as a sexual invitation. Projecting responsibility on the analyst, the dream replies that, if she insists on interposing herself as object of his sexual wishes, he is ready to accept her invitation. Nevertheless, even with such encouragement, he feels inadequate and expects her husband to appear any moment.

When we now translate literally the symbolism in which these thoughts are imbedded, we find an even clearer portrayal of the two infantile fantasies that we found in the symbolism of the flood dream (115): First the patient is filling a hole in front of a house with water, and then a woman gets into the hole; this we interpret as a fantasy of giving the mother a child by urinating upon her. Then the patient follows the woman into the hole, which, when literally translated, is an intrauterine sharing fantasy.

1. See especially chap. xliv of this volume.

CHAPTER XVI

Historical Background of the Water Symbolism

In an early paper (1912), Rank pointed out that, in the same dream, water often represents urination at one "level" and pregnancy, intrauterine existence, and birth at another "level." Rank did not work out the dynamic interrelations between these two meanings of the water symbolism but contented himself with the mere fact of overdetermination.

To complete our reconstruction of the historical background of our patient's water dreams, we turn to the question suggested by this observation of Rank's: Why are impulses to urinate so closely associated with the theme of pregnancy in water dreams?

The simplest hypothesis to account for this association is the one suggested by the flood dream (115) and the dirty hole dream (205): that the water symbolism is based on a urinary theory of impregnation.

The Amniotic Fluid Theory.—Before elaborating this hypothesis further, we shall first examine another hypothesis that is popular in the psychoanalytic literature.

Being in the water, as a symbol of the intrauterine state, is sometimes thought to be based on prenatal memory of the amniotic fluid. Of course, this theory must reckon with the fact that the unborn child can know of the amniotic fluid only in terms of kinaesthetic and tactual impressions.[1] According to the amniotic fluid hypothesis, the postnatal kinaesthetic impressions of the infant in his bath reactivate and are identified with kinaesthetic memories of the intrauterine state, and thus bring these intrauterine memories into association with the notion of being in the water.

It is not improbable that kinaesthetic and tactual memories of the intrauterine state may play some part in the water symbolism. Yet in the dreams of many persons, as in those of the patient whom we have been studying, the intrauterine fantasy is por-

1. And perhaps also by swallowing and aspirating it.

trayed in terms that imply visual imagery. It is difficult to conceive how memories of the intrauterine state could contain visual or conceptual imagery such as the notion of being inside an inclosed space. It is much more reasonable to assume that this notion of being in an inclosed space is derived not from intrauterine memories but rather from the earliest period of sexual investigation, from the discovery that there is another child inside a woman's body.

It is still more difficult to account for the *motivation* of these intrauterine fantasies in terms of an amniotic fluid theory of the water symbolism. We know that the function of dreams is to preserve sleep by quieting pressures that arise to disturb sleep. It is difficult to conceive how a spontaneously arising longing for an undisturbed intrauterine state could be the source of a disturbing pressure. When we study actual dreams, we find rather that the wish for the intrauterine state is motivated by a need to quiet sleep-disturbing pressures from other sources. Sleep itself is frequently identified with the intrauterine state; and the wish for a refuge inside the mother's body regularly appears not as a sleep-disturbing pressure but as a desire to escape from disturbing stimuli of other kinds. We conclude, therefore, that a craving for the intrauterine state cannot furnish the motive power for dreaming but serves rather to neutralize pressures from other sources.

Historical Background of the Water Symbolism.—We return now to our *hypothesis that the water symbolism is based on a urinary theory of impregnation.* With this hypothesis as a starting point, we can make a reasonably adequate reconstruction of the historical background of our patient's water dreams.

In the water dreams that we have just been studying, the motivating pressure has arisen from wishes that were originally stirred up by the mother's pregnancies and by the sexual investigations of early childhood. These investigations and discoveries were sexually exciting. Sometimes the patient reacted by fantasies of emulating his notion of the father's role, of giving the mother a child by urinating upon her. Yet soon his jealous hatred of brother and sister transformed these impregnation fantasies into hostile ones. The fertilizing flood became a hostile one. Instead of giving the mother children, he then fantasied using his "water" to drown the unborn children. It was the need to escape from these destructive wishes and from the consequent danger of estrangement from the mother that drove him to the fantasy of sharing with his rivals their place inside the mother. By such a fantasy of sharing the mother, he struggled to diminish the intensity of his jealous hatred and the real danger of losing his mother's love. Yet the attempt thus to quiet the disturbing pressure was not always successful. Behind his fantasies of peace in the intrauterine state, there lurks always the fear of drowning in the threatening flood of his own hostile wishes. Fundamentally, water means danger for this patient, not peace and repose; and he cannot return to the refuge of inclosed spaces without finding that others are already there before him.

SECTION IV

Other Recurring Patterns

CHAPTER XVII

Another Recurring Pattern

Significant past events exert their influence on later behavior not only once but repeatedly. For this reason, recurring patterns of behavior are particularly useful as starting points for inquiry into a patient's past. Our patient's water dreams illustrate a pattern that recurs at intervals and gradually unfolds throughout his treatment. We shall next study a pattern that is repeated frequently in a long sequence of consecutive dreams:

In the bridge dream (10*a*) the patient pinches a girl in the back, then escorts her home to her mother.

In the anvil dream (12) the iron bar has a hook on the end of it, used to remove clinkers from a furnace. The bar is being beaten.

In the pencil-stealing dream (25) he steals pencils and a pad, then wakes up with asthma after the watchman appears.

In the 32d hour he tells childhood memories, once of stealing a nickle from his father's cashbox and another time of taking a knife from a neighbor's house. In each case he felt guilty afterward, with the result that he confessed, in the one case, and gave the knife back, in the other.

In the Mexican woman dream (44) he is scrubbing a little boy's arm. His associations identify the little boy with himself and the scrubbing with a somewhat punitive concept of his treatment.

Each of these episodes, with one exception, implies an act, contemplated or actual, in which the patient reaches out his arm and hand to grasp or take something, then reacts with some evidence of guilt, such as renunciation (e.g., in the bridge dream), confession, or need for punishment. The one exception, in the anvil dream (12), differs only in the fact that it is an iron bar with a hook on the end of it that grasps the clinkers and gets beaten for it.

The significance of this disturbing impulse cannot be guessed from the emotional context of any one of these episodes alone. We propose, accordingly, to review systematically the dream sequence in which they occur in the hope that the psychological contexts of a number of these dreams may supplement one another.

Pinching the Girl in the Back in the Bridge Dream.—In the bridge dream (10*a*) we first interpreted the patient's pinching the girl in the back as an erotic gesture. Later we realized that this erotic gesture was the erotized expression of a hostile impulse. We do not know why this erotized hostile impulse should have taken just this form, why the dream should have chosen pinching instead of any number of other possible impulses that might have given the same playful expression to either his erotic urges or his latent hostility.

We do have one hint. At the end of the dream the patient receives a glass of milk from the mother—another act that involves his reaching out his hand to grasp something. Perhaps the grasping hand that is reached out to receive from the mother is ready to be turned against brother and sister if they threaten to come between him and the mother.

The Iron Bar with the Hook To Remove Clinkers.—The anvil dream (12) is motivated by the patient's need for punishment on account of his sexual wishes toward the analyst. The usual significance of a rigid bar as symbol of an erect penis is consistent with this interpretation. Since the patient needs punishment on account of his sexual wishes, it is fitting that a phallic symbol should submit to the beating.

What does it mean that the mother is shaping a hook on the end of this phallic symbol? A hook suggests a hand, and grasping clinkers to remove them is the function of a hand.

When we translate bar as penis and hook as hand, we arrive at a very plastic way of expressing the interpretation that we have already made. The patient is in conflict between sexual wishes and his need for the mother's love. In order to retain her love, he must renounce his sexual wishes. The anvil dream (12) pictures his mother beating down the erect penis that so offends her, bending it and shaping it into a hand! In order to retain the mother's love, he must have the sexuality beaten out of him. The erect penis must be beaten into shape and converted into the grasping hand of a dependent child.

Yet we are still in the dark about the significance of removing clinkers from the furnace of a locomotive.

Stealing Pencils from a Boxcar.—The next dream in which the hand is being used for a forbidden purpose is the pencil-stealing dream (25). In this dream (25) the patient is testing out whether he can trust the analyst's apparent tolerance for forbidden impulses; but the impulse chosen for this test is a rather trivial symbolic one.

What is the really significant impulse for which this trivial one has been substituted?

The analyst suspects that the pencils and pad that the patient wishes to steal are those that she uses to take notes during the analytic sessions. He himself does not accept this suggestion. He protests that they resemble rather the pencils that the railroad furnishes. The motive for this substitution is evident from the associations. Not only the pencils but also the office, the boxcar, the expression, "Bring it into the office," the switchman and the watchman—all are references to his work. As in previous dreams, he is attempting to get rid of the seductive implications of being alone in a room with a woman and to emphasize the professional or business-like character of the relationship by substituting his situation at work, where there are no women and he deals only with men.

Yet even after we have recognized the motive for this substitution, we are still not much nearer to the real significance of stealing pencils and a pad from a boxcar. To steal the analyst's pencils and pad is still a rather trivial temptation. The forbidden impulse that is really disturbing the patient must be a much more significant one.

CHAPTER XVIII

Several Interrelated Patterns

In this chapter, elaborating further our method of following out the literal implications of the dream symbolism, we shall compare and analyze fantasy patterns as we would superimpose lines, angles, and figures in a geometrical demonstration.

Readers who have not acquired some tolerance of psychoanalytic reasoning may already have experienced some difficulty in following this kind of argument. Since the sexual and hostile fantasies that usually underlie the dream symbolism tend to call forth emotional reactions of disgust or disbelieving repudiation, it is often not easy to study them with detachment. Yet such detachment is necessary if we are not to be distracted from the task of comparing and analyzing their patterns.

Fantasy patterns are cognitive fields. The interrelations between the different fantasies that have helped shape a dream constitute its cognitive structure. In this chapter we shall take as our starting point fragments of cognitive structure that recur in two or more dreams and shall then proceed to compare ways in which the same cognitive pattern is elaborated in different dreams.

Two Boxcar Dreams.—The boxcar symbol appears in two dreams that we have studied. The pencil-stealing dream (25) and the pig dream (43), which have this symbol in common, are also motivated in part by the same conflict, by a conflict about confessing forbidden thoughts to the analyst. In the pencil-stealing dream (25) the patient is unable to accept the opportunity to confess that the watchman offers him; he wakes up with an acute attack of asthma instead. Similarly in the pig dream (43) we have recognized an attempt at confession which disintegrated into angry protest and then into asthmatic wheezing.

The two dreams (25 and 43) also differ, both in their actions and in their symbolism. In the pencil-stealing dream (25) the opportunity for confession follows a symbolic act to which the watchman has tempted him, whereas the action of the pig dream

(43) is completely preoccupied with talk. In the symbolism the boxcar contains pencils and pads ("merchandise") in the earlier dream (25); pigs in the later dream (43).

In view of their similarities, we shall now treat these two dreams as parts of a single psychological context. We shall postpone attempts to account for the differences between them.

In his associations to the pig dream (43) the patient tells us that a pig is a dirty child. In discussing the dream he is eager to identify himself with a dirty, greedy pig. We first interpreted[1] this dream as a reaction to the sexual wishes toward the analyst which he confessed in the 41st hour. According to our first interpretation, he pictures the analyst as protesting because he is such a dirty pig. Later the "two carloads" of pigs that had been ordered suggested another interpretation, that the patient, too, is protesting because his mother presented him with so many brothers and sisters. This latter interpretation, based on the emotional context, fits closely the interpretation suggested by the dream symbolism: that the boxcar with the pigs in it is a symbol of pregnancy. The patient's resentment of being presented with so many dirty pigs is resentment of the mother's many pregnancies.

This symbol interpretation receives further support from the fact that it brings our two earlier interpretations into close and understandable relation to each other.

When we first interpreted this dream (43), it was not clear just how guilt about his sexual wishes and protest against having so many brothers and sisters are related to each other. Our symbol interpretation now supplies the necessary link between these two conflicts. We need only assume that the patient has spun out his fantasy one step further. If he should act on his sexual wishes toward the analyst, the possibility of pregnancy would involve him once more in rivalry with a younger child for a mother's love.

If pencil-stealing dream (25) and pig dream (43) belong to the same psychological context, then the boxcar must represent the pregnant mother in the pencil-stealing dream (25) also, even though this boxcar contains pencils and pads instead of pigs. If we now translate this symbolism literally, we arrive at the interpretation that taking pencils and pads from the boxcar must have the

1. See chap. vi of this volume, pp. 45–46.

significance of attacking the pregnant mother to take her child from her.

We assume that this hostile impulse toward the pregnant mother belongs to a very early version of the text of this dream (25). We must reconstruct later versions in order to explain how a boxcar came to be substituted for the mother, and pencils and pads for babies.[2]

Fire-tending Dream and Anvil Dream.—We have already discussed[3] the fire-tending dream (45a) and the confirmation that it gives to the phallic significance of the iron bar in the anvil dream (12). The associations to the fire-tending dream (45a) make it clear that the lady's request that he stir up the fire symbolizes a sexual invitation. In this context the stove symbolizes a woman, fire is symbolic of sexual excitement, and stirring up the fire, of coitus. The role of the penis is presumably played by a poker held in the patient's hand.

Literal interpretation of this symbolism has some further implications. In the dream text (45a) the patient is requested not only to stir up the fire but also to remove the ashes. If the stove is a woman, cleaning out the ashes must be taking out something that is inside her body. Perhaps the stove clogged with ashes, too, is symbolic of pregnancy; and cleaning out the ashes, of getting rid of the mother's unborn child.

Yet there is an obvious objection to this interpretation. Ashes are a strange symbol to represent a child. As a waste product they are more suitable to represent a stool. In fact, the patient's associations dwell on the thought that ashes are waste. It is also easier to bring this last suggestion into relation with the other interpretation suggested by the psychological context. We have interpreted[4] the stove clogged with ashes as a pictorial representation of the dreamer's own resistance against responding to sexual temptation. When translated into physiological imagery, this picture looks more like constipation than like pregnancy.

There is still one more possibility: that both interpretations are correct. Perhaps the dream is equating a baby with a stool, as in

2. See chaps. xxiv and xxvii of this volume.
3. See chap. viii of this volume.
4. See chap. vi of this volume, p. 48.

the anal theory of birth, one of the commonest infantile sexual theories. To think of a baby as a waste product would be entirely in accord with the desire to get rid of him that we postulate.

In the anvil dream (12) we have already recognized that the iron bar is both a phallic symbol and the symbol of a grasping hand. Since the two dreams (12 and 45a) belong to the same context,[5] removing clinkers from a locomotive furnace in this dream (12) presumably has the same significance as removing ashes from a stove in the fire-tending dream (45a). This interpretation of the iron-bar symbol fits well into our earlier interpretation of the anvil dream (12)—that the patient is being beaten both for sexual wishes and for hostile wishes toward a brother-figure. The symbol interpretation merely designates the hostile wish more precisely as an aggressive wish against the mother's pregnancy.

Anvil Dream, Mexican Woman Dream, and Broom Dream.— Recurrence of symbolism is not the only way in which two dreams may resemble each other. The Mexican woman dream (44) makes use of a different set of symbols but resembles the anvil dream (12) closely in its pattern for dealing with the patient's guilt and with his need for rapport with the analyst or mother. In the anvil dream (12) an iron bar receives the beating that the patient feels he deserves; in the Mexican woman dream (44) a little boy gets a scrubbing because the patient's thoughts are "dirty." The parallel goes further. In both cases there is a sense of co-operation between the patient and the mother-figure in administering the punitive therapy. In the anvil dream (12) the patient is admiring the mother's work; in the Mexican woman dream (44) he is actively co-operating in scrubbing the child. These parallels with the much franker Mexican woman dream (44) confirm our earlier impression[6] that in the anvil dream (12) the iron bar gets a beating that the patient would like a brother to get instead of taking it himself.

The parallel structure of the two dreams also helps in the reconstruction of the Mexican woman dream (44). Except for the hint that the arm is the guilty organ, we do not know for

5. See chap. viii of this volume.
6. See I, 111–12.

what impulse the little boy is being scrubbed; but the parallel with the iron bar that is being beaten in the anvil dream (12) suggests that it is the same impulse that is symbolized by removing clinkers from a furnace—to attack the pregnant mother and take her child.

We can check this reconstruction by comparing the Mexican woman dream (44) with the broom dream (26), whose symbolism is suggestively similar. In the broom dream (26) the brush on both sides of the road corresponds perhaps to the woods of the later dream (44); the squirrel partly covered with leaves to the shack half-buried in the ground; the broom to the scrubbing brush; but the suggested act of hitting a squirrel is not homologous to the act of scrubbing the little boy—since hitting the squirrel is a suggested act that the patient is repudiating, whereas scrubbing the child's arm is a therapeutic procedure with punitive implications, in which the analyst (as Mexican woman) and the patient are co-operating. Hitting the squirrel in the broom dream (26) corresponds not to scrubbing the child in the Mexican woman dream (44) but to the impulse for which the child is being punished in this dream (44) and to the removing of clinkers from a stove in the anvil dream (12). In the broom dream (26) this impulse is not punished but repudiated. It is the repudiation of the disturbing impulse that parallels most closely the scrubbing of the little boy in the Mexican woman dream (44).

We have already suspected[7] that the squirrel in the broom dream (26) represents a child; and, if so, the fact that it is partly covered with leaves suggests a rather vivid symbolization of pregnancy. If we now follow out the implications of the parallels between the two dreams (26 and 44), we must suspect that the half-buried shack in the Mexican woman dream (44), which is homologous with the squirrel half-covered with leaves in the earlier dream (26), is also a symbol of pregnancy; and the impulse for which the little boy is getting a scrubbing in the Mexican woman dream (44) again turns out to be homologous with an act symbolic of attack on the pregnant mother, i.e., with the suggested act of hitting the squirrel half-covered with leaves.

Pubic Hair Symbolism in Four Dreams.—One more interpreta-

7. See chap. vi of this volume, p. 43.

tion, suggested by the literal implications of the dream symbolism, may help us bring the pattern of these two dreams (26 and 44) into relation with later dreams. If the half-buried shack is a uterine symbol, the woods around presumably represent pubic hair; and the underbrush on both sides of the road in the broom dream (26) probably has the same significance.

When we now examine the two dream texts more closely, we discover that in each dream (26, 44) the hair symbolism is duplicated. Not only the vegetation but also the bristles of the broom and brush are hair symbols. Since both broom and brush are grasped in the patient's hand, this symbolism suggests that we should interpolate another intermediate version between the impulse to attack the mother's pregnancy and the actual dream texts. In this intermediate version we must assume that the impulse to take the unborn child from the mother has been replaced by a less disturbing fantasy of pulling out her hair.

In two later dreams we find this fantasy portrayed in a more direct symbolism. We have already reported one of these dreams. After the flood dream (115) and just before the whiskey dream (116b) the patient reported a dream (116a) in which he was pulling up the weeds in a neighbor's yard.[8] We shall soon report an earlier weeding dream.[9]

8. According to our earlier interpretation of this dream (116a), the weeds growing in another man's yard represent the patient's guilty sexual wishes toward the analyst, who is another man's wife. Thus if our suggested interpretation of the symbolism is correct, this weeding dream (116a), like the Mexican woman dream (44), is masking a hostile impulse (pulling out hair, getting rid of a child) behind the rationalization of getting rid of his own guilty sexual impulses. A similar mechanism is equally clear in the earlier weeding dream (55).

9. See dream 55 reported in chap. xx, pp. 128–29.

CHAPTER XIX

Sex and Sibling Rivalry in a Long Sequence of Dreams

By piecing together the psychological contexts of six different dreams, we have found evidence in each of them of the patient's resentment of his mother's pregnancies and, in all but one, of an impulse to reach out his hand to take the child from her. This interpretation is consistent with our psychological understanding of each of these dreams, but it is still possible that the dreams that we have compared have been arbitrarily chosen. As a further check we should like to know how well our interpretation of this symbolism fits into our understanding of this whole period of the analysis.

Except in the symbolism, we do not find direct reference to the mother's pregnancies in the patient's associations and manifest dream content during this period. In the absence of such direct evidence we shall focus our attention, first, upon two questions:

1. Do hostile impulses toward children play a continuously significant role in this patient's behavior?

2. Are there other indications of an identification of children with waste products, such as is suggested by the ashes symbolism?

From Bridge Dream to Borrowed Book Dream.—We first recognized this patient's hostility to a child in the threat to his son implied by his playing with a snake in the snake dream (14).[1] With this hint from the snake dream, we next recognized the presence of the girl's brother in the bridge dream (10*a*) as a reference to the patient's hostility to brother and sister, and the playful pinching of the girl as a mitigated or erotized substitute for a hostile impulse.[2] A basic conflict between need for a mother's love and both sexual wishes toward mother and sister

1. See I, 91–93, reprinted in the Appendix to this volume (p. 349).
2. See I, 92–93, reprinted in the Appendix to this volume (p. 349).

and hostile wishes toward brother and sister proved to be the problem with which each one of the patient's first five dreams was struggling.

Our study of the water dreams has since shown that the water symbolism, too, is an elaboration of sexual wishes toward the mother and of hostile wishes toward brother and sister and in particular toward the mother's pregnancies.

In the next sequence of dreams we are best able to follow[3] the patient's reactions to the analyst's encouragement of forbidden impulses; but, except in the fireplug dream (19a), in which erotic impulses become manifest, the nature of the forbidden impulses that are being encouraged can be read only from the dream symbolism. Water symbolism, with its sexual and hostile implications toward the pregnant mother, plays the central role in the rowing (18a) and fireplug (19a) dreams. Then came two dreams (25 and 26) that we studied in the last chapter. The hostile impulses toward pregnancy that we read out of the symbolism of the pencil-stealing dream (25) and broom dream (26) are evidently a continuation of the conflict about hostility to children that has run through all the previous material. In the pencil-stealing dream (25), if we accept the boxcar as symbol of a woman, reaching into the boxcar should also have an erotic significance, with the arm serving as a phallic substitute. Such a condensation of phallic and hostile meanings of the outstretched arm and grasping hand is evidently continuous with the similar condensation of erotic (phallic) and hostile (grasping hand) significance of pinching the girl in the bridge dream (10a) and of the iron bar with a hook on the end of it in the anvil dream (12). In the broom dream (26) playing golf, as an admired masculine activity, may continue the phallic significance of the symbolic acts that we have just mentioned; but this admired phallic activity is now for the first time distinguished from (instead of being condensed with) the hostile impulse toward the mother's pregnancy symbolized by hitting the squirrel with a broom, which is now energetically repudiated.

Next comes a dream whose symbolism we have not yet deciphered. In this borrowed book dream (27), we have recog-

3. See Vol. I, chap. xxxiv.

nized[4] that the patient's need to repudiate the analyst's gift must be motivated by guilt toward her; but our only hint of the reason for his guilt is his laughing use of the word "mistreated" in describing the crumpled and worthless stocks that she gives him. Since it is not customary to speak of objects but only of living creatures as being "mistreated," it is perhaps not too hazardous to guess that "mistreated" stocks may have the same significance as hitting a squirrel, thus continuing the theme of hostility to a child symbolized in the dream just preceding. This, of course, is a guess that should be checked by further study of the worthless-stocks symbolism.

In our last chapter we suspected that the ashes symbolism gives expression to the wish to get rid of a child in two ways: not only by the act of removing the ashes from the stove but also by identification of the child with a waste product. If this interpretation is correct, we might expect the same identification of a child with a waste product to appear also in connection with this patient's other symbolic representations of pregnancy. This expectation is confirmed by the three consecutive dreams (25, 26, 27) that we have been studying.

In association to the broom dream (26) the patient tells of sweeping up in the basement after putting coal in the furnace. Since a broom is the tool that is to be used on the squirrel too, this association puts the squirrel in the same class with the patient's sweepings in the basement, in the same class with coal, ashes, and waste.

An association to the borrowed book dream (27) brings this dream, too, into relation with waste products. The patient tells us as an afterthought that someone threw the stocks into the wastebasket.

In the pencil-stealing dream (25) we have only a hint of this identification of what is inside the mother-symbol with something worthless, to be gotten rid of. After taking pencils and a pad, he throws back the pad as something cheap and worthless.

The pencil-stealing dream also calls what is inside the boxcar "merchandise." This perhaps puts these contents of the boxcar in the same class with the stocks of the borrowed book dream

4. See chap. vi of this volume, p. 43.

(27). In any case, we have in the borrowed book dream a significant association of two contrasting concepts—stocks, "merchandise," possessions, on the one hand, and waste, something worthless, to be thrown away, on the other hand.

From Dirty Food Dream to Burning Logs Dream.—After the long resistance period in which the patient is repudiating the analyst's help, there follows a sequence of dreams in which his conflict begins to appear in less disguised form.

In the dirty food dream (39) and the pump dream (41) we find the patient struggling with the same two conflicts that preoccupied him in the first period of his treatment and which we have continued to recognize in the symbolism since then. In the dirty food dream (39) the six men around the camp fire and the reference to "food enough for a regiment" show that the problem to which he is returning is again one of sharing the mother with rivals, with brother and sisters. From his confessions after interpretation of the pump dream (41) we learn that he has also been preoccupied with sexual thoughts about the analyst, to which the dirty food in the dirty food dream (39) as well as the dirty water of the pump dream are allusions.

In the dreams of the next four hours (43, 44, 45a, 46a and b) the patient continues preoccupied with the same two conflicts as before.

The sexual conflict is nearer the surface. In discussing the pig dream (43), he is eager to appease the analyst by calling himself a dirty pig. In the Mexican woman dream (44) he pictures himself co-operating with the analyst (Mexican woman) in scrubbing the dirty little boy who represents himself. In both cases it is his sexual wishes that are characterized as dirty. Continuing the same theme underneath a transparent symbolism, the fire-tending dream (45a) is reacting to the treatment as a sexual seduction and the burning logs and penis envy dreams (46a and b) give evidence of the patient's longing for instruction from a father to tell him what to do about his sexual impulses.

Under cover of this sexual conflict hostile impulses toward rivals for the mother's love emerge. In the pig dream (43) the "two carloads" of dirty pigs that have been ordered betray the fact that it is the patient who feels cheated because his mother presented him with so many brothers and sisters. As we have already pointed out, scrubbing the dirty little boy in the Mexican woman dream (44) is a fitting sequel to calling the children dirty pigs in the pig dream (43). After condemnation comes punishment. By attributing to his sibling rivals his own guilt on account of sexual impulses, he has found an excuse for giving vent to his hostility toward them. It is this rationalization that has made it possible for his hostility to emerge in the overt act of scrubbing the little boy. The little boy, whom the patient first identifies as his own son, is really hated not because he is dirty but because he is a rival for a mother's love.

As soon as this rationalization ceases to perform this function, we must expect that hostility toward the child will be denied direct expression and permitted outlet only in some symbolic act. If our suggested interpretation of the symbolism of the fire-tending dream (45a) is correct, then this expectation is fulfilled. Hostility toward his sibling rivals is now finding outlet in the symbolic act of cleaning out ashes from a stove.

CHAPTER XX

Two Dreams and Two Memories

In the last few chapters we reasoned from the dream symbolism that the symbol of the grasping hand that keeps recurring in a long series of this patient's dreams is symbolic of an impulse, dating from the patient's early childhood, to attack the mother while she was pregnant in order to get rid of the child. In confirmation of this reasoning, review of the patient's material during this whole period revealed the fact that impulses to get rid of children and implied identification of children with objects that are to be gotten rid of or thrown away are not only encountered in a few isolated dreams but also constitute a central theme throughout this whole period of analysis.

If we still have doubts about the importance in this material of the need to get rid of a child, let us now review the course of the patient's analysis after the short period of resistance that followed the burning logs (46a) and penis envy (46b) dreams.

In the 50th hour the patient reports that he wheezed the night before after doing some varnishing. Then he reports the following dreams:

Dream 50a.—One horse and a buggy with crooked wheels and axles. Horse not hitched. The buggy just stood there. The horse had small ankles and bright eyes. I wanted to know whether it was male or female, and it was female.

Dream 50b.—About two family doctors. Either I was with them or I saw them. They were together.

In association he thinks that the doctor represents some sickness, weakness. Both doctors were jolly and laughing. They were walking into a big porch. The patient has actually called these doctors when he was sick. The older man was their family doctor until six years ago. He was the doctor of a fraternal order to which the patient belongs. Then the younger man got the job. The analyst comments that these two doctors are brothers. The patient reports that the older one brought both of his boys. The analyst points out that the problem of sickness is associated with children. The patient inquires if that has anything to do with his asthma. He sure was pleased with the boys! He confirms the analyst's comment that his asthma came back after the birth of his boy. After that he had asthma for three years, after which there was relief for four years more. The analyst reminds him that his asthma came back once before after he discovered that a woman with whom he was intimate was pregnant.

In association to the buggy in the dream the patient says it was like an old farmer's buggy: "Horse and buggy is a pleasure." He went in them for a good time. Then he inquires whether it might be a baby buggy. To the crooked axles he remarks, "Kind of out of shape. I didn't have a good view of it." He liked the way the horse was built; "thin legs, long neck, face good, good proportions, good eyes." He was interested whether it was male or female. It represents a woman. Hair reddish and shiny. When the analyst inquires what woman, the patient says, "Any woman." He was interested in the beauty of the horse. People look at a woman's hips, face, and chest. The analyst suggests that a horse is a woman toward whom the patient feels sexual attraction. She suspects that the misshapen buggy may represent a pregnant woman. The patient replies, "My wife's hair is black, but two women who come to the house have chestnut hair." The patient is not interested in them. In answer to the analyst's question, he does not remember the color of his mother's hair, perhaps it was chestnut. . . . "I admired mother's build. She was tall and slender. She was a well-built woman and had beauty with it. She was tall, not skinny and not too fat either. She always looked young." He remembers on Sunday mother and father came to see him at school. Other boys saw him with mother and asked him if mother was his sister. She must have looked young. He wonders about the buggy. Was it a baby buggy? "We had an old buggy at home," but he "doesn't see any sense in it."

"Well, maybe there is." Once he was left to mind his brother. He was supposed to take care of him. The buggy was outside on the lawn. The patient pushed him down the hill, and he fell out. He doesn't know what possessed him. He never did get along well with the brother. The brother was left at home, and the patient was sent away. He thought he was a better son than the patient. The patient was always jealous of him, all right. He was luckier than the patient was. The patient begins to see that that was reflected in his dream. He did like him to some extent, but the patient was always pushed away from home, and the brother could stay. The patient went away to learn a trade . . . then couldn't get along at home. He was always away from the mother and missed her more than anyone else. . . . He cannot see why that should stir up asthma. The first woman with whom he was intimate . . . he didn't know she was pregnant until his sister told him. Then he had asthma when he found out.

Four days later, in the next hour (51), the patient complains that he has that feverish feeling again but "no fever on the thermometer." It makes him sick all over like a high fever. But his asthma is better. He has had a tongue lashing from his wife. He "blew off" twice but tried to control himself. The feverish feeling began yesterday at work. He and his wife were quarreling about money and the children last night. He again dreamed about the same horse and buggy, but it was very faint, like a picture passing before his eyes. He does not know whether it scared him. It was more like a camera picture. When the analyst reminds him of the memory of pushing the baby down the hill, the patient replies that he got a good trimming for it because he could have killed the brother; but he did not mean to. He did not want to take care of him and wanted to get rid of him and so let the buggy go. He wonders why he pictured his mother like a horse. He liked horses and he liked his mother too . . . he never did like babies right after birth, not until they began to crawl or talk. Not even his own. . . . He may have felt the same way toward his brother, but he doesn't remember it. His brother is like the analyst's child. . . . His burning sensations are like the sensations that follow the use of adrenalin. When the analyst mentions the connection between adrenalin and anger, he replies that he was angry yesterday. His wife does not talk like a human being. It was wild, hard language. The children are tremendous offenders. The patient went out and did not come home until 1 o'clock. He played poker and had two glasses of beer. The quarrel started when his wife needed money, and the patient told her to wait until the next day, which was pay day. She thought he had money and wouldn't give it to her. The patient told her to take the boys to the dentist and she didn't do it yet. . . . He feels he would like to kick somebody and himself too. . . . He insists he has no love for his wife.

In the next hour (52), two days later, the patient is thinking about breaking up the home. He wheezes badly as he discusses it. He is stuck because he has the house. It costs a lot, but in the main it is his feeling toward the children. Still the condition at home is not good for the children. If he separated from his wife, it would set him back to where he was twenty-five or thirty years ago. . . . The analyst remarks that his asthma comes whenever he is afraid that sex or hostility will interfere with his relationship to his mother. . . .

In the next hour (53), the next day, he is critical of political speeches that he has heard. Then he asks if it would help for his wife to see a social worker. . . . In childhood he used to be depressed whenever he was scolded. He took a scolding hardest from his father and next hardest from his teacher. He was depressed when someone was dressed better than he or got along better in school. . . . He inquires what is the best way to get away from these conditions. If the home doesn't improve, the boys might become criminals, and the patient will be responsible. He wheezes badly as he says this and cries a little.

In the next hour (54), four days later, he reports that there has been little wheezing, but he spends most of the hour discussing illnesses he has had. He admits that he has a resistance to digging deeper in the analysis.

Two days later (55th hour) he reports a dream:

Dream 55.—The patient is in the back yard picking out wild grass from lawn. He pulls up about one bushel basket full.

In association he wonders whether the wild grass refers to his wild life. He was cleaning up the lawn; maybe cleaning up his mind, cleaning out the bad thoughts. In the back yard around the house (in the dream) there was some kind of weed with long roots which was spreading. He pulled out the roots and all. But green grass is something pleasant and clean. The bad thoughts, he thinks, relate to his home. They have deep roots and have been spreading for years. These thoughts killed everything good in him, his ambition and self-respect. He was pulling it out and throwing it into the waste basket . . . last night he was angry because his wife kept the children at a bunco party until after twelve. He did not want the children to attend this party. It is starting the children early to shake dice. He was angry all right and expressed his thoughts and raised hell about it. He likes to be home alone. The wife and children irritate him when they are home, but he was not angry when he was left alone. He is surprised that he is not wheezing today. When the analyst suggests that weeds grow in the mother-earth and may represent a strong attachment to the mother, the patient again dwells on how deep the roots were (in the dream). Some roots were about eleven feet long. He was surprised when he got hold of the weed and it came out so easily and the root didn't break off. He was thinking what a clean job of it he was doing. Usually weeding is boring, but he was doing such a clean job of it. It is difficult for him to accept the analyst's suggestion that he has such a deep attachment to her.

In the next hour (56) the patient is wheezing again and is irritated when the analyst presses her interpretation that the patient is afraid of separation from her and that he wants to be a baby to his wife. But he does admit that he leaves everything to his wife around the home.

In the 57th hour he reports having been awakened with asthma by a dream, but he has forgotten it. He is so miserable and unhappy about the house. . . . He is ashamed of "that woman." She is so sloppy and dirty. He began to wheeze when a woman remarked how fat his wife was. He complains that he has no backbone. He cannot understand why he puts up with his situation at home. All he does is to lie down and cry. In answer to the analyst's interpretation of his self-punishing tendencies, he says he is dragging a ball and chain. . . . He is like a criminal. He starts to wheeze.

In the 58th hour he says that he did dig up some criminal guilt all right and reports a memory of sneaking home late one day and coming upon father and mother in intercourse. As he sneaked into the house, something attracted his attention. He peeked in the window and saw that his mother was getting the worst of it. He shouted "Murder" and rushed around the house. His mother came out. The patient thought that the father was chasing her, but she said it was all right, that they were just fooling around. He hated the thought of that for many years. . . . He breathes hard as he tells how his illness has given his wife the power to dominate him.

In the 59th hour he is again wheezing. He complains chiefly of indigestion after eating green onions. He cannot account for it. He played poker the night before and won. Nothing upset him at home because his wife and children were out. He wonders if it was because he had to prepare his own supper. He was dissatisfied with his supper. There was no butter on his bread, and a fellow offered him two onions when he exploded about it. He was angry with his wife and showed it. . . . Yes, he is constipated.

In the 60th hour, after reporting continued wheezing, he tells the following dream:

Dream 60a.–Dug excavation on Michigan and Randolph. Great big hole. Someone said they used an elephant to lift big stones, and elephant went wild and had to be shot.

In association he says there was a crowd of people around; someone told him about the elephant. An elephant does not make any sense. An elephant is power and is used for power. The corner of Michigan and Randolph reminds him of nothing. He has been there many times. There is a subway there, and there was an excavation there a few years ago. The analyst reminds him that Michigan and Randolph is on his way to the Institute. . . . Then he reports another dream:

Dream 60b.–Four of us at work, inspectors, we were dissatisfied. We were going to quit Nickel Plate and go to I.C. One man went first. The rest of us undecided. Perhaps we'd better stay where we were. Didn't want to lose position we had already.

The patient agrees that there is an I.C. station at Michigan and Randolph and that the I.C. is near the analyst's apartment (where the analyst is seeing the patient this time). Then the analyst remarks that in the dream text the patient was in conflict about changing his job. The patient adds, "We were all set. Two fellows had changed already." The patient used to work for the I.C. The analyst suggests that he is transferring his conflict from his home to his work, that he wishes to transfer his interest from his wife to some earlier interest or to the analyst. In answer to this interpretation he says that he was undecided. He talked the other man out of it; he held back. "We had seniority here, and over there we would start as new men." He had some fear about it. He was more satisfied when he worked for the I.C. One year after his marriage he lost his job during a strike. That one year of marriage was pleasant. He thinks his work represents security; there is more pleasure than there is around home. When the analyst suggests that the patient is afraid to give up his dependent relations to his wife, the patient recalls that there has been a murder near the analyst's home. The police think that a boy did it. The patient is afraid for his own children. He energetically rejects the analyst's interpretation that he resents the children because they come between him and his wife. Then he reports another dream:

Dream 6oc.—I was in Cook County Building. I was sitting on the floor in a corridor. Don't remember what I was doing. Along came a real estate man I know (a Jew down the street from us). He pulled out a $20.00 bill and put it on my shoulder in the back. Then he said, "Take it, it's yours," and walked away. I got up and walked away. Forgot about the $20.00. Then after I got out of the building, I went back to look for it and didn't find it.

In association the patient is astonished that the Cook County building is also on Randolph Street. The man in the dream is again the real estate dealer with whom the patient worked years ago, who tried to cheat the patient out of his commissions. The patient had to report it to the Real Estate Board. The patient was mixed up in politics years ago and met this man in the County building. Sitting on the floor, the patient says, is like a child. . . . He always felt guilty about real estate deals. There is crooked stuff in it. He would rather lose the deal than be involved in it.

The next hour (61), on the following day, he is still wheezing. He reverts to the real estate man. He cannot see why he has been wheezing so much this last week. When the analyst remarks that the dream was about cheating, the patient says in business it's always one man trying to get another. A lot of men have no heart. There is no limit to their desire to beat a man just for profit. The patient would tip off the one who was getting the worst of it and would lose business. In association to the $20.00, the patient remarks that it was quite a bit of money and he was so careless. "I never had any faith in that man. Why didn't he hand it to me instead of putting it down my back?"

Being a child reminds him of his brother. No doubt he did wrong to the brother. The brother was younger. He was jealous of the brother. He was angry that the brother could stay home. The patient was shoved away in the city. He missed the open spaces in the country. He was caged in a room. The patient remembers that it is harvest time. Now everything is in bloom. He recalls another accident. He lost his brother. His brother was just crawling or walking. He went away into the field of rye. "We couldn't find him. We looked all night." The patient was worried because he was to blame. The next morning someone heard the brother cry. He was missing all the afternoon and night. It may have been a put-up job. They were afraid someone might have kidnapped him. The patient was worried all night and didn't sleep. When the analyst suggests death wishes against the brother, the patient insists it was an accident. It caused trouble for mother and the rest of them. There were always gypsies around. He recalls the Bible story of Joseph but protests he did love his brother, only he was jealous of him when the patient was sent away from home. When the analyst points out the conflict between hate and love, the patient wheezes. Now he recalls that he was the one that carried his brother Joseph into the field and remembers that it was harvest time and that his mother was busy preparing meals for the harvesters.

CHAPTER XXI

Anal Interpretation of Pregnancy

Interpretive Comment. The $20.00 Bill Dream.—In the $20.00
bill dream (60c) the patient walks off and leaves behind him a
$20.00 bill; in the childhood memory reported in the next hour
(61) he walked off and left his baby brother in a rye field. Just as
in the dream (60c), he went back but could not find the $20.00
bill, so in the childhood memory they went back and could not
find the baby. The baby remained lost all night in the rye field.

This dream (60c) occurred at a time when the analyst's repeated interpretations of his dependence on her and on his wife
and mother were increasingly activating his hostility to her child,
to his own two children, and toward his brother. The crooked
wagon dream (50a) had alluded to his memory of pushing his
brother's baby buggy down the hill; and his impulses to do something violent were finding projected expression in his fear that his
children would become criminals, in the elephant's going wild in
the elephant dream (60a), and in his references to a murder near
the analyst's home.

The $20.00 bill dream (60c) is a dramatic protestation of his
childish innocence. Like an innocent child, he is sitting in a corridor of that den of crooked politicians, the Cook County building! And he does not know enough to take the $20.00 that his
politician friend slips him from behind. Only afterward does he
go back to look for it—in vain. In other words, he is thinking
rather regretfully what an innocent fool he was, not to have taken
advantage of the chances to get money that this politician and
real estate dealer put in his way. He was so innocent that, instead
of profiting, he got cheated by this man.

This protest of childish innocence fits well into the context of
the memory reported in the next hour. His mother should have
known that he was just a child! She should not have intrusted him
with responsibility for his brother! Now he would like to make
the same protest to the analyst. The analyst should not talk so

much about his dependence. He is still too much a child to be expected to take responsibility for his children!

This is not the first time that this patient has substituted money for a child toward whom he is hostile. In the borrowed book dream (27) we have already suspected that the two "mistreated stocks" that he receives from the woman are symbols of his impulse to "mistreat" his own two children. The borrowed book dream (27) and the $20.00 bill dream (60c) run parallel in a number of points: In each dream (27 and 60c) he receives a gift. The two stocks correspond to the $20.00 (both are probably references to the fact that he has two children). The fact that the two stocks are worthless and that someone throws them into the waste basket in the earlier dream (27) is paralleled by the patient's walking off and leaving the money in the later dream (60c).

In both dreams (27 and 60c) the patient's depreciation and rejection of the proffered gift is motivated by guilt. In the earlier dream (27) his sense of guilt is intensified by feelings of obligation because he is receiving help from the analyst. In view of his hostile wishes toward her child,[1] how can he accept the help that she is offering him! The dream (27) attempts to mitigate this feeling of obligation and guilt by depreciating the value of the analyst's gift, by transferring over to the "stocks" that he is receiving from her the hostility that he feels toward her child (or his own two children). In the $20.00 bill dream (60c) he punishes himself, by losing the proffered money, for his desire to be rid of the brother[1] who was intrusted to him in childhood (or of the two children for whom he is now responsible).

We ordinarily think of money as something of value, something to be held onto, not thrown away; and the fact that this patient can be punished by losing money is a sign that he, too, values money. Yet, because his guilt compels him to substitute money for a child, he must transfer over to money his hostile im-

1. In the dream work and in other unconscious reactions, situations that are dynamically similar are not sharply distinguished and are often fused together (condensed) like a composite picture. In these dreams (27 and 60c), for example, the patient's reactions to the analyst's child, to his own two children, and to his brother in the childhood memory are closely identified (for further discussion of this point, see chap. xxix).

pulses toward the child. His impulse toward the child is a complex one, first to take it from the mother, then to throw it away. This double impulse is transferred over to money and possessions. In the pencil-stealing dream (25) he takes pencils and a pad but throws back the pad. In the borrowed book dream (27) he receives the book and stocks from a woman, but the stocks have been "mistreated" and somebody throws them into the waste basket. In the $20.00 bill dream (60c) he receives the money but walks off and leaves it.

This paradoxical attitude toward money explains this patient's fascination for gambling and for playing cards. Both gambling and card playing consist largely in taking objects and throwing them away. In the 65th hour, which we shall report later in this chapter, the patient specifically relates his guilt toward his pinochle partner (a woman to whom he was sexually attracted) to the fact that in losing a card game he was taking money from her children.

Anal Interpretation of Pregnancy.—In the psychoanalytic literature we are familiar with such ambivalent attitudes toward money. Money is not the first object that the child wants both to hold onto and also to get rid of. Freud has made us aware that an infant treats his stool as an erotic object and derives pleasure not only from expelling it at a time of his own choosing but also from retaining it. Freud (1908) also pointed out the anal-erotic significance of money, the fact that the child's interest in the stool is regularly transferred to money; and in a later paper[2] he shows how, in the symbolism of the Unconscious, stool, child, penis, and money are often interchangeable. Even though undisguised references to the anal functions have not yet appeared in our patient's dreams and associations, we must suspect, as a result of our psychoanalytic knowledge, that his close association of a child, ashes, money, and (as we shall show later[3]) a tool are based on these "symbolic equations" that Freud has demonstrated.

Our study of the symbolism of the fire-tending dream (45a) has already suggested that the pregnant mother's unborn child is being identified with a stool in this dream. The parallel symbol-

2. S. Freud, 1916.
3. See chap. xxiv.

isms of "merchandise" (25) and of dirty pigs (43) in a boxcar, of a squirrel half-buried in the leaves (26) and of two "stocks" in a book (27), are also suggestive of the symbolic equation of child and money (possessions).

Another bit of confirmatory evidence is the frequently recurring reference to approach from behind in this patient's dreams. In the bridge dream (10a) the patient is pinching the girl in the back (i.e., from behind). In the burning logs dream (46a) the snakes threaten from behind. In the first weeding dream (55) the patient is pulling up the weeds in his back yard. In the $20.00 bill dream (60c) the money is given him from behind. If impregnation and getting rid of a child are both thought of as taking place per anum, then we have a clue for the understanding of these dream details.

Babies and Cow Manure.—To check these interpretations, we skip ahead to a dream reported four months later, a couple of weeks after the patient's return from the summer interruption of his analysis.

During the summer months the patient had been free of asthma, but he developed an attack after telephoning for his first appointment. His asthma became severe in the two weeks immediately following his return to analysis and was accompanied by indigestion, constipation, and "chills." His symptoms developed after his partner at a pinochle game reproached him for losing money which she needed for her children. In the next two hours (67th and 68th) he confessed to having been sexually interested in this woman.

In the 67th hour he is wheezing hard. He reports a dream:

Dream 67.—Man showing me gutter on the roof. It was full of ice. He said it was a poor layout and poor spout.

In association he mentions that this house is next door to the patient's house, has been empty all summer, and has just been redecorated, just as the analyst's house has been. The analyst interprets the dream as an attempt to "freeze up" his sexual interest in her.

In the following (68th) hour also, there were interpretations of the sexual transference. At the end of the hour he reported that he felt better, that his bowels had moved, and that his appetite was better.

In the next (69th) hour he complains that he was sick in his stomach and vomited up milk and pudding he had eaten before coming to the hour. Then he reports a dream of the night before:

Dream 69.—About a lot of feminine horses. All had little ones. Stable like a lying-in hospital, for women. Nice and broken-down ones, all kinds, and colts alongside. Men and women there. Don't know who they were. One woman stepped right into the manure, like cows', not horses' manure. She stood right in it all slopped up. Stables were government or army stables. In another room someone opened the door. I could see horses having colts. Some man, all dressed in white, said, "Don't look in there, it's not for you to look in there."

In association the patient recalls that he had a dream about horses once before (dream 50*a*) and compared them to women. In the stable there were two rows of horses. He saw lots of horses in the army when he was in the hospital but never was in the stable there. Another thing, in the old country there was a government stable for breeding horses. It was on the other side of the river where he dreamed about meeting the girl.[4] The stable was alongside this bridge. The horses there were for breeding only. He was never inside but only saw the horses outside.

In association to the woman stepping in the cow manure: "She was right in the dirt. Her shoes and stockings all dirty. My wife? She walked right through the dirt." The analyst points out that she walks into dirty subjects and that a cow is an animal that gives milk. Later she suggests that the patient wishes to dirty the mother because she had babies and gave milk to them, that he is peeping at the mother having a baby. The patient responds that he never saw the mother but was curious about babies. He never saw a woman having a baby, not even his own. He protests that (in the dream) he didn't dirty the woman. She was just standing in it. He protests that he never complained because his wife had babies. He admits that he never did love her since then, but that wasn't the cause. He felt a sharp pain in the left side and back like left

4. See dream 10*a*, reported in I, 79, and reprinted in the Appendix (p. 335).

kidney and felt funny all day. He continues to ruminate over the analyst's suggestion that he was angry at the mother for having babies. The analyst reminds him that he has a conflict about her "baby," too, and recalls that two weeks previously he had seen her child. Then she had had to cancel the appointment the next day. The patient agrees it is possible and thinks again of the dream about the horse, which the analyst reminds him was identified with his mother. The patient agrees he never did like a little baby. He doesn't like to see a newborn baby, even his own. He didn't like to see the baby take the breast. His mother was sick with one baby, and a strange woman came, but he didn't like that either. He notes that he is no longer wheezing and remarks that he sure did raise hell for one week (i.e., with his asthma and other symptoms).

In the next hour (70) he reported that he had slept very soundly, though he wheezed some but still had a sick feeling in his stomach. Thinking about the milk he vomited before his last dream (69), he recalled that it would make him sick as a child if the woman serving food had dirty clothes or hands. The woman in the dream (69) was taller and slenderer than his wife; she was more like the analyst.

Interpretive Comment.—This dream is again a reaction to the analyst's interpretation of the patient's sexual wishes toward her. The dream retorts that she is just like all sorts of other women, that she puts herself on a level with horses and cows, that she steps right into the dirt. In contrast to her, the dream pictures a man in a (clean) white uniform, presumably a physician in the hospital, who warns him that this sight is not for his eyes. In this we recognize the patient's ever recurring wish for a male physician, who, instead of tempting him sexually, would treat him medically and warn him gently to keep away from sexual topics. A few days later he reports that he has acted on this wish by going to the asthma clinic and that the doctor there had expressed his disapproval of psychoanalysis.

Of particular interest is the fact that this dream deals with childbirth, whereas the interpretation that served as the dream stimulus dealt with the patient's sexual wishes rather than with his reactions to pregnancy. The most probable explanation is that the dream is a warning to the analyst. Projecting his own sexual wishes, he attributes them to the analyst and warns her that her fate will be the same as that of all sorts of other women, or of horses and cows; that pregnancy and childbirth follow inevitably on the gratification of animal desires.

In the preceding material we have seen repeated indications of his wish to regard children as dirty pigs, dirt, ashes, waste, something to be gotten rid of. This stable dream (69) expresses this attitude without disguise and reduces it to the simplest possible terms. The child is equated[5] with cow manure, childbirth with defecation.

The stable dream (69) and the material leading up to it show clearly the patient's tendency to defend himself against sexual wishes by giving them displaced outlet in the symptom of constipation. In the frozen gutter dream (67), just preceding the stable dream, the ice clogging up the gutter is symbolic of his need to "freeze up" his sexual interest both in the analyst and in his pinochle partner; and during this whole period he had been suffering from constipation. In the hour (68) just previous to the stable dream (69) his last association was his expression of relief that the period of constipation was over and that he was now able to move his bowels. Then the stable dream (69) implies that a woman is having a child and equates childbirth with defecation.

In the fire-tending dream (45a) we suspected that the stove clogged up with ashes was a projected representation of the patient's own tendency to constipation. At the time of the stable dream (69) we know that the patient has just recovered from a stubborn constipation. In the context of the stable dream (69) it is clear that the patient's constipation of the preceding weeks must also have expressed a protest against the fantasy of a child's being brought into the world.

5. We base this interpretation on an implied parallelism in the manifest dream: A lying-in hospital is a stable—a place where women have babies, horses have colts, and cows produce cow manure.

CHAPTER XXII

Present Dynamic Influence of Past Conflicts

Some Doubts.—We have been treating the dreams and associations of one whole year (69 hours) of this patient's analysis as a single psychological context. Whenever the emotional context of one dream proved inadequate for the interpretation of some detail, we searched through the patient's whole material for similar details, hoping to fill in the gaps in our understanding by putting together the two or more contexts in which these similar details occurred. In this way we pieced together a consistent picture of the patient's resentment of the mother's many pregnancies, of impulses to do violence to the expected child, of fears of losing the mother's love as a consequence, and of attempts to avoid estranging the mother by substituting trivial or harmless symbolic acts for these violent impulses.

Before elaborating these conclusions, we shall first consider some doubts about the reliability of our procedure: Common sense teaches us that a person's behavior is usually a reaction to present situations or recent events. We should expect dreams, too, to be reactions to recent events; and we know that we cannot really understand a dream until we discover the dream stimulus, the precipitating situation to which it is reacting. In a year's time many things happen. Yet in nearly every one of this patient's dreams we have found evidence of hostile impulses toward his mother's pregnancies. Can we believe that this patient's life has been so monotonous that he could continue preoccupied every night with this one theme?

One more fact makes this conclusion extraordinary. At this time the only mother-figures in this patient's life are his wife and his analyst. Neither one of them is pregnant. Since the theme of pregnancy has so little actuality just now, what could be keeping him preoccupied with it?

A Present Problem Reactivates the Memory of Past Failures.—

We have already discussed[1] how present situations and memories from the past interact in the integration of behavior. When confronted with a present problem, one reactivates memories of how similar problems were solved in the past. If problems similar to the present problem have never been solved, then memories of previous failure are called up.

In terms of this principle we can understand why this patient is preoccupied with his childhood rivalry with brother and sister for his mother's love. Just now he is similarly rivalrous with his own two children and with the analyst's child. His own two children are a threat to his dependence on his wife, just as his brother and sister were once a threat to his dependence on his mother; and just as his aggressive impulses toward brother and sister threatened to estrange him still further from the mother (in childhood), so now his aggressive impulses toward his own two children and toward the analyst's child threaten to estrange him still further from his wife and the analyst. The problem of adjusting to rivals for a mother's love is an unsolved problem now as it was then; and whatever now stirs up this problem at home or in the analysis tends also to reactivate memories of the same unsolved conflict in the past.

But Just What Is Reactivating Memories of the Mother's Pregnancies?—These considerations account adequately for the repeated reactivation of memories of rivalry with brother and sister. They do not account specifically for the ever recurring references to the mother's pregnancies in the dream symbolism.

In search of a clue let us consider carefully the implications of certain facts to which we have given only passing attention.

The pig dream (43) was precipitated by the analyst's first direct interpretation of the patient's sexual transference in the 41st hour. Much relieved by this interpretation, he had confessed that "keeping that secret" had had "an awful effect" on him. When he discusses the pig dream (43), he is eager to continue his newly won sense of reconciliation with the analyst by condemning himself as a dirty pig.

We wish now to call attention to one perplexing detail of this reaction: Although this dream (43) is reacting to an interpreta-

1. See Vol. I, chaps. xxxii and xxxviii.

tion of the patient's sexual wishes toward the analyst, both the dream symbolism and the dream thoughts are preoccupied with reactions to the mother's pregnancies.

We should prehaps be less impressed with this observation if it were not duplicated in later material. The precipitating stimulus for the stable dream (69) was again an interpretation of the patient's unconscious sexual interest in the analyst. In the text of the stable dream (69) the detail of the woman's stepping into the cow manure is a specific reference to this interpretation. The patient dwells on the fact that she "walked right through the dirt," "stood right in it all slopped up"; that her shoes and stockings were all dirty. All this the analyst correctly interprets as a reaction to her walking into a dirty topic. Yet the central preoccupation of this dream is again with pregnancy and childbirth.

Sex and Babies.—How are we to account for the fact that this patient twice reacted to an interpretation of his sexual wishes by a dream about pregnancy? The answer to this question is a fact of everyday knowledge: that children are the product and consequence of sexual activity. Projecting responsibility for his sexual wishes on the analyst, who has called his attention to them, the dream is warning her that the result of acting on sexual impulses is the same as it would be for any animal, that gratification of animal desires is likely to be followed by pregnancy and childbirth.

This interpretation is indicated so clearly in the dream context (69) that we need not fear being led astray when we find it again in the dream symbolism. The dream text characterizes the analyst's talking about sex as a woman stepping into cow manure. The imagery chosen for this characterization suggests a depreciatory and inverted symbolic representation of coitus (a woman putting her foot into cow manure instead of a man inserting his penis into the vagina). When we fit this symbol interpretation into its place in the dream text (69), we recognize that the dream is dramatically recapitulating the patient's first discovery that the birth of his numerous brothers and sisters is somehow the result of the sexual activity of the parents. The dream text takes us back directly to the atmosphere of these early sexual investigations. Children are being born. He is puzzled. (In the dream text he does not know who all the people are.) Then follows the explanation.

If our interpretation of the woman's stepping into the cow manure is correct, he recalls at this point the coitus of the parents.
His disgust and resentment are openly expressed. The fact that
the stables are government stables for breeding horses emphasizes
again the theme of his sexual curiosity in childhood. By condensing a lying-in hospital and a stable, the dreamer gives expression
to the thought that there is not much difference between the
breeding of horses and the breeding of babies. In the dream text,
his curiosity continues until he is warned by the man in white;
"It is not for you to look in there."

Fixation on a Disturbing Discovery.—It is not extraordinary
that this patient knows that sexual intercourse may result in pregnancy; but it is strange that he is reacting to this fact as though it
were a discovery that he is making for the first time. He is still
reacting with strong emotion to this fact. His disgust and resentment are still sufficient to freeze up his sexual interest in women,
to inhibit his sexual curiosity, and to make him dream of a man in
a clean white suit who tells him that such things are not for his
eyes.

Evidently the conflict stirred up by discovery of the procrea-
tive significance of sexual intercourse is another one of the unsolved problems of childhood that is still exerting a profound
influence on the patient's behavior. Why is his curiosity not yet
satisfied? After so many years why must he still be dreaming
about the problem of where children come from? To account for
this fact, we must inquire into the emotional reactions stirred up
by this discovery.

The patient is still in conflict about this discovery because he
can neither rid himself of sexual impulses nor tolerate children as
rivals for his mother's love. There are only two possible realistic
and satisfying solutions for this problem. Either he must use con-
traceptives, or he must reconcile himself to sharing with the children their mother's love and to himself accepting responsibility
for them. It is evident from this dream (69) that he has been unable to make the emotional adjustment necessary for either of
these solutions. He is still attempting the impossible task of trying
to freeze up his sexual cravings, of trying to find outlet for his
sexual pressures in the regressive symptom of constipation.

In normal development this problem should have been struggled through to a fairly satisfactory solution in the few years following puberty. The reason for this patient's continued failure to solve it is indicated in his dream (69). In the dream text he is not even struggling wholeheartedly to find a solution. He is inclined rather to accept the advice of the man in the clean white uniform, that these dirty animal processes are not for his eyes. He has failed to work the conflict through to a satisfactory solution because he long ago withdrew from the task of struggling to solve it.

A Person's Whole Life Is a Single Psychological Context.—At the beginning of this chapter we entertained doubts about the reliability of our procedure of treating the dreams and associations of a whole year of analysis as a single context. In criticism of such a procedure we cited our usual common-sense impression that behavior is predominantly a reaction to present situations and recent events. Since life involves us in so many different kinds of situations, how can it possibly make sense to treat the events of a whole year of this patient's life as a single emotional context?

To this doubt we now have an answer. Problems in the present cannot profitably be distinguished sharply from the similar problems in the past. Every reaction to a present situation is based on patterns acquired by past experience;[2] and in the hierarchy of motivation every important problem in the present has a past problem as its background or is a derivative of a past problem of finding satisfaction for the same fundamental needs. Yet the fundamental needs that motivate behavior are relatively few in number; and very early life-experiences bring these few fundamental needs into vital dynamic interaction.

Especially the unsolved problems left over from traumatic memories of the past have intimate dynamic relations with one another. In this patient's case his dependent need for a mother's love has stirred up hostile impulses toward younger children. Not only these hostile impulses but also sexual impulses bring him again into conflict with his need for a mother; and his sexual impulses threaten him still further in his need for exclusive possession of the mother by bringing more children into the world.

2. See Vol. I, chap. xxxviii.

Yet, at times when he is more secure in the mother's love, he becomes capable of sharing her with brother and sister, or his hostile impulses may be mitigated into erotic ones.[3]

It is true that when we are interested only in an individual's superficial motives, his behavior seems to be split up into many small contexts; but when we study fundamental motivations and unsolved conflicts, a person's whole life becomes a single psychological context.

3. See Vol. I, chaps. xx and xxi.

SECTION V
Physiological Pattern and Interpersonal Field

CHAPTER XXIII
Physiological Pattern

We have discussed the patterns of organization and the historical backgrounds of dreams. In the next few chapters we shall study two other aspects of a dream's cognitive structure: (1) the functional significance of the patterns of physiological excitation of which the dream gives evidence; and, more specifically, (2) the physiological patterns involved in its cognitive grasp of interpersonal situations (real or imaginary).

Motivational Pattern and Physiological Pattern.—We have reconstructed two different memory patterns, in each of which the patient reacts with both erotic and hostile impulses to memories of his mother's pregnancies. The two patterns differ chiefly in the bodily organ involved: In one the fantasy is by urinating on the mother either to give her a child or to drown her child; in the other it is one of reaching out with the hand either to give her a child or to take her child from her.

It is evident that we must distinguish between the motivational pattern and the physiological pattern of a person's behavior. We define "motivational pattern" as the hierarchy or constellation of motives that activates behavior at a given moment. "Physiological pattern" is the pattern of distribution of actual physiological excitations that corresponds to this motivational pattern.

Making use of Freud's concept of erotic zones, psychoanalytic literature has long been interested in noting what organ or physiological function figures most prominently in a person's behavior or in a particular dream or other bit of behavior. For example, a dream of eating is characterized as "oral erotic," and a dream of holding onto money may be called "anal erotic." Our notion of "physiological pattern" is an attempt to refine this method of analyzing behavior; we recognize that behavior involves the activity not of one physiological function only but rather of an integrated pattern involving a number of different physiological activities.

149

The physiological activities that constitute a physiological pattern are, of course, not associated by mere chance; they are functionally interrelated. This fact, which is obvious for most behavior, has not always been recognized in the case of dreams. In the following chapters we shall show that the physiological patterns of dreams, too, have functional significance. We try to understand the functional significance of a dream's physiological pattern by studying how it is related to the dream's motivational pattern.

Physiological Pattern of the Anvil Dream.—It is difficult or impossible to make extensive physiological tests without interfering with the behavior that we wish to study. Accordingly, since we do not have a better method, we shall try to get some notion of the physiological pattern of our patient's dreams by the simple device of taking note of the bodily organs whose activity is implied in the successive steps in the pattern of dream organization. Such a reconstruction of the physiological pattern of a dream will be necessarily incomplete, because it does not take account of the activities of internal organs of which the dreamer is unaware. However, it is possible that the method which we shall now illustrate, which is admittedly a crude first approximation, can later be supplemented by psychosomatic studies which take more account of internal physiological functions. As an example of our method we shall first consider the physiological implications of the pattern of organization of the anvil dream (12).

This dream is in reaction to conflict between sexual and hostile impulses, on the one hand, and fear of offending the mother, on the other. From the condensed symbolism of the iron bar we conclude that the sexual impulse involves genital excitation (iron bar = erect penis) and that the hostile impulse involves excitation of outstretched arm and hand (bar with hook on end of it).

Being beaten, which is the fantasy with which the patient first reacts to this conflict, would involve painful sensations in muscles and joints.

Finally the dream text, in which the patient is watching the mother beat the bar, implies visual excitation.

Presumptive and Actual Physiological Patterns.—Does such a reconstructed physiological pattern correspond to an actual sequence of physiological excitations during the course of the dream work? Of this we cannot be sure. Sometimes a man who dreams of beating someone will find himself beating the pillow when he wakes up; or, after looking intently at something in a dream, he may wake up with tired eyes or a headache. The anvil dream (12), which we are now studying, was followed by painful sensations in muscles and joints, but only after an interval of two or three days. If these muscular pains were really continuous with physiological excitations corresponding to beating and being beaten, then we should expect to find evidence of such excitation[1] during the three-day interval also. And, in general, it is always possible that physiological activities that seem to be implied by our reconstruction of a dream may be illusory.

Yet even hallucination of an organ's activity probably involves excitation of a closely associated cerebral area. For our present purposes we shall regard an organ and its cerebral projection as two parts of a single physiological system. When our reconstruction of the pattern of organization of a dream implies the activity of a particular organ, we shall assume tentatively that excitation either of the organ designated or of its cerebral projection or of both has occurred; or, if we wish to be particularly cautious, we may call our reconstruction the "presumptive physiological pattern" of the dream.

A Gap in Our Reconstruction.—Before we can fully appreciate the functional significance of the anvil dream's (12) physiological pattern, we must first fill in a gap in our reconstruction of its pattern of organization.

As a first test of our reconstruction, we expect that each step in a dream's pattern of organization must be intelligibly moti-

1. From our analysis of the symbolism of grasping and throwing away (in chaps. xviii and xxi of this volume) it seems probable that the poker playing reported in the 13th hour was continuous with the motor pattern symbolized by the iron bar used to remove clinkers from a furnace in the anvil dream (12). In the text of the anvil dream, the patient's admiring description of the mother's work shows that the feeling tone of this dream was not painful, but pleasant. We have interpreted this to mean that the painful pressure of the fantasy of being beaten was deflected away from the muscles and absorbed in a pleasurable visual hallucination (see Vol. I, chap. xxvii). This deflection of pressure away from the muscles is the probable explanation of the two-day delay in appearance of his muscle pains.

vated. As a more rigorous test, we should insist also that our reconstruction should take account of all the motives which should be expected as reactions to each version of the dream text.

Measured by this criterion of complete motivation, our first reconstruction of the pattern of organization of the anvil dream (12) was incomplete. According to our interpretation, the iron bar in this dream is a penis that is being beaten and bent into the hand of a child. It would be remarkable if the dreamer could accept such castration without protest. What has happened to the dreamer's protest against castration?

Until now we have failed to find this protest only because we did not look for it. We have recognized the dreamer's need to prove that a woman can do a man's work. We have interpreted this as a need for reassurance that his analyst is competent to treat him. But why has the dream projected this reassurance back into the patient's past? In the dream text why is it the mother, rather than the analyst, who is doing a man's work so well? Evidently his need to prove that a woman can do a man's work must be one that dates back into the patient's childhood. Now we know where this need comes from. For fear of offending the mother, he is imagining himself submitting to a symbolic castration; but he cannot accept castration without protest. It is not only on the analyst's behalf but also on his own behalf that the dream protests that a woman can do a man's work. In protest against his fantasy of castration, he would like to prove that even a castrated woman can do a man's job like the father. Emulation of the father's strength and skill as a blacksmith offers a good compromise. Without running the risk of incurring the mother's displeasure by sexual activity, he can hope to prove his masculinity by wielding a hammer like his father in the blacksmith shop (see Fig. 14).

Further Reconstruction of Physiological Pattern of Anvil Dream.—This expanded interpretation gives us a vivid picture of the physiological pattern of this dream and of its significance. In the dream text (12) the mother is beating a hook on the end of an iron bar. This we interpret to mean that the patient's fear of offending the mother is struggling to inhibit genital excitation and to transfer exicitation away from the genital to an impulse to grasp something with his hands. Yet the bar is pictured as rigid. This implies a stubborn persistence of his genital erection in defiance of his inhibiting fear.

This interpretation of the dream symbolism is in accord with our understanding of the dream as a whole. It is not only in the dream symbolism that the grasping hand is being substituted for the genital. The whole action of the anvil dream (12) has been shifted away from the genital to a projected representation of energetic muscular activity performed with a tool grasped with the hands. The events of the next few days prove that this shift in physiological pattern is significant; for the patient develops pains not in the genital but in muscles and joints. In the dream text he is merely looking at this activity and admiring it; yet the pains that follow later suggest that the dream probably was accompanied by tension in the muscles, based on a strong urge to emulate the activity that he was observing, and reflecting his childhood wish to emulate the father's strength and skill by working upon the anvil (see Fig. 14).

In the dream text (12) he is doubly identified with the scene in the blacksmith shop. Predominantly, he feels himself to be the bar that is beaten upon the anvil. Like the bar, he knows what it is to feel the force of the father's blows. Yet in contrast to this submissive fantasy is the childhood wish that he, too, might one day wield the power of that blacksmith's hammer.

Evidently, this anvil dream (12) has been shaped by an active struggle between two conflicting reactions. On the one hand, his need to retain the mother's love constrains him to fantasy his erect penis beaten down into the grasping hand of a child; but pride and fear join in resisting this threat of castration and in driving him to assert his masculine power. The hand shall no longer be a symbol of infantile helplessness! With the father's powerful tool in his hand, he will convert his hand into a symbol of masculine power. Although, to appease the mother, he must try to transfer excitation from his erect penis to his arm and hand, his masculine pride must also struggle to transform his hand into a symbol of identification with the powerful father.

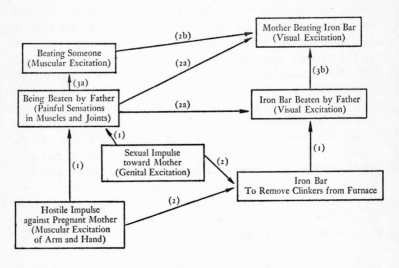

KEY TO MECHANISMS AND MOTIVATIONS

(1) Turning to father for punishment

(2) Visual projection supplemented by deanimation of
conflict (see chap. xxvi of this volume)
  (a) Role of being beaten projected
  (b) Role of beating projected

(3) Aggressive protest
  (a) By substituting beating for being beaten
  (b) By substituting mother for father in beating role

FIG. 14.—Physiological pattern of anvil dream

CHAPTER XXIV
Hand and Tool

Retiring into the Role of Observer.—The text of the anvil dream (12) does not picture the patient either as being beaten or as wielding the hammer but as watching the mother beat an iron bar. We can best indicate the functional significance of this projection mechanism by saying that the dreamer *has retired into the role of an observer.*

This projection mechanism has both advantages and disadvantages for the integrative function. There are two kinds of advantages:

1. It protects the patient from the real consequences both of his need for punishment and of his aggressive wishes. (*a*) Projected fulfilment of his need to be beaten is not so painful as a real beating would be; in this dream (12) he has even a fascinated delight in watching the bar beaten on the anvil. (*b*) Similarly, by giving projected and symbolic, instead of direct, expression to his wish to beat someone, he avoids the dangerous consequences that might result from acting upon this wish.

2. Projected representation has the further advantage that it permits the vicarious living-out, at the same time, of two roles that are incompatible in real life. Watching the beating of an iron bar, he can unconsciously identify himself both with the bar that is being beaten and with the one who is doing the beating.

Transfer of excitation from the sense organs and the muscles to the visual apparatus has also one disadvantage. Watching someone else is usually only temporarily satisfactory as a substitute for an impulse to do or experience the same thing one's self. One cannot be satisfied indefinitely with merely looking at an admired activity. After just looking for a time, there is usually an urge to participate in some way in the observed activity. In accordance with this principle, our patient's fascinated admiration of the mother's beating an iron bar in the anvil dream (12) was followed after a time by pains in his muscles and joints.

Learning by Identification.—In the rational behavior of waking life, this alternation of looking and doing is often successfully integrated into a learning process. By observing the skilled activities of his parents or others, a child can learn how to perform the same acts himself.

In the anvil dream (12) and in a number of the dreams that follow it, the patient is not able really to do what the father does; but these dreams give evidence of an unconscious awareness of this discrepancy and of a number of rudimentary substitutes for learning by identification.

Hand and Tool.—The anvil dream (12) is polarized about two conflicting wishes. In order to retain his mother's love, he tries to renounce sexuality and become a child again; but his pride demands that he be a man like his father. In the light of this discrepancy the symbol of the hand grasping the hammer acquires a new significance. *What one cannot accomplish with the naked hand one can perform by means of a tool.* The tool grasped in the hand becomes a means of overcoming the patient's inadequacy, of bridging the gap between his dependence on the mother and his desire to prove himself a man. Grasping a hammer, his hand seems to be no longer a symbol of dependence but the possessor of a mighty power.

In order to understand the cognitive structure of this dream (12), we must recall again the thesis on which we insisted in Volume I:[1] that wishes are not omnipotent even in dreams or neurotic symptoms, that the dream work must struggle with a persisting tendency of unacceptable desires or of disturbing facts to reassert themselves and must find satisfying memories or reassuring present opportunities on which to base its illusions of wish-fulfilment. In accordance with this thesis, the anvil dream (12) has been unable to ignore the discrepancy between the patient's aspiration to play a man's role and his dependence on a mother. To combat his sense of inadequacy, the dream work has made use of one present fact and one memory: His admiring recognition of the analyst's interpretive skill is the

1. See chap. xiii.

present fact; he has also the reassuring memory that he himself once worked as a blacksmith in his father's shop. On these two facts is based the reassuring thought to which the dream text gives expression: Even though he feels himself to be a (castrated) woman, he still can do a man's work.

Yet this reassuring thought is not an adequate answer to the discrepancy that is really disturbing him. What is really disturbing him is the inhibition of his genital function. The physiological pattern of this dream is trying to bridge the gap between his inhibited genital function and his desire to be a man like his father. It is this gap that the dream is trying to bridge by means of a tool held in the hands.

In a series of dreams that follow this one we find evidence of a similar realization of discrepancy between infantile helplessness and a masculine or other ideal and of attempts to bridge the gap by means of a tool or other devices.

In the snake dream (14) there is an implied contrast between the helpless child and the dangerous snake. Yet the snake has become harmless, and the child is demonstrating his power over it by grasping it and pulling it out of the pillowcase. In this case, a hand, even without a tool, is asserting mastery over a symbol of masculine power.

In the latent thoughts of the rowing dream (18a) the patient thinks of himself as a sick man and wishes to be rowed upstream by a father; but in the dream text, he is entertaining the thought of himself playing the father role, by rowing a sick old man upstream. The discrepancy between his wish to be cared for as a sick man and his need to prove himself adequate as a man is to be bridged by the act of rowing—i.e., by means of oars, which are tools grasped in the hands.

Tools are used for many purposes. In the fireplug dream (19a) the gap is one between a little girl and a grown woman, and the tool is a water can. In the dream text (19a) the little girl grows up to be a mature woman but then responds to her mother's call like a little girl again. Yet, before she grows up physically, she and the patient grow up symbolically by carrying the five-gallon water can, which we recognize as a symbol of pregnancy. The water can, too, is a tool grasped with the hands.

In the pencil-stealing dream (25) the patient's taking pencils and a pad suggests a wish to take the pencils and pad that the analyst uses to take notes during the interviews. We suspect that this impulse is a reaction to an aspiration to play the analyst's part instead of accepting his own role of a patient. Since he cannot really play the role of the analyst, he would like to bridge the gap by stealing her tools.

The distinction which this dream (25) makes between pencils and pad probably symbolizes a distinction between masculine and feminine roles. In the dream text (25) the patient takes the masculine symbol but rejects the pad (the feminine symbol) as "cheap" and throws it back. This symbol interpretation is confirmed by the next dream (26), in which the distinction between masculine and feminine tools is more sharply emphasized. In the broom dream (26) he is complaining that he has been given not a golf stick, which he admires, but a broom, a woman's weapon. Evidently he is disturbed by the discrepancy between impulses which he regards as feminine and his masculine aspirations; and he wishes to have the gap bridged for him by being given the proper tools.

The Wish for Instruction or Encouragement.—Playing with the father's tool may be a first step toward learning by identification. A child may fondly hope that by taking the father's tool he can appropriate the father's skill and power. The patient's irritation in the broom dream (26) is a sign that he is no longer satisfied with this illusion. He is complaining that he is not being given the right kind of tool. Such dissatisfaction is necessary if learning is to occur. The next step must be to watch and learn how to use the tool; or he may hope that some older person will teach him to use it. The book that the patient is receiving in the borrowed book dream (27) is probably a symbol of the patient's desire for instruction from the analyst about how to solve his problem.

If the obstacle to learning is fear as well as lack of skill, then the child may long for someone to encourage him, for moral support. In the pencil-stealing dream (25) this theme of encouragement to a forbidden activity appears for the first time. This dream (25) records the patient's first positive response to the analyst's actual role of encouraging forbidden wishes into consciousness. The switchman, calling his attention to the open door of the boxcar, seems to be tempting him to take something.

Yet the patient is too frightened to accept this encouragement. It is only after his long period of resistance that he can again find reassurance and help from the analyst's moral support. In the text of the Mexican woman dream (44) he is playing a paternal role, helping a mother-figure scrub the arm of a boy whom he identifies as his son. But the associations to this dream (44) identify the boy also with the patient himself. Evidently in the dream thoughts there is a gap between the patient's sense of being a guilty child and the role of punishing parent to which he aspires. In this dream (44) the patient's sense that the analyst is encouraging him to co-operate in the treatment has made it possible for him to bridge this gap and imagine himself helping her in her parental role.

In the fire-tending dream (45a) the "lady" who represents the analyst is playing a frankly encouraging role, which the patient is again interpreting as seductive.

The penis envy dream (46b) of the next hour calls attention frankly to the discrepancy between the genitals of father and son. The real discrepancy to which both dreams (46a and b) in this hour are reacting is between the dreamer's own underlying need for help in solving his sexual problem and the parental role that he pictures himself as playing. In the associations of this hour, as well as in the burning logs dream (46a), he indicates how he feels that the gap between child and father should be bridged. The sexual instruction that he is giving his son is an inverted expression of his own wish to be instructed by a father.

Phallic Significance of Tool and of Outstretched Arm.—In this whole series of dreams the patient is struggling to bridge the gap between his infantile helplessness or feminine submissiveness and his aspirations to play a male role. In the penis envy dream (46b) this discrepancy is pictured directly as the difference in size between the genitals of a child and those of a man.

We can now better appreciate the significance of the double meaning of this patient's grasping-hand symbolism. In the anvil dream (12) the iron bar with a hook on the end of it represents both an outstretched arm with a hand on the end of it and a penis. Stretching out his arm and tool to take "clinkers" from a "furnace," the little boy would like to imagine that his arm and tool (iron bar) are an erect penis. Similarly, his arm stretched out to pinch the girl in the bridge dream (10a) and the act of stealing the pencils from the boxcar in the pencil-stealing dream (25) both have this double significance. After the pencil-stealing dream (25) the two impulses are no longer condensed in a single symbolic act but are distinguished as two separate acts. The broom dream (26) contrasts hitting a golf ball as a masculine aspiration with hitting a squirrel with a broom, which symbolizes his (infantile) hostile wish toward a child; and in the fire-tending dream (45a) the "lady" requests the patient both to remove the ashes (get rid of a child)[2] and to stir up the fire.

However, the patient's hostile impulses toward the mother's pregnancies have a kind of "actuality" that his genital fantasies do not have. The dependent and hostile impulses symbolized by his grasping hand are an expression of his real emotional relationship to the mother, but his coitus and impregnation fantasies are make-believe play. Hence the need, throughout this whole series of dreams, to bridge the gap between his actual dependence (and hostility) and his masculine aspirations.

2. See our discussion of the symbolism of this dream (45a) in chap. xviii of this volume.

CHAPTER XXV

Cognitive Aspects of Social Integration

Interchanging Roles in Our Concepts of Interpersonal Relationships.—In both the dream work and the process of symptom formation, one person or even an inanimate object may be substituted in a role that originally belonged to another person. We distinguish several kinds of substitution. If someone or some other object is substituted for the dreamer, we speak of "projection." The iron bar that is being beaten in the anvil dream (12) is a projected representation of the patient's own need to be beaten. Similarly, we speak of "identification" or "introjection" when the dreamer takes over the role of someone else. In other substitutions the person of the dreamer is not involved at all. For example, in the text of the anvil dream (12) the mother has been substituted for the father as the one who is working upon the anvil.

These mechanisms have important implications not only for psychopathology but also for our concept of how we understand the motives of other persons. The fact that we can interchange roles so readily proves that our concept of a role in an interpersonal relationship is like a role in a play, which remains the same role regardless of who plays it.

How do we learn to know that another person is angry, or what another person is likely to do when he is angry? We base such a conclusion on two kinds of experience. We have observed the frowning face, the clenched fists, the loud voice, the energetic, jerky movements, and the destructive behavior of an angry person. We have also experienced anger in ourselves and the destructive impulses that accompany it; and we have recognized in ourselves some of the signs of anger that we have observed more clearly in others. Our concept of anger is based on a condensation into a single complex of these two sets of impressions. In our habitual and intuitive conceptual picture of the behavior of ourselves and of others, memories of being angry are fused with memories of seeing others angry. *This fusion of self-observation with observation of others explains the fact that my own anger can be represented in a dream as the anger of someone else.*

Our concepts of all kinds of motivated behavior are based on a similar condensation of what we have experienced ourselves with what we have observed in others. The structure of language also testifies to this fact. As directly perceived experiences, "I hit him," "He hits me," and "He hits her" have little in common; yet we use the same word "hit" to describe all three of them. Verbs are one-act plays whose dramatis personae can be interchanged at will. Evidently we must have acquired very early in life a habit of condensing and identifying the concept of what I do with that of what others do with the same parts of the body.[1]

Following an early analogy of Freud's, we often think of the substitutions in the dream work as displacements of psychic energy from one mental content to another, comparable to the diversion of a fluid from one channel into another in a hydraulic system. Yet this hydraulic analogy is applicable only to the simplest cases. It fails to take account of the fact that a more or less complex pattern in the original mental content usually persists in the substitute.

We shall again use the anvil dream (12) as an example. In this dream first a fantasy of the father's beating an iron bar and then the manifest dream of the mother beating an iron bar were substituted for the original fantasy of the patient being beaten by the father. In these substitutions the pattern of someone beating something has been retained throughout. To say that energy has been displaced from the patient to the iron bar and from the father to the mother would be an incorrect description of this process. This hydraulic analogy fails to take account of the persistent pattern.

A much better analogy is that of a drama in which each of the several roles is taken successively by different actors. In this analogy the persistent pattern is the drama, and the successive substitutions are the shifting roles of the actors.

1. It is well known that the infant's preoccupation with feeling, looking at, and manipulating his own body has this significance.

Resonance between Integrative Fields.—The fact that a fantasy of beating an iron bar and one of watching the father beat an iron bar are interchangeable in the dream work has the same significance as the use of the same word "beat" in the two sentences, "I beat an iron bar" and "Father beats an iron bar." Both imply that there has been a condensation and identification of memories of himself working as a blacksmith upon the anvil with other memories of watching the father's work upon the anvil. Similarly, the fact that a scene in which the father is beating an iron bar has been substituted for a memory of himself having been beaten by the father has a significance similar to that of the use of the same word "beat" in the two sentences: "Father beats an iron bar" and "Father beats me." Both imply a condensation and identification of memories of watching or seeing iron bars being beaten by the father with other memories of himself being beaten by the father.

But just what do we mean in physiological terms by these words "condensation and identification"? In psychological terms we are familiar enough with the experience. We go to a movie and experience an illusion as though the events were really happening to us that we see happening to the hero on the screen. We call this "identifying with" the hero. We would like to form some concept in physiological terms of how this is possible.

We return to the anvil dream (12). Physiologically, watching the father beat an iron bar involves the functional activity of the visual apparatus. If the patient himself beats the iron bar, it is the musculature of the whole body that is functionally active. If he conceives of himself as being beaten, he must anticipate painful stimulation and will probably try to protect himself by tonic contractions of the body musculature. In the text of the anvil dream the patient is watching the mother beat an iron bar, but not long afterward he experiences intense pains in muscles and joints. This fact confirms our suspicions that his dream of watching the mother beat the iron bar was accompanied both by tensions in the muscles and by stimulation such as later gave rise to his intense pains in muscles and joints. We also suspect that the intense muscular activity in this dream implies activation[2] of the motor patterns involved in beating a bar upon the anvil.

Thus we sense a kind of resonance between the visual pattern of observing an activity and the motor pattern involved in imitating that activity. In everyday life observing an activity often does give rise to an impulse to imitate that activity. When watching someone kick a football, one often feels a strong impulse to kick one's own foot vigorously into the air. Similarly in the mechanism of hysterical identification, seeing or knowing of pain being inflicted on another person often gives rise to similar pain in the observer. There are also many well-known instances of projected representation of one's own activities during sleep by the visual image in a dream of someone else performing a similar act. Such facts make it clear that there is a "resonance" also in the opposite direction, by virtue of which a motor pattern may activate the visual pattern of observing a similar activity.

We have already[3] made use of the concept of resonance or mutual induction between integrative fields in our account of the integration of purposive behavior. In order to account for the subordination of means to an end, we have postulated that there is a need to maintain equivalence of pattern between a plan for achieving a subordinate goal and the corresponding part of the more comprehensive plan for achieving the end-goal.

The same concept of resonance between integrative fields is necessary to account for co-operation between different physiological systems in the guidance of behavior. For example, to account for one's being able to find his way in the dark in a

2. We do not mean that this dream was necessarily accompanied by violent muscular activity. This hypothesis, if applied to the double identification in this dream, would lead to a clear contradiction: The dreamer obviously could not at the same time tense up his muscles in anticipation of being beaten and also engage in violent muscular activity. Our hypothesis is rather that both these patterns were activated but that one or both of them were also inhibited from muscular expression; in other words, that there were conflicting innervations. Certainly, if there was painful stimulation, the pain corresponding to this stimulation must have been repressed, inasmuch as the affect in the manifest dream is one not of pain but of fascinated admiration of the mother's activity. Later we shall present evidence in support of the hypothesis that the motor symbolism of this dream is based on a conflict between two kinds of motor pattern (see chap. xlviii of this volume).

3. See chap. i of this volume and also Vol. I, chap. xliv.

familiar room, we must assume induction of a kinaesthetic integrative field by a visual one. We remember how the room looked and translate this visual picture into a kinaesthetic one. In so doing, we transfer over to the kinaesthetic field by which we guide ourselves in the dark much of the complex structure of the visual field in terms of which we remember the position of objects in the room.

We return to our study of the mechanisms of the dream work. We have spoken repeatedly of successive versions of the dream text as though it were a manuscript and have assumed that no version is entirely new, that every version can be traced back, step by step, to patterns arising out of the dreamer's past. This analogy with the history of a manuscript has one defect. It does not represent vividly enough the dynamic character of the "documents" that we are studying. Making use of our concept of psychological induction, we now recognize that each of the "versions" of our dream "text" is an integrative field or plan of action, polarized either by an incentive to achieve a single dominant goal or by conflicting incentives to achieve more than one goal. The substitution of one "version" of the dream "text" for another is now sensed as the activation of one integrative pattern by another. As we have just reminded ourselves, such activation of one integrative field by another is part of the normal hierarchy of end and means that constitutes the mechanism of purposive behavior. The concept of induction of one integrative field by another thus makes it possible for us to understand the displacements characteristic of symptom and dream formation in terms comparable to those by means of which we understand the mechanisms of purposive behavior. The only difference lies in the fact that in purposive behavior the successive induction of integrative fields occurs systematically and under the dominance of the more comprehensive integrative pattern of the end-goal, whereas in the mechanisms of symptom and dream formation the integrative patterns corresponding to conflicting goals interact and fuse with one another in ways that often lead to paradoxical behavior and to confused and irrational cognitive patterns.

The mechanisms of the dream work are related more closely to the mechanisms of integration of social behavior than they are to the integration of purposive behavior. We return again to the anvil dream (12) for illustration. The pattern of the manifest content of this dream is a visual one; the patient is watching the mother beat an iron bar. With this observed scene, the dreamer is doubly identified. He is identified both with the bar that is being beaten and with the mother who is wielding the hammer. In our proposed physiological terminology this means that the figure of the mother in the visual pattern is in resonance with the motor pattern of beating the bar, whereas the iron bar in the visual pattern is in resonance with the pattern of sensory stimulation and self-protective motor tension corresponding to a fantasy of being beaten. Except for the fact, which we neglect for a moment, that an iron bar rather than a person is being beaten, this observed scene can illustrate for us, roughly, the mechanism by means of which one understands a social relationship or interaction between two people by identifying with both of them.

The Problem of Subordinating Resonant Patterns.—Such analyses of the mechanisms by means of which we understand the motives of other people have often been made.[4] They are of little value unless we can carry the analysis further and inquire what dynamic factors determine whether a person shall be able to understand the motives of other people correctly or whether his understanding of the motives of others shall be distorted in one way or another.

We may now illustrate a first approach to this problem by attempting to analyze the differences between the mechanisms of this dream (12) and those involved in a true grasp of how two other people feel toward each other or interact with each other. For an objective understanding of an interpersonal relationship it is necessary that the identification with one or both persons in the observed scene be not too intense, that it be, as it were, only a token or sample identification. For the purpose of objective understanding, the two patterns of identification must be kept separate, each condensed or in resonance with the visual image of the person to whom it corresponds. The observer must remain in the role of observer, the visual pattern serving

4. See especially G. F. Mead, 1934.

as a cognitive pattern, portraying the two persons as actors in an interpersonal relationship. The two patterns of identification, on the other hand, remaining separate and in resonance each with the visual image of the corresponding person, endow the visual image of each person with a projected sense of how the observer would feel if he were playing this person's role. Thus, if the observed scene is one of a father beating a child, the visual image of the father, in resonance with the motor pattern of the act of beating, is endowed with a sense of how the observer would feel if he himself were doing the beating; whereas the visual image of the child, in resonance with the pattern of painful stimulation and protective muscular tension corresponding to the fantasy of being beaten, is endowed with a sense of how the observer would feel if he were himself being beaten.

What will happen if the intensity of activation either of the pattern of beating or of the pattern of being beaten increases? In such a case the role of the observer will tend to become less that of an observer and more that of an active participant. If the intensity of both patterns of identification increases, then the two patterns can no longer be kept separate but will come into active conflict with each other. This is what has occurred in the anvil dream (12), in which we sense an active conflict between the need to be punished by being beaten and the compensatory ambition to wield the hammer. In the dream text the roles of beating and being beaten are not kept separate. In the latent dream thoughts it is clear that the submissive role of being beaten is regarded as feminine, as the role of the mother, and that beating is regarded as the masculine role of the father. In fact, the patient explicitly tells us that the mother never worked upon the anvil. Yet in the dream text the roles are reversed: The mother is wielding the hammer; and a phallic symbol, the iron bar, is being beaten. In other words, the two roles are not being kept separate, but each of the two figures is a projected picture of the patient's own conflict between the patterns corresponding to the two roles. The beater is being beaten, and the beaten one is doing the beating!

Of course, the patient is dreaming, not observing an actual scene; yet a dream might conceivably reproduce an actual memory. This particular dream (12) is evidently based on the reactivation of childhood memories in which the patient did play the role of observer, memories of watching the father at work upon the anvil, and probably also memories of the primal scene. In these memories, as in the dream, the patient was probably not at all an objective and understanding observer; he was probably in conflict between intense needs to identify with both father and mother in the primal scene, and, in the blacksmith shop scene, both with the father who was wielding the hammer and with the object that was being shaped upon the anvil. He was not only an observer but also a participant in both roles; and this double participation results in a fusion or condensation of the two roles in each of the figures in the dream text.

In the case of an objective observer, the visual pattern "Father beats child" must be a superordinated pattern, able to restrain the two patterns, "I beat child" and "Father beats me," from involving him too much as a participant to the detriment of his role as an understanding observer. This is the essential point in which the integrative pattern of the anvil dream (12) differs from that of the understanding observer. In the anvil dream the visual pattern, "Mother beats iron bar," is no longer a superordinated pattern that makes use of the identification patterns, "I beat iron bar" and "Mother beats me," for the purpose of objective understanding of a really observed scene. In this anvil dream, on the contrary, the conflict between the two patterns, "I beat" and "I am beaten," is dominant, and the visual pattern has arisen by displacement of the energy of these two conflicting patterns to the visual apparatus, in order to protect the dreamer from the full impact of this conflict.

CHAPTER XXVI

Functional Significance of Deanimated Symbols

Diminished Resonance with an Inanimate Object.—Often in the dream work an inanimate object is substituted for a person. For example, in the anvil dream (12) the dream text has substituted an iron bar to be beaten in the patient's stead.

Now we can understand the functional significance of this substitution. The dream work has first substituted a visual image to absorb the painful pressure of the fantasy of being beaten. But what if the patient had dreamed of watching another person being beaten? If so, the dreamer would have tended to identify with the person receiving the beating. The observed role of a woman or child being beaten, remaining in resonance with a physiological pattern corresponding to the dreamer's fantasy of himself being beaten, would have tended to reactivate this painful fantasy. By substituting an inanimate object to be beaten, the dream work has diminished this resonance and is protecting the patient from identifying himself too strongly with the one who is receiving the beating. Thus the selection of a deanimated substitute to receive the beating supplements the mechanism of projection by erecting another barrier against reactivating the painful fantasy.

Comparison with Another Dream.—We can test this formulation by comparing this dream with another dream in which the same conflict is less intense. The Mexican woman dream (44) and the anvil dream (12) are motivated by need for punishment for the same sexual and hostile impulses; and in both dreams this need for punishment is projected; but the fact that the punitive therapy is milder (a scrubbing rather than a beating) and the fact that the patient himself participates in administering it indicate that his conflict is less intense in the later dream (44). According to our formulation, we expect that in this dream (44) there should be less need to protect the patient against identification with the object that is receiving punishment. Comparison of the two dreams (12 and 44) confirms this expectation. In both dreams the punishment is inflicted on a substitute object; but in the Mexican woman dream (44) a child receives the scrubbing. In this dream it has not been necessary to supplement the projection mechanism by substituting an inanimate object to receive the painful treatment.

Deanimation without Projection.—Substitution of deanimated symbolism need not always supplement a projection mechanism. Sometimes an inanimate object is substituted for the object of an aggressive impulse of the dreamer, as, for example, in the fire-tending dream (45a), in which a stove has been substituted for the woman who is the object of the dreamer's sexual impulses. Similarly, in the pencil-stealing dream (25), stealing small objects from a boxcar has been substituted for sexual and aggressive impulses against the pregnant mother. In this way in both cases the dream work has protected the dreamer against too intense identification with the woman against whom these sadistic impulses are directed.

The tool symbolism involves another kind of use of the deanimation mechanism, in which there is only a partial projection of a disturbing act, accompanied by deanimation of the offending organ; the interposition of the tool to execute the act diminishes the dreamer's sense of direct participation.

Need for Deanimated Symbolism Correlated with Intensity of Conflict.—We shall conclude this chapter with further examples of the principle that the need for deanimated symbolism diminishes when the intensity of the conflict centering about the symbolized act diminishes.

In the bridge dream (10a) the hope of pleasing a mother has made it possible to substitute a playful erotic gesture for the hostile and sexual impulses that are so disturbing in later dreams. The gesture of pinching the young girl is already harmless enough to make the use of deanimated symbolism superfluous; but in the anvil dream (12), after the intensity of the patient's conflict has increased, the disturbing impulse must be both projected and deanimated. In the symbol of the iron bar to remove clinkers from a furnace, the iron bar is a deanimated and projected symbol of the patient's arm and hand, and the furnace is a deanimated symbol of the woman who is the object of the dreamer's aggressive impulse.

Again in the fireplug dream (19a) the patient's initial hope of the analyst's approval has made possible an erotization of his conflict and has made it unnecessary to replace the girl who is the object of his erotic interest by an inanimate symbol. Only the genital sexual impulse, with its implications of resulting pregnancy, would give rise to a conflict too intense to permit of undisguised representation. At this point in the dream work the water can, filling it at the fireplug, and carrying it are introduced as deanimated symbols of pregnancy and of the act of impregnation.

At the end of the fireplug dream (19a) the patient's erotic impulses undergo sudden inhibition.[1] The effects of the resulting increase in the intensity of conflict are seen immediately in the dreams that follow. In the brake dream (19b), not only are the patient's disturbing impulses projected,[2] but the woman who is the object of them has also been replaced by an inanimate symbol —a milk truck. Similarly, in the pencil-stealing dream (25) a boxcar has been substituted for the mother and small inanimate objects for the children.[3] The increase in intensity of conflict is also reflected in the fact that the disturbing impulse is no longer erotized, which is indicated by the fact that the symbolism of taking small objects from a boxcar emphasizes the hostile impulse toward the pregnant mother (to take the child from her) rather than the erotic impulse.

In the broom dream (26), in contrast to the pencil-stealing dream (25), the impulse to attack a child re-emerges almost undisguised in the suggestion that the patient hit a squirrel half-buried in the leaves. In this case the disturbing impulse has been neither erotized nor deanimated. The explanation is as follows: In the pencil-stealing dream (25), the patient is committing himself

1. As indicated by the sudden interruption of the patient's embrace of the girl when her mother calls and also by the excessively powerful brakes referred to in the next dream (19b).

2. I.e., the brakes are being put, not on the patient, but on a symbol representing the woman who is tempting him—the milk truck.

3. See chap. xviii of this volume.

to the disturbing act. Recognition of his own impulse to attack the pregnant mother would involve a conflict too great for his integrative mechanism to span. In the broom dream (26), he is repudiating and projecting responsibility for the act to which he feels tempted. Since he does not recognize the impulse as his own and is actively struggling to repudiate it, it is less disturbing to delineate its content[4] more clearly.

4. See F. Alexander, 1925.

CHAPTER XXVII

Complementary Substitution Mechanisms

We cannot usually understand the significance of one substitution mechanism alone. When we study the dream work as a whole, we find a pattern of complementary substitutions.

Our discussion of the anvil dream (12) has already illustrated this principle. As another example we turn to the pencil-stealing dream (25).

Process of Organization of Pencil-stealing Dream.—The stimulus for this dream (25) was the patient's doubt whether the analyst's apparent encouragement of forbidden impulses could be trusted. The dream is putting this question to the test, but only cautiously, by picturing what might happen if he should act upon a very trivial substitute for his really disturbing impulses. Our study of the dream symbolism[1] has suggested that stealing small objects from a boxcar is a trivial substitute for sexual and hostile impulses against the mother's pregnancies. How did the dream work arrive at this symbolism?

We suspect that the pencils and pad represent those that the analyst uses to take notes during the analytic sessions. For the sexual and hostile impulses that so disturb the patient's relationship to the analyst, the dream thoughts have substituted curiosity about what she is writing and an impulse to steal her writing materials.

Yet the patient does not accept this suggestion.[2] He protests that the pencils and paper resemble rather the pencils that the railroad furnishes. The motive for this substitution is evident from the associations. Not only the pencils but also the office, the boxcar, the expression "Bring it into the office," the switchman, and the watchman—all are references to his work. As in previous dreams, the patient is trying to get rid of the seductive implications of being alone in a room with a woman and to emphasize the

1. See chap. xviii of this volume.
2. See chap. xvii of this volume.

173

professional or business-like character of the relationship by sub-stituting his situation at work, where he deals only with men.

Thus the substitution of an impulse to take objects from a box-car for aggressive impulses toward the pregnant mother is only part of a more comprehensive reorganization of integrative pat-tern whose motive is to turn away from the disturbing conflict in relation to the analyst (mother) and to find refuge in the less dangerous situation on the job. Yet the patient is already deeply emotionally involved in, and committed to, his conflict in relation to the analyst. It is impossible for him really to turn away from the analytic situation to seek relief in the job situation. For this reason he cannot turn his interest away from the analysis to find real satisfaction on the job, but, continuing his preoccupation with his conflict in the analysis, he can do no more than translate this conflict into symbols borrowed from his job.

In this translated version the analyst (mother) has been re-placed by three different objects. The switchman gives him the encouragement that he craves and receives from the analyst. In the role of prohibiting parent she is represented by the policeman or watchman. As the object of his forbidden destructive impulses, she has been replaced not by a person but by a boxcar, by an in-animate object which resembles a pregnant woman only in being a container, in being something that holds something else inside it.

Significance of the Boxcar Symbolism.—Substituting a boxcar for the analyst is part of this dream's attempt to substitute the im-personal job situation for the patient's dangerously personal rela-tionship to the analyst. Of the boxcar the men on the job say jokingly, "Bring it into the office." A boxcar is an impersonal object, just part of his job, not a person of central importance in the patient's life. It is a deanimated as well as a depreciated substi-tute for the mother on whose love he is dependent; it cannot feel pain or approve or disapprove.

Thus, by substituting a boxcar, the dream is trying to diminish both sides of the patient's conflict. Instead of attacking the mother, he is merely taking a cheap pad and some paltry pencils. "Besides," the dream seems to say, "who is this woman anyway? I am here only on professional business, and she is just a bit of the office furniture."

Complementary Substitution Mechanisms.—We have just interpreted the *motive* for this dream's substituting a boxcar for the analyst; but we must again remind ourselves that wishes are not omnipotent. How can we account for this dream's *capacity* to substitute a boxcar for the analyst?

It is easier to make light of one's need for another person if there is someone else to whom one can turn as a substitute. In this pencil-stealing dream (25) the patient has found two substitutes to whom he can turn. The boxcar is only one of the objects substituted for the analyst in this dream. The boxcar represents her only in so far as she is the object of his disturbing hostile and sexual impulses. In her role as a mother, encouraging and prohibiting, the dream has replaced her not by a depreciated impersonal object but by two men on the job. In real life the patient has rather satisfying relations with the men on the job, who treat him indulgently. In the dream (25) he is turning away from this woman, who is stirring up such a disturbing conflict, to find satisfaction for his dependent needs from two men who have taken over this part of her role. Because he finds satisfaction for his dependent needs from these two men on the job, the dream can depreciate the analyst's importance in his life by picturing her as a boxcar.

The Problem of Discharge of Pressure.—But what has happened to the other side of the patient's conflict? By what means is the dream able to minimize his impulse to attack the mother, representing it as nothing more than a paltry temptation to steal a pad and a few pencils?

We find the answer to this question in the acute attack of asthma with which the dreamer awakened. As the dream ended, the dreamer was evidently under pressure to say something in answer to the watchman's question but was unable to utter more than the single word, "No." His asthma attack evidently resulted from physiological disintegration[3] of his need to talk.

Let us review the accumulation and discharge of pressure in this dream. In the background there is a conflict of considerable

3. For explanation of the concept of physiological disintegration see Vol. I, chap. xxvi. We have postulated a similar disintegration of speech into asthmatic wheezing in the pig dream (43) (see chap. vi, p. 47, of this volume).

intensity between sexual and hostile impulses and fear of offending the mother; but much of the pressure of this conflict is probably absorbed at first by sleep,[4] while motor discharge is inhibited by fear of losing the mother's love. Then, encouraged by the analyst's indulgence of forbidden wishes, the dream tries cautiously to release some of the accumulated pressure through the symbolic act of stealing the pad and pencils; but the dreamer dares not yield to his really strong urge to attack the analyst, and his petty symbolic act of stealing the pencils permits only a very inadequate motor discharge of the accumulated pressure. The real discharge[5] of pressure occurs as he wakes up—in his acute attack of asthma.

4. See Vol. I, chap. xl, for discussion of "absorption of pressure by sleep."

5. We are using the word "discharge" somewhat loosely at this point. In Vol. III we shall discuss at greater length the distinction between "absorption" of motivating pressure and "discharge" of pressure. As we use the terms, "absorption" of pressure by a somatic symptom or other physiological activity is a temporary event, lasting only so long as the symptom persists, whereas "discharge" implies also a relief of pressure after the symptom has subsided. In the case of the pencil-stealing dream (25) we have no report about how long the dreamer's asthma attack lasted and no evidence to indicate whether or not it was followed by relief of pressure.

SECTION VI

The Span of the Interpersonal Field

CHAPTER XXVIII

Dreams and Rational Behavior

Having reconstructed the cognitive structures of a number of dreams, we are now ready to consider again how the cognitive structure of a dream is related (1) to Freud's concept of the primary process and (2) to the cognitive structure of rational behavior.

Primary Process and Process of Dream Organization.—When we study the chains of associations that lead from the latent dream thoughts to the manifest dream, we cannot avoid the impression, which Freud formulated, that energy is displaced along any available pathway, without regard for reality or logic and guided only by the pleasure principle. This impression has tended greatly to discourage attempts like ours to find a logical structure underlying every dream. Yet the better we understand any dream, the more we are impressed with the fact that the dream work is an organized process.

Encouraged by this impression, we have approached the study of the dream work in another way. We study it not as a tangled network of chains of association but as a reaction to the total situation created by the dreamer's conflict. We have suspected[1] that the seemingly chaotic implications of the primary process are in part an artifact, resulting from the study of chains of associations in the dream work. We shall now try to check this impression by inquiring what remains of the appearance of free displacement of energy when we study the reorganizations of cognitive pattern in the process of dream organization.

Dreams and Rational Behavior.—Our working hypothesis is that the differences between the integrative processes in dreams and in rational behavior can be reduced to two: (1) the modifying influence of sleep and (2) the fact that most dreams are struggling with conflicts and that the dreamer's capacity to understand his

1. See chap. ii of this volume, p. 11.

conflict situation is usually inadequate and often fluctuates during the course of the dream work.

We have already discussed[2] the modifying influence of sleep on the integrative processes of goal-directed behavior. We concluded that the sleep state, in proportion to its depth, absorbs the pressure of unfulfilled wishes or of conflicts. This absorption of pressure by sleep permits the dreamer to be better content with wish-fulfilling hallucinations than he would be in waking life. His much diminished need to bring his wish-fulfilling fantasies into relation with external reality can usually be satisfied by allusions to facts remembered from the preceding day; and, instead of acting, he is usually content to dream of acting on his dream wishes. According to our hypothesis, denial of disturbing reality by wish-fulfilling hallucinations is most successful at the beginning of a dream, when sleep is deepest; but disturbing pressures tend to re-emerge as the dream progresses.

In our next chapter we shall discuss some differences between chains of associations and reorganizations of cognitive pattern. Then we shall return to the task of tracing the effects of the dreamer's inadequate and often fluctuating grasp of his conflict situation. In this way we hope to account for important differences between dreams and rational behavior, as well as for some of the apparently senseless displacements and condensations in the dreamer's chains of associations.

2. See Vol. I, Sec. VI.

CHAPTER XXIX

Associative Chains and Reorganizations of Pattern

When we study the dreamer's reactions to his conflict situation as a whole, we find the dream work repeatedly substituting one picture of the conflict situation for another. In these substitutions much of *the pattern of each successive picture* of the dreamer's conflict *is continued into the next picture*. It is *this continuity of pattern* that *gives the dream work its organized character*.

In the dreamer's associations, the pictures in the dream's pattern of organization are often broken down into fragments. For this reason, when we trace chains of association, we can easily lose track of the continuity of pattern in the underlying cognitive structure. In the dreamer's associations we often find links between fragments instead of the reorganizations of cognitive pattern that are really significant.

Does this fragmentation of cognitive pattern account fully for the peculiarities of the primary process? In Freud's account of the chains of associations in the dream work, the two most important mechanisms are displacement and condensation. The dream work, Freud believes, disregards the sense of the latent dream thoughts and displaces energy along any available associative pathway; and the energy of two or more entirely different dream thoughts may be concentrated (condensed) on a single middle term of a long chain of associations. Our question now is: What do we find that corresponds to the displacements and condensations in the dreamer's chains of associations when we study the reorganizations of total cognitive pattern in the dream work, instead of studying links between fragments of these patterns?

We shall be interested also in two other questions: Do the reorganizations of cognitive pattern in the dream work have functional significance? Are they analogous to reorganizations of integrative pattern that also occur in rational behavior?

Reorganizations of Cognitive Pattern.—As we have just pointed out, the substitutions in the process of dream organization correspond only very roughly to the displacements in Freud's account of the dream work. In the process of dream organization, instead of associative links between fragments or elements of cognitive patterns, we find reorganizations of a total cognitive pattern.

The successive pictures in the process of dream organization may be related to one another in several different ways.

In the simplest case, new elements are substituted for old ones in a pattern that remains otherwise unchanged. The substitution of a $20.00 bill for the dreamer's two children and of the Cook County building for the rye field in the $20.00 bill dream is an example of this mechanism.

In other cases the new pattern is formed by rearrangement of elements of the old pattern. (This mechanism may or may not be accompanied by the introduction of new elements or by the substitution of new elements for old ones.) For example, in the flood dream (115), instead of the patient's urinating on (into) the young woman, he and the young woman are walking in dirty water that has entered the basement.

In the most radical reorganizations of cognitive pattern, one or more features of the underlying pattern itself may be reversed or otherwise modified. For example, in the bridge dream, fear of offending the mother by sexual and hostile wishes toward her daughter has been replaced by hope of pleasing the mother by returning her daughter to her.

Condensation of Dynamically Equivalent Patterns.—The condensations in the chains of association in the dream thoughts may correspond to a number of different kinds of relations between cognitive fields in the process of dream organization.

One of the most familiar forms of condensation in the dream work results from the fact that present behavior is based on patterns from the past. For example, our patient's conflict between sexual wishes toward the analyst and his dependent need to be loved by her has been patterned on a similar childhood conflict in relation to his mother; and in his dreams, accordingly, the same woman often represents both the analyst and his mother. Similarly, this patient's conflicts resulting from his rivalry with the analyst's child for the analyst, from his rivalry with his own two children for his wife, and from his rivalry with his brother for his mother are all dynamically equivalent and are usually reacted to as a single problem in his dreams. For example, the $20.00 bill dream (6oc) may be understood equally well either as a reaction to his memory of losing his brother in the rye field, to which his walking away from the money is an allusion, or as a reaction to his wish to repudiate responsibility for his own two children, to which the "2" in the $20.00 is a specific allusion.

Such condensation of dynamically equivalent situations is characteristic of the normal learning process, especially when learning has not yet been completed. For example, one recalls learning to drive an automobile as a single learning process, not as a series of particular attempts to drive, each one of which is remembered separately. And, even if one used two different cars in the process, one tends later to condense what was learned from the two into a single pattern of driving. If the two cars had different kinds of gear shift, *one might* for a time *try to manipulate the new gear shift in the way that was appropriate for the old one. When our patient does not distinguish sharply between his analyst and his mother, he is reacting according to a similar mechanism.*

Condensations Resulting from Continuity of Pattern.—The kind of condensation just discussed is only one example of the principle of continuity of pattern in the process of dream organization.

For example, in the $20.00 bill dream (6oc) we find a condensation of two memory patterns: (1) the patient's childhood memory of walking off and leaving his baby brother in a rye field and (2) a later memory of a friend with political influence who put opportunities in his way for making money dishonestly. The dream (6oc) is modeled on a fantasy of walking away from his own two children as he once walked away from his brother. In the manifest dream, he is still a child, but a $20.00 bill has been substituted for his two children and the Cook County building for the rye field.

This substitution is evidently part of a self-justifying argument. The dream work has converted the childhood memory, in which the patient was guilty of abandoning a child, into a self-justifying dramatization of the later memory: The dream excuses him by picturing him as a child so innocent that he did not know enough to take the money that "someone" in the Cook County building tried to slip him from behind his back.

But the point that now interests us is the fact that the pattern of walking away from something has been retained even after the brother and the rye field of the childhood memory have been replaced by allusions to the later memory. This retention of an essential feature of the earlier memory in the self-justifying fantasy that has been substituted for it results actually in condensation of the two memories.

Sometimes, as we have already pointed out,[1] successive versions of a dream text are like a drama which remains the same while its several roles are played successively by different actors. This is the case, for example, when a $20.00 bill takes the place of two children in the dream (60c) just discussed. In other cases the pattern or plot of the "drama" is modified, but the modification affects only one part or aspect of the original pattern and leaves other parts unchanged. For example, in the flood dream (115), a fantasy of being urinated upon has been replaced by one of walking in the dirty water, but the notion of being urinated upon is still retained in the detail of dirty water having entered the basement room where the patient is. Similarly in the bridge dream (10a), escorting the girl home in the dusk has been substituted for the sexual and hostile impulses toward her which this dream is trying to master. But the negative of a photograph is still recognizable as the same photograph in spite of the reversal of shades; and in the bridge dream the underlying pattern of fear of offending the mother by sexual and hostile wishes is still discernible after it has been replaced by the hope of pleasing the mother by returning her daughter to her.

As a result of this continuity of pattern in successive versions of the dream text, we can usually recognize the manifest dream itself as a composite picture of the memories and fantasies that have contributed to its formation. In the flood dream (115) and its symbolism, for example, we found allusions not only to the memory of making sexual advances to the girl in the mother's home but also to memories of wetting the bed, to fantasies of uri-

1. See chap. xxv of this volume.

nating on the girl and on the mother, to the mother's pregnancies, and to fantasies both of having given her her child and of destroying the child, and also to fantasies of sharing with brother and sister their position inside the mother. Thus it is evident that the successive substitutions that we find in the pattern of organization and in the historical background of a dream result in far-reaching condensations as well as displacements in the final dream text.

Condensation at the Periphery of Interest.—In many cases condensation has another kind of functional significance. When a cognitive pattern is shifted from the center to the periphery of the dreamer's field of interest, its more or less complex structure tends to be condensed into a simpler one. For example, in the rational behavior of waking life, if I have once decided to build a house, I shall probably begin working out detailed plans with an architect; but if I am merely considering building a house as one of a number of possibilities, I shall probably content myself with a much less detailed notion of what is involved in such a project.

This kind of condensation is illustrated by the symbol of the iron bar in the anvil dream (12). In the text of this dream interest centers not on the impulses for which the patient feels he needs a beating, and not even on the beating, but rather on the analyst's (mother's) skill in performing her task. In other words, in this dream the impulses for which the dreamer feels guilty are on the periphery of his field of interest. Corresponding to their peripheral position in the dreamer's field of interest, the disturbing impulses are represented in the dream text by a single condensed symbol—an iron bar, which is both a phallic symbol and a bar used to remove clinkers from a furnace.

In two later dreams (26 and 45a) the impulses symbolized by the iron bar of the anvil dream have moved into the center of the dreamer's field of interest; and in these two dreams we find the content of these impulses elaborated in greater detail. In the broom dream (26) hitting a squirrel with a broom *is contrasted with* hitting a golf ball with a golf-stick. In the fire-tending dream (45a) cleaning out the ashes (corresponding to the bar's being used to remove clinkers in the anvil dream) and stirring up the fire (corresponding to the phallic significance of the iron bar in the anvil dream) *are mentioned separately*.

In the light of our analysis of the water symbolism, the river in the bridge dream (10a) is an even more striking example of the same principle. In the bridge dream the dreamer's interest is centered on winning a mother's thanks by returning her daughter to her. The river, which plays only a very peripheral role as one detail of the setting of the manifest dream, is a highly condensed symbol. The constellation of enuretic fantasies to which this symbol of the river is an allusion emerges into clearer view, step by step, in the later water dreams, as one group of these fantasies after another becomes central in the dreamer's interest.

Summary.—Thus our examples illustrate our thesis that the actual process of dream organization is a meaningful and intelligibly motivated series of reorganizations of cognitive pattern, which resemble in a number of ways the reorganizations of cognitive pattern upon which our waking behavior is based. The displacements and condensations in the dreamer's chains of associations reflect some features of these reorganizations of cognitive pattern; but by breaking down total patterns into fragments and then linking fragments together, they tend to destroy, or at least to obscure greatly, the nature of the transformations that are occurring in the underlying cognitive structure.

CHAPTER XXX

Consequences of Inadequate Integrative Capacity

Alternation of Conflicting Motivations.—The bridge dream (10*a*) has been our favorite example of subordination of behavior to purpose in a dream; but in many dreams, instead of subordination of means to an end, we find an alternation of conflicting motives in successive steps of the process of dream organization. For example:

In the process of organization of the anvil dream (12) (we shall consider only our first and simplest reconstruction), a sexual wish toward the analyst-mother gives rise to a need for punishment; then the dream work protects the dreamer from excessive pain by substituting an iron bar to be beaten; and, finally, by picturing his mother skilfully performing the father's work, the dreamer reassures himself against his doubts about his analyst's competence to beat him into shape.

In the pencil-stealing dream (25), substitution of a trivial symbolic act for a really disturbing temptation situation is followed by the re-emergence of the fear of offending the analyst, resulting, first, in appearance of the watchman and then in the dreamer's waking up with an acute attack of asthma.

In the process of organization of the fire-tending dream (45*a*), the patient first turns away from the seductive analyst to the company of men, then turns back to a harmless substitute (stirring up the fire) for the heterosexual temptation situation.

Similarly in the flood dream (115) the symbolism suggests that the dreamer first turned away from heterosexual temptation in the therapeutic situation to a fantasy of feminine submission to a father but that he then reacted to this submissive fantasy with a masculine protest in which he and the analyst together walk in the dirty water and wash their faces in it.

In fact, our analysis of the water symbolism has led us to the conclusion that, in all this patient's water dreams, a hostile impulse against the pregnant mother has activated fear of offending her, resulting in the aggressive impulse being turned back against himself, but that then the dreamer reacts to his fantasies of being drowned with fantasies of aggressive protest, climbing on a boat, walking in the water or on a bridge over the water, etc.

A Series of Partial Integrations.—In order to account for the fact that a person often tends to become "rattled" or to "lose his head" under the pressure of excessive conflict, we have proposed the concepts of integrative task, integrative capacity, and integrative span of a guiding integrative field.[1] Effective efforts to achieve a goal, we postulate, are possible only when motor activity is guided by insight, by an integrative field. "Losing one's head" can best be accounted for by the hypothesis that, when motivating pressure is excessive, the necessary guiding insight cannot control motor discharge. The amount of motivating pressure that must be controlled by an integrative field is its "integrative task." To account for the fact that an integrative field sometimes cannot exert effective control over motor discharge, we assume further that the integrative field itself has a quantitatively limited "capacity" to bind motivating pressure.

Disintegration of goal-directed behavior may manifest itself either by loss of control of motor discharge, as we have just postulated, or by diminution of integrative span—by which we mean diminution in the number of aspects of the situation that the guiding integrative field can take account of.

Making use of the concept of diminished integrative span, we can now suggest the following hypothesis to account for the alternation of conflicting motivations in the dream work:

Subordination of behavior to purpose is possible only when the integrative capacity of the guiding integrative field is adequate to span the whole of the dreamer's problem. When integrative capacity is adequate, we find the overdetermined motives of a dream linked together in relationships of end and means or of alternative means to the same end, as in rational behavior. But when integrative capacity is not adequate to span the whole of a dreamer's problem, the process of dream organization becomes a series of partial integrations, in which motives that have been left out of

1. See Vol. I, chap. xii.

account in one attempt at integration are reacted to in the next attempt.[2]

Conflict in Excess of Integrative Capacity.—As a check on this explanation, we make use of our hypothesis that integrative capacity is based on hope of success and satisfaction, whereas the integrative task is proportionate to the sum of the pressures of conflicting needs. In accordance with this hypothesis, we should expect the subordination of means to an end-goal to be more successful when satisfying memories or present opportunities give reason for hope of satisfaction. On the other hand, we must expect alternation of conflicting motivations to increase when the dreamer's conflict is more intense.

In accordance with this latter expectation we find that alternation of conflicting motivations usually reflects the persisting dynamic effect[3] of a traumatic memory. For example, even in the bridge dream (10*a*), which we have so often cited as an example of successful subordination of behavior to purpose, the process of organization of the water symbolism shows an alternation of conflicting motivations similar to that underlying the water symbolism in the patient's other dreams. We can readily deduce the explanation from our analysis of the water symbolism: This patient's water dreams reflect the reactivation of a traumatic memory. By definition a traumatic conflict is a problem that the dreamer has never been able to solve. When such a conflict is reactivated, it gives rise to pressures too great for the integrative mechanism to span; otherwise the problem would have been solved long ago. Consequently, the integrative mechanism, with its inadequate integrative capacity, can achieve only a series of partial integrations, in accordance with the principle of complementary substitutes.

We may now contrast the patient's reaction to a traumatic memory in the first episode of the bridge dream with his response to hopes of pleasing a mother-figure with which this dream ends. After playfully pinching the girl, the patient renounced his sexual and hostile impulses, thus turning away from his traumatic

2. This is in accordance with the principle of complementary substitutes (see Vol. I, chap. xlvi).

3. See chap. xxii of this volume.

conflict to hopes of pleasing the girl's mother by returning her daughter to her. Such a turning-away from a traumatic memory and emergence of reassuring hopes should result in an increase in the integrative span, with resulting diminution in the alternation of conflicting motivations. In accordance with this expectation, this last episode of the bridge dream is the one that illustrates most clearly the subordination of means to an end-goal, as in rational behavior.

If reactivation of a traumatic memory results in an alternation or succession of conflicting motivations, we must expect further that resolution of such a traumatic conflict will diminish or eliminate the alternation (or succession) of motivations caused by the conflict. In Volume III we shall discuss this principle at greater length and utilize it to measure progress toward resolution of a conflict in the therapeutic process.

CHAPTER XXXI

A Sudden Shrinkage of Integrative Span

Fluctuating Integrative Span in the Cognitive Grasp of Interpersonal Relations.—We shall now examine some evidence that suggests that fluctuations of integrative span occur during the process of dream organization. Such fluctuations involve most frequently the dreamer's cognitive grasp of interpersonal relations.

For objective understanding of an interpersonal relationship, we postulate,[1] identification with the several actors in the observed (or contemplated) scene must be subordinated to a cognitive grasp of the situation as a whole, to an understanding of how the motives of these several persons are related to one another. This understanding of the roles of the several interacting persons in relation to one another we shall call the "interpersonal cognitive field" or the "interpersonal field," whereas the physiological pattern corresponding to each particular role will be called an "identification pattern." For the purpose of objective understanding, the several patterns of identification must be kept separate and each recognized as the feelings and motives of the particular person to whom it belongs.

If one of the patterns of identification, becoming too intense, begins to escape from the control of the interpersonal field, then the understanding observer becomes less an observer and more an active participant. When two or more patterns of identification escape from cognitive control, then the need to participate actively in several different roles brings the several patterns of identification into conflict with one another. They can no longer be kept separate as the roles of several different persons but struggle with one another to control and shape the previously dominant interpersonal field, thus fusing into some kind of composite picture.

We have already studied[2] the end-result of this process in the

1. See chap. xxv of this volume.
2. See chap. xxv of this volume, pp. 167–68.

text of the anvil dream (12); and we have already suspected that it is because of their too great intensity that the conflicting patterns of beating and being beaten are dominating and shaping the visual pattern of the dream text (12), instead of being controlled by this visual pattern and each being relegated to its appropriate role in the observed scene.

The concept "too great intensity" implies a comparison. What we mean is intensity in excess of the capacity of the visual pattern which is the interpersonal field in this dream. Again we are dealing with a relationship of integrative task and integrative capacity. In order to subordinate patterns of identification to their role of contributing to the understanding of the observed scene, the integrative capacity of the interpersonal field must be adequate to span the sum of the pressures of the identification patterns.

Shrinkage of Integrative Span in the Pig Dream.—To illustrate these relationships, we shall re-examine the pig dream (43).

In the text of this dream (43) the lady feels "cheated." What are the implications of this word "cheated"? "Feeling cheated" implies being disappointed in something that was hoped for and expected. An intense feeling of being cheated implies acute disappointment, implies that hopes have been high and disillusionment sudden. The text of the pig dream uses the word in just this sense. The lady expected two carloads of pigs but received only half a carload: she feels cheated. The vehemence of her protest indicates that her disillusionment is intense.

Since integrative capacity is based on hope, we expect acute disillusionment to result in loss of integrative capacity and disintegration of integrative pattern. Our reconstruction of the process of organization of this dream (43) confirms this expectation. According to our reconstruction, an attempt at confession has degenerated, first, into an angry quarrel and then into prolonged asthmatic wheezing. This is a good example of physiological disintegration[3] of a goal-directed striving such as we expect to occur after loss of hope of achieving the goal.

The dream text (43) shows us an intermediate stage in this process of disintegration. In the dream work, as we reconstruct it,

3. See Vol. I, chap. xxvi.

we can follow the shrinkage of integrative capacity that we should expect to accompany the patient's feeling of being "cheated." Encouraged by the relief resulting from the patient's accepting the analyst's interpretation of the pump dream (41), the dream work (43) started with hope of reconciliation with the analyst by means of confession. The integrative capacity arising from this hope was at first sufficient to span both the patient's own sense of being cheated by the prospect of more children and also a realization that the analyst or mother could not help feeling cheated by the nature of his feelings toward her. Yet this insight soon destroyed the hope that made it possible. The fantasy of an angry quarrel into which the patient's fantasy of confession degenerates is still a superordinated cognitive field, spanning both the patient's' own feelings and those ascribed to the mother; but the dream text has already abandoned the task of keeping the two quarreling figures separate. As integrative capacity shrinks, the superordinated cognitive field has become unable to span the sum of the pressures of the patient's feelings and of those ascribed to the mother; and, adapting its span to its diminished integrative capacity, the dream text has abandoned the task of keeping the roles of the two quarreling persons separate and has replaced them both by the composite picture of a single protesting "lady."

CHAPTER XXXII

Expansion and Shrinkage of Goal
in Social Behavior[1]

The Integrative Mechanism of Taking Responsibility for Others.—In our first discussion of the bridge dream (10*a*), we considered the integrative task to be one of subordination of behavior to purpose. In socially oriented behavior the integrative task also has another aspect. For example, in the bridge dream (10*a*) the patient's purpose to please the mother implies that he has some notion of how she will react to his escorting her daughter home. The wish to please the mother implies that his behavior is guided by an integrative field that includes not only his own sexual impulse toward the girl but also the mother's anxiety to have her daughter returned to her. In fact, the integrative field that guides the bridge dream also includes a sense that the young girl, too, needs the protecting love of her mother; on this realization are based his impulse to share the mother's love with a sister and brother and his hope of pleasing the mother by so doing.

In this way we arrive at a notion of what is involved in taking responsibility for the needs of another person. Taking responsibility for another person requires an integrative capacity adequate to span not only one's own needs but those of another person, too.

The Integrative Mechanism of Dependence.—This definition of taking responsibility for others suggests a complementary definition of dependence on others. Dependence on another person is an attempt to lighten one's own integrative burden by transferring the whole or a part of the integrative task to someone else to solve.

To illustrate this concept of dependence, we recall our patient's reaction after he had begun to realize, in the broom dream (26), the inadequacy of his efforts to please the analyst. In the bor-

1. The argument of this chapter has already been presented briefly in T. M. French, 1945.

rowed book dream (27), which immediately follows, the book
that the woman is giving (returning to) him gives evidence of his
desire for instruction from the analyst. He feels the need to please
her, but, since his attempt to renounce and deny his sexual and
hostile impulses has failed to impress her, he does not know how
to make his impulses acceptable to her. The helplessness resulting
from his loss of hope of pleasing her threatens to increase greatly
the unneutralized pressure of his need to be loved. He protects
himself from this increase in his integrative task by a simple
device: The analyst shall solve this problem for him. Trusting in
her therapeutic interest in him, he protects himself with the hope
that she will teach him how to make his impulses acceptable to
her, that she will instruct him how to bridge the gap between his
own actual impulses and what he thinks she requires of him. Thus
he is trying to make his integrative task lighter by relegating part
of it to the analyst to solve.

*Further Analysis of the Disintegration of Integrative Pattern
after the Bridge Dream.*—These concepts of the nature of dependence and of responsibility for others now help us round out and
complete our understanding of the disintegration of the goal-
seeking mechanism that occurred after the bridge dream (10*a*).[2]

The basic goal that gives rise to the patient's conflict is a dependent one—to be loved and fed by the mother. This goal takes
account only of his own needs and requires the help of the
mother to satisfy them. To this goal-directed striving, brother
and sister are only obstacles. Yet the impulse to get rid of brother
and sister soon stirs up fear of offending the mother, which had
originally been left out of account but which now increases
greatly the patient's integrative task.

In the bridge dream (10*a*) the patient has turned away from
this impossible task to a new hope. With integrative capacity increased by the hope of pleasing the analyst (mother), he has been
able to expand the goal of his strivings to take account of all three
persons concerned, integrating his hope of pleasing the mother
with the hope of sharing her protective love with his sister. After
the bridge dream (10*a*), when loss of hope of pleasing the analyst-

2. See Vol. I, chaps. xix, xx, and xxi.

mother[3] results in diminution of integrative capacity, this expanded goal can no longer be maintained. With interest centered on the patient's own needs, brother and sister again become merely obstacles to his exclusive possession of the mother; and conflict re-emerges between hostile impulses toward brother and sister and fear of estranging the mother.

We now have an additional explanation of the mitigation[4] of a hostile impulse into a playful erotic gesture in the pinching incident in the bridge dream (10a). With his goal expanded to include the mother's and sister's need as well as his own, not only has the sister ceased to be an obstacle, but the patient's protective interest in her safety and welfare tends to exert a mitigating influence on whatever remnant of the original hostility may still be present.

3. See Vol. I, chap. xix, for explanation of this loss of hope of pleasing the analyst.

4. See Vol. I, chap. xxi.

CHAPTER XXXIII

Fluctuations of Integrative Span Earlier in the Process of Dream Organization

In the pig dream (43) acute disillusionment, resulting in shrinkage of integrative span, occurred as a last step in the process of dream organization. Shrinkage of span that has occurred earlier in the dream work is more difficult to reconstruct in detail. But hopes and fears probably fluctuate often in the course of the dream work, and we expect to find corresponding fluctuations in integrative capacity, integrative task, and integrative span.

Number, Intensity, and Divergence of Roles in an Interpersonal Field.—As a preliminary guide for study of these fluctuations, we reason tentatively as follows:

In the understanding of interpersonal relations the integrative task is to span and keep separate the identification patterns corresponding to each of the roles in the observed scene. From our discussion of the pig dream (43) we should expect the difficulty of this task to depend on several factors: (1) on the number of roles to be spanned; (2) on the intensity or pressure of each identification pattern; and (3) on the amount of contrast or divergence between the roles that must be kept separate. The greater the intensity of any two identification patterns and the greater the divergence between them, the more difficult will be the task of the interpersonal field to keep them separate.

Shrinkage of Integrative Span in the History of the Water Symbolism.—As an example we shall consider again the genesis of our patient's water symbolism. According to our reconstruction: The fantasies underlying his water dreams were originally stirred up by his mother's pregnancies. At some time in the course of his sexual investigations in early childhood, he came to realize that the mother's pregnancies were the result of sexual relations between his parents. Interpreting what he observed in terms of his own sexual excitement, he arrived at a urinary theory of impregnation and fantasied himself emulating his notion of the father's role, giving the mother a child by urinating upon her. Unfortunately, this proud fantasy was soon disturbed by the threat of the expected child as a rival for the mother's love. Jealous hatred of brother and sister transformed his impregnation fantasies into hostile ones. Instead of giving the mother children, he imagined himself using his water to drown the babies inside the mother's body. Yet this wish only increased the danger of estrangement from the mother. To forestall this catastrophe, he tried to get rid of his jealousy by picturing himself as sharing the intrauterine position with his rivals; but, when this sharing fantasy failed to quiet his rising resentment, it culminated in the threat of all drowning together in the destructive "flood."

When we review this reconstructed sequence, it is evident that it is one of progressive disillusionment: First, his hope of pleasing the mother by giving her a child must give way before the threat of brother and sister as rivals; and then he must realize that his hope of getting rid of his rivals involves the danger of even greater estrangement from the mother.

According to our hypothesis, the integrative mechanism adapts to disillusionment by shrinkage in integrative span. We find evidence of such shrinkage when we compare the first and the last of the fantasies in our reconstructed sequence. In the urinary impregnation fantasy the interpersonal field must keep separate three different roles: (1) the role of the patient urinating on the mother; (2) the coveted role of being inside the mother, which this fantasy must project (renounce), ascribing it to the child; and (3) the role of the mother, pleased by the patient's sharing her protective attitude toward the child. To this complexly articulated fantasy we now compare the text of the capsized boat dream (187b) in which we find only one really significant role—that of the lady in danger of drowning and struggling to save herself by climbing on top of the boat. From this role of the "lady" in danger of drowning we can hardly distinguish that of the patient as observer, since, in his anxiety for the "lady," he is so closely identified with her struggles.

Thus, in accordance with our expectation, the disillusionment involved in his infantile conflict has resulted in a shrinkage of integrative span. A field that was spanning and keeping separate three different roles has shrunk to a fantasied scene in which only one distinct role can be recognized.

Subsequent Expansion of Interpersonal Span in Some Water Dreams.—In several of our patient's water dreams, present hopes of the analyst's approval or indulgence have temporarily increased the integrative capacity available to deal with his infantile conflict. According to our hypothesis, we expect such an increase in integrative capacity to be reflected in an increased span of the interpersonal field. In the bridge dream (10*a*), in accordance with this expectation, although the river is still an allusion to the fear of drowning arising out of his infantile conflict, the interpersonal field has expanded to include: (1) the patient's own needs, (2) those of the young girl, and (3) those of her mother.

In other words, at any given moment, the span of the interpersonal field depends on the quantitative relation between its integrative capacity, on the one hand, and the intensity of the conflict that constitutes its integrative task, on the other. We continue with this patient's water dreams as our example. If the integrative task is excessive, the cognitive structure may disappear, and the patient may be completely preoccupied with sensations of suffocation, as in a severe asthma attack. When the integrative task is less overwhelming, we find the suffocation sensations imbedded in an elementary cognitive pattern in which a single person is struggling against being drowned, as in the capsized boat dream (187*b*). In the erotized water dreams, with integrative capacity increased by hope of the analyst's indulgence, the cognitive structure is more complex: In the flood dream (115), for example, three persons (the patient, a sister-figure, and a brother-figure) are sharing the role of the child (being in the basement room and threatened by the flood); and the girl, making up the cot for the child, is playing the role of the mother (which had previously disappeared, having been replaced by the inanimate symbol of the basement room). In the dirty hole dream (205) even the patient's original hostile impulse has found its way back into his integrative span, in the partially erotized and partially inhibited form of half-filling a hole with water from his hose.

CHAPTER XXXIV

Internal Strains Determining Reorganization of an Interpersonal Field

In this chapter we shall try to answer another kind of question about reorganizations of cognitive fields.

When disillusionment occurs, we expect the nature of the dreamer's conflict to determine how shrinkage of integrative span is to be achieved. For example, in the pig dream (43) two techniques for diminishing integrative span are employed. These are related, respectively, to the dreamer's two conflicting motives:

1. In everyday life, if one wishes to inflict injury on a hated person, he must "harden his heart"; he must inhibit any tendency to identify with the injured person, lest his hate be restrained by pity. By substituting an inanimate boxcar for the analyst and for the mother whose pregnancies he resented, the dreamer has symbolically achieved a "hardening of heart" in the pig dream (43).

2. However, this dreamer also longs for reconciliation with the mother. For this desire for harmony, too, the manifest dream (43) has achieved an illusion of fulfilment—by means of the composite picture of the "lady," who represents both the dreamer and the mother-analyst, as though they were one person.

Cleavages and Strains in the Interpersonal Field in the Pig Dream.—For understanding a reorganization of cognitive pattern in the dream work, the notions of cleavages and of strains in an interpersonal cognitive field are useful concepts. Two different roles in an interpersonal cognitive field may be either in close harmony or in sharp conflict with each other. Roles that are in conflict with one another we think of as separated by sharp lines of cleavage. Usually the sharpest cleavage is one between "ego-syntonic" and "ego-alien" roles. The "ego-syntonic" roles include both the dreamer's own role and other roles with which the dreamer is closely identified; "ego-alien" roles are roles with which the dreamer is in conflict.

In the successive steps in the process of dream organization, not only do the several roles often undergo modification, but the lines of cleavage between them may also shift their positions. For example, in the process of organization of the pig dream (43), the fantasied quarrel between the dreamer and the mother-analyst implies a sharp cleavage between their two roles; but in the dream text this line of cleavage has disappeared and another has taken its place: In the manifest dream (43) the line of cleavage is no longer between the patient and the analyst-mother but between the "lady," who represents them both, and the boxcar with dirty pigs in it, that symbolizes the theme of controversy between them (see Fig. 15).

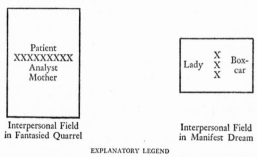

Interpersonal Field
in Fantasied Quarrel

Interpersonal Field
in Manifest Dream

EXPLANATORY LEGEND

XXXXX = Line of cleavage (i.e., conflict between roles)

FIG. 15.—Reorganization of cognitive pattern in pig dream

This realignment in the dreamer's interpersonal field can be easily understood as a direct consequence of the dreamer's conflict between resentment of his mother's pregnancies and his longing for reconciliation with her. It is as though the dreamer and the analyst-mother were uniting to turn their hostility away from each other and against an indefinite somebody, not even explicitly mentioned in the dream text, who is responsible for their both being cheated.

To understand the details of such a reorganization[1] of cognitive pattern, we now postulate that the dreamer's conflict is causing internal strains in his cognitive field. For example, in

1. Kurt Lewin (1935) speaks of "restructuring" of the cognitive field.

the fantasied quarrel, we assume that the patient's longing for harmony with the analyst tends to pull their two roles together, to fuse them with each other, but that the dreamer's resentment of the mother's pregnancies tends to push their two roles farther apart. Then, in the dream text, we can recognize the combined effect of the action of these two forces. Torn between conflicting forces, the role of the mother-analyst has been split into two parts, one of which, based on memory of the mother's many pregnancies, is repudiated; while the other, in accordance with the patient's desire for reconciliation with the analyst in the therapeutic situation, is fused with the patient's own sense of being cheated.

Modifying Effect of Resonant Physiological Patterns in the Water Dreams.—According to our hypothesis, each role in an interpersonal cognitive field is in resonance with an underlying physiological pattern—its identification pattern. If so, we must expect that reorganization of an interpersonal field will be resisted by the resonant identification patterns, unless these, too, can be correspondingly modified. In the fantasied quarrel in the pig dream, both the dreamer's role and that of the mother are roles of verbal protest because of feeling cheated. Since the physiological patterns corresponding to these roles are so similar, the two roles can be condensed or fused without essential modification of the underlying physiological pattern of either. However, in other cases, the roles that are being pulled together by the strains in the interpersonal field may correspond to radically different identification patterns.

For example, in the water dreams, according to our reconstruction, the fantasy of being drowned arose in reaction to a conflict between an impulse to drown the child inside the mother's body and fear of estrangement from the mother. This conflict implies an interpersonal field that spans and keeps separate three roles: (*a*) the patient's own hostile impulse to urinate on the pregnant mother; (*b*) the suffocating sensations of the child; and (*c*) the offended reaction of the mother, protective of the child. In this interpersonal field the patient's desire to be loved by the mother pulls toward fusion of his own role (*a*) with that of the mother (*c*). Yet the physiological patterns corresponding to the dreamer's hostile role (*a*) and to the mother's protective encompassing role (*c*) are so different that either the one or the other must be radically changed in order to permit fusion of the two roles.

In the fantasy of being drowned there has been just such a radical modification of the dreamer's impulse to urinate on the pregnant mother. The dreamer's fear of offending the mother has turned back against himself his impulse to urinate upon her. In our physiological terminology this means that a large part of the pressure activating this impulse to urinate (corresponding to role *a*) has been deflected to augment the sensations of suffocation that correspond to the role (*b*) of the child.

Resulting Reorganization of Interpersonal Field.—We can study the resulting realignment of forces in the interpersonal field by examining the capsized boat dream (187*b*). In the manifest content of this dream, we find the sharpest line of cleavage no longer between the dreamer and the pregnant mother, as it was in the underlying conflict, but between the "lady," with whom the patient is identified, and the water of the lake, which threatens to drown her.

In this reorganization the most important step has been extrusion of the role (*a*) of urinating on mother and child, across the line of cleavage that separates ego-syntonic and ego-alien roles. The impulse to urinate has become ego-alien and has been replaced by a deanimated symbol, water. We assume that this has been made possible by the change that we have already mentioned in the underlying physiological patterns, by deflection of the greater part of the pressure of the impulse to urinate. In other words, the impulse to urinate can be represented by the deanimated symbol, water, only after the greater part of its activating pressure has been diverted elsewhere.

We postulated that the pressure deflected from the impulse to urinate has augmented the sensations of suffocation corresponding to the role (*b*) of the child. In the manifest dream this increased pressure of the suffocating sensations is reflected by the dream's vivid portrayal of the "lady's" struggles against drowning, by the dreamer's anxiety for her, and by his wheezing all night.

In the dream text the patient's own (manifest) role has become one of watching anxiously and sympathetically identifying with the lady's struggles against drowning. This sympathetic anxiety for the "lady" may be regarded as a rudimentary equivalent of the mother's protective attitude (role *c*) toward her child in the underlying conflict. In other words, *this dream (187b), too, has achieved an illusion of harmony with the mother —by the dreamer's taking over a part of her role.* In terms of the dynamics of the interpersonal cognitive field, the dreamer's need for the mother's love has pulled the roles (*c* and *b*) of mother and child, which were originally ego-alien, across the line of cleavage that previously separated them from the dreamer's role, thus making them ego-syntonic.

Degradation of the Mother's Protective Role.—Our chief remaining problem is to account for the degradation of the mother's role (*c*), for the substitution of the sympathetic anxiety of a mere observer for the protecting encompassing love implied by the mother's pregnancy. In the dream text only the boat remains as a deanimated substitute for the mother's pregnancy, and even the boat has tipped over.

In the light of the preceding discussion we can now recognize this degradation of the mother's protective role as a consequence of the shrinkage of integrative capacity resulting from the excessive intensity of the dreamer's conflict. The protective role symbolized by the mother's pregnancy is one of protective responsibility for her child, implying an expanded integrative span. With his integrative capacity curtailed by the excessive intensity of his conflict, the dreamer can no longer form a notion of what a mother's protective love can be like. The helpless anxiety of a sympathetic onlooker is all that can survive at the moment of his notion of protective love.

Summary.—Thus the processes of organization of both these dreams illustrate our thesis that the pattern of each reorganization of the interpersonal field in the dream work is determined by internal strains in this field, which are themselves determined by the nature of the dreamer's conflict. In the water dreams we see also the modifying effects of the physiological patterns that are resonant with the several roles in the interpersonal field.

CHAPTER XXXV

The Process and the Pattern of Dream Organization

In this chapter we shall make several attempts to reconstruct the actual "process" of dream organization.

Ignoring time as a factor, we have not always distinguished carefully between the "process" of dream organization and the cognitive structure that results from it. The cognitive structure of a dream is a constellation of cognitive fields in resonance with one another at the moment of dreaming. Yet we sometimes describe the "pattern of dream organization" as though we were reconstructing the history of a manuscript. We speak[1] of "a series of pictures or fantasy patterns that starts with the dreamer's practical understanding of his conflict situation and leads, by intelligibly motivated substitutions, to the manifest dream content." Later (in our diagrams) we speak of "intermediate versions" of the "dream text." All this sounds as though we were describing not a "pattern" but a "process" of dream organization.

We should distinguish between the order of dominance of cognitive fields in an already formed cognitive structure and the chronological order of the steps by which that cognitive structure was arrived at. In the cognitive structure that guided me as I started to drive to Cleveland,[2] "polarization" of the "expected landscape" by my desire to go to Cleveland was "transmitted" through the interstate map and the street map to the actual streets of Chicago in the observed landscape. This was the order of dominance in an already formed cognitive structure; in this case this order of dominance in the final cognitive structure just happened to correspond to the (chronological) order of my consulting the maps.

Actually, the cognitive structure of behavior is continually changing. On my trip to Cleveland, I no longer needed the

1. See chap. ii, p. 11.
2. See chap. i, pp. 5–7.

street map of Chicago after I reached Route 20. When I reached Route 20, the street map of Chicago dropped out of my cognitive structure.

When a goal-directed effort gives rise to conflict or frustration, more radical reorganizations occur. Since most dreams are struggling with conflicts, we find more profound reorganizations of cognitive structure in the process of dream organization than we do in rational behavior. We have already discussed a number of examples of reorganization of cognitive pattern in the process of dream organization.

As soon as we distinguish carefully between "process" and "pattern" of dream organization, we are confronted with questions like the following:

What happens to the fantasy patterns that are activated in the process of dream organization? Do they persist as part of the pattern of dream organization? Or does each new fantasy replace the one that preceded it?

We can ask a similar question about the memories and fantasies that constitute a dream's historical background: Do these memories and fantasy patterns continue active until the moment of dreaming? Do they then become a part of the final pattern of dream organization?

In this chapter we shall consider whether the evidence permits us to answer questions like these. We assume that the answers may differ for different dreams.

Degrees of Reactivation of a Traumatic Memory.—We shall discuss, first, what happens to disturbing patterns from the past. Let us compare the bridge dream (10*a*) with the capsized boat dream (187*b*).

In the capsized boat dream (187*b*) the patient identifies with the lady who is in danger of drowning; he is anxious for her and wheezes all night. In this dream it is evident that his childhood fantasy of being drowned is still active at the moment of dreaming. On the other hand, in the bridge dream (10*a*), there is no evidence of anxiety; both the patient and the girl are safe on the bridge, looking down at boats on the river. But if there is no anxiety, why does the river remain in the dream text, and why does the dream lift the dreamer up on a bridge above the river? Evidently, in the bridge dream, too, there must have been some slight reactivation of the impulses and fears symbolized by the river.

Freud (1926) has pointed out that in many cases castration fear (or other fear of consequences) needs to be activated only slightly in order to serve as a warning signal. If the integrative mechanism is able to give heed to the warning, it will avoid activating the disturbing impulse and thus prevent further activation of the fear of consequences. This is evidently what occurred in the bridge dream. Even though the disturbing memories underlying the water symbolism were only slightly activated, they nevertheless exerted a significant inhibitory effect on the dreamer's behavior, causing him to renounce his emerging sexual wishes and escort the girl home to her mother.

But what determines whether the integrative mechanism will be able to heed such a warning signal? For example, why could not the capsized boat dream (187b) avoid reactivating the patient's drowning fantasies?

Our previous discussion of the bridge dream[3] has already suggested the answer to this question: In this dream it was not fear of offending the analyst but hope of pleasing her that made it possible for the dreamer to renounce his sexual wishes and thus avoid the consequences that he feared. In this dream the hope of winning the mother's thanks and a glass of milk was attractive enough to deflect the dreamer away from his dangerous sexual impulses.

In general, a warning signal alone is not enough to deflect pressure away from a disturbing impulse. If the warning is to be effective, it must be supplemented by hope of substitute satisfaction, and this hope of substitute satisfaction must be attractive enough to absorb and channel the pressure of the underlying need. If hope of substitute satisfaction is not adequate, then the integrative mechanism will not succeed in deflecting pressure away from the disturbing impulse, and fear of consequences will emerge in an intensity far in excess of what is needed for

3. See Vol. I, chap. xxi.

a warning signal. This, we assume, was what occurred in the capsized boat dream (187*b*).

Thus our comparison of bridge dream (10*a*) and capsized boat dream (187*b*) dramatizes an assumption that has been implicit in much of our preceding discussion—that the patterns of disturbing events from the past exist in varying degrees of activation. At any given moment (except perhaps in the most severely neurotic behavior) most of these traumatic memory patterns are in a state of latency.[4] At other times they may be slightly activated as warning signals. They are more intensely activated only when the integrative mechanism is unable to heed their warning signal.

Questions about the Process of Dream Organization.—We return now to our questions about what happens to fantasy patterns that are activated for the first time in the present. When fantasies are activated during the process of dream organization, do they persist as part of the pattern of dream organization? Or does each new fantasy replace the one that preceded it?

Our notion of shrinkage of integrative span during the process of dream organization seems definitely to imply transformation of one integrative field into another.

According to our reconstruction, the process of organization of the pig dream (43) started with an interpersonal field that spanned both the patient's own and the analyst's (mother's) feelings of being cheated; but then, when his disillusionment resulted in rapid diminution of integrative capacity, his picture of himself and the mother as two quarreling figures was unable to maintain itself; it was replaced by a field in which the patient and the analyst were fused into a single figure, the "lady" of the dream text. The question we are now asking is: Was the picture of the two quarreling figures really *replaced* by the composite picture of the single "lady"? Might not the picture of the two quarreling figures have *persisted* as part of the pattern of dream organization, *in resonance with* the condensed picture in the dream text?

4. See Vol. I, chap. xxxii.

The reasoning on which our reconstruction is based seems to leave little room for this possibility. Since integrative capacity was inadequate, how could such an expanded interpersonal field have maintained itself?

Our reconstruction of the genesis of the drowning fantasies underlying our patient's water dreams has similar implications. These fantasies, we believe, arose in reaction to impulses to urinate on the pregnant mother and drown her child. According to our reconstruction, fear of offending the mother by these impulses soon involved the patient in a conflict which his integrative capacity was unable to span; and then, when the integrative span shrank, the dreamer's fantasy of himself being drowned arose by fusion of his own role with that of the child whom he wished to drown. In the capsized boat dream (187b), for example, we now ask (as we did in the case of the pig dream): Did the picture that originally spanned both sides of the dreamer's conflict *persist, in resonance with* the condensed picture in the dream text? It is difficult to conceive how this could have been possible. With an inadequate integrative capacity, how could such an expanded picture, spanning both sides of the dreamer's conflict, have maintained itself?

On the other hand, when a dream reacts successively to different parts of the same (focal) conflict situation, then we must assume that the dreamer's (unconscious) grasp of the whole situation must have remained active in some form during the whole process of dreaming.

For example, in the pencil-stealing dream the patient was in conflict between hopes of the analyst's permissiveness and fear of offending her. In the manifest dream this conflict seems to have been fragmented: First, the switchman tempted him, and then the watchman appeared to question him.

But we must again ask the same question that we did in the case of the pig dream: We suspect that the dreamer's understanding of his conflict situation has undergone fragmentation because his integrative capacity was inadequate to span his problem all at once. If his integrative capacity was inadequate, how is it possible that "the dreamer's (unconscious) grasp of the whole situation" should have remained "active in some form" while the dreamer was reacting successively to different parts of it?

However, on closer examination of the pencil-stealing dream (25) it is evident that the dreamer's understanding of his conflict situation did not really undergo fragmentation. First, in deference to his fear, he tested the analyst's permissiveness only cautiously, by stealing a few pencils; and then, after the appearance of the watchman had brought his fear to the surface, the door of the boxcar was still open as a symbol of the analyst's permissiveness. In other words, both his hope and his fear were active throughout the process of dreaming. In this dream (25) it was possible for the integrative mechanism to span both sides of the dreamer's conflict because the really disturbing conflict was never fully activated during the process of dreaming. Our hypothesis is that the dreamer's traumatic memories of sexual and hostile impulses toward his mother's pregnancies were at first only slightly reactivated, but served as a warning signal, causing him to turn away to the hope of testing the analyst's indulgence by a trivial symbolic act. Testing the analyst's permissiveness required from the beginning an integrative field that could span both his hopes of indulgence and his fears; and, as long as his disturbing impulses were only slightly reactivated, the integrative capacity was adequate for this task. When the underlying conflict began to be more intensely activated, physiological disintegration occurred, and he awoke, wheezing.

SECTION VII

Pattern of the Water Dreams

CHAPTER XXXVI

Plan To Survey Relations between Dreams

Study of Recurring Dream Patterns.—When we trace back to their historical sources the thoughts that have contributed to the shaping of a dream, we find a constellation of compactly interrelated situations and fantasy patterns. This constellation is the cognitive structure of the dream's historical background.

When we compare the cognitive structures of different dreams of the same person, we find parts of the historical background of each dream repeated in the historical background of other dreams. We have been using comparisons with other dreams to check our reconstructions of the process of organization of single dreams. In the rest of this volume we shall also use our comparisons of dream structure for another purpose—to study how the cognitive structures of different dreams are related to one another.

We have been studying the cognitive structures of single dreams. Now we shall try to reconstruct the "cataloguing system" or "road map" of which the historical background of each particular dream is a part.

In attempting this reconstruction we shall use two kinds of comparisons: (1) comparisons of successive recurrences of similar or homologous cognitive structures and (2) camparisons of sequences of consecutive dreams.

Homologous patterns are somewhat easier to compare. Our comparison of the anvil dream (12) and the fire-tending dream (45*a*) is an example,[1] and both the water dreams and the grasping hand dreams offer us many opportunities for comparison of parallel cognitive structures.

Our starting point for comparing consecutive dreams is the fact, which we have already illustrated, that in consecutive be-

1. See chap. viii of this volume.

havior a basic problem persists[2] while different attempts to solve it succeed one another. Our task will be to analyze the reorganizations of cognitive structure that occur in the course of attempts to solve a persisting underlying problem. We call these "functional transitions."

Study of Choice Points and Alternative Reactions.—Our basic conceptual scheme in the comparisons that follow is one of alternative reactions at choice points.

In previous chapters we have been studying how fantasy patterns succeed one another under the modifying influence of continually changing motivations, much as one might study the "textual history" of a manuscript. When we compare different dreams or different parts of the same dream, we often find that two or more alternative chains of reaction may take origin from the same fantasy pattern. In other words, our reconstructions of the cognitive structure of a dream or of two or more homologous dreams often take the form of a branching tree. A choice point is a point from which two or more possible alternative reactions diverge.

We can improve our understanding of possible reactions at choice points by postulating quantitative differences in the degree to which alternative reactions replace one another. Let us assume, for example, that there are two possible alternative reactions, A_1 and A_2, to the same reactivated memory pattern, M. Under appropriate circumstances the patient may react first with A_1 and then with A_2. The replacement of the one alternative by the other may be complete, or it may be incomplete in varying degrees. In Figure 16 we indicate schematically possible quantitative variations in the relations between M, A_1, and A_2.

Returning to our road-map analogy—in this kind of analysis we are studying not only how the roads are situated and intercommunicate but also how traffic is distributed among them at a given time.

However, we should not forget that our "road map" is only an imperfect analogy. It is adequate to represent some, but not all, of the relations between cognitive fields in a cognitive struc-

2. See Vol. I, chaps. ix and xix.

ture. The difficulty with this analogy arises from the fact that the points on our "road map" represent not points but patterns— cognitive fields. The contractions and expansions of integrative span that we discussed in the last few chapters are, therefore, difficult to picture in terms of this analogy.

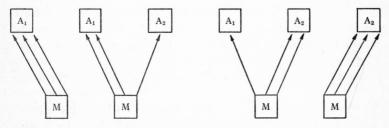

FIG. 16.—Possible quantitative distributions of pressure between two alternatives.

CHAPTER XXXVII

Sharing and Reversal of Aggression

In the next few chapters (Sec. VII) we plan to summarize and analyze the relations between the fantasy patterns that we encounter in the water dreams. Later (in Secs. VIII and IX) we shall explore the relations between the water dreams and other dreams of this patient.

A significant feature of the capsized boat dream (187*b*) is the fact that the dream reacts to the "lady's" danger of drowning not with guilt but with anxiety. In the dream (187*b*) the "lady" is struggling to climb on top of the boat, and the patient is anxious for her. Yet he shows no sign of guilt either in the dream text or in the associations. Since the "lady's" drowning is in fulfilment of the dreamer's wish, why does he not feel guilty? The reason for the absence of manifest guilt seems to be that the "lady" represents himself as well as the "sister" whom he wishes to drown, that he is expiating his guilt by identifying with her danger and her anxiety.

In a number of other dreams of this series the same pattern of identification with the objects of his hostile wishes takes the form of his sharing the role or threatened fate of the fantasied victims of his aggression. For example, in the bridge dream (10*a*) both the girl and the patient walk over the bridge that lifts them above the river. In the fireplug dream (19*a*) he helps the girl carry the water can. In the flood dream (115) he and the girl and the eleven-year-old boy are all in the flooded basement together. In the train wreck dream (154*a*)[1] the number of cars that tip over corresponds to the number of children in the parental home. Since this number, six, includes the patient himself, we must assume that in the underlying fantasy he pictured himself as sharing the fate that he wished for his younger brothers and sisters. In the dirty hole dream (205) he follows his "sister"

1. See chap. xiv of this volume, pp. 90–91 and 99–100.

into the hole, which is already half-full of water and dirt from his hose.

We encounter also another kind of sharing fantasy in these dreams. In the bridge dream (10*a*) the patient is able to win the mother by sharing her love with brother and sister. In the dirty food dream (39) there is "food enough for a regiment." In the flood dream (115) he shares the basement room as well as the dirty water; and in the dirty hole dream (205) he gets into the hole with the sister-figure. Even in the train wreck dream (154*a*) there are many soldiers in each car.

In the bridge dream (10*a*) the function served by these fantasies of sharing the mother's love is particularly clear. When the patient can be content to share the mother with brother and sister, then the disturbing rivalrous impulses become unnecessary, and he need no longer fear offending the mother by them. We assume that his intrauterine sharing fantasies perform a similar function. By imagining himself sharing the mother, he makes hostility to her unborn child superfluous.

Yet this mechanism is not always successful. His intrauterine sharing fantasies are usually disturbed by the threat of water penetrating into the protecting room or train or boat.

We can best account for the variations and fluctuations in these fantasies in terms of the hypothesis[2] that integrative capacity is based on hope. If hope of the mother's indulgence or approval is adequate, then the fantasy of sharing her may have integrative capacity sufficient to neutralize and channel the pressure of his need for love; but when hope wanes, the integrative capacity diminishes, and unneutralized pressure emerges in the form of hostile impulses toward rivals. In the fantasies underlying the water symbolism the hostile impulse takes the form of a wish to drown brother and sister, which promptly reawakens the patient's fear of offending the mother.

There are a number of possible ways of reacting to this conflict; but we shall first consider only one of these: turning back the hostile impulse against the patient himself. This leaves us to consider two possible alternative reactions to the reactivated memories of the mother's pregnancies: (1) sharing the mother

2. See chap. xxx of this volume and Vol. I, chaps. xii and xix.

with brother and sister and (2) suffocating sensations embodied in a fantasy of being drowned.

When hope fluctuates, first one and then the other of these reactions may be activated, or the replacement of one alternative by the other may be incomplete in varying degree.[3] The two alternatives are an intrauterine sharing fantasy (Sh) and a fantasy of being drowned (Dr). By postulating quantitative differences in the extent to which the first of these alternatives (Sh) has been replaced by the second (Dr), we can account for a number of the variations in the intrauterine symbolism of these water dreams (with water threatening a uterine symbol increasingly as activation of the drowning fantasy increases; see Fig. 17).

3. See preceding chapter and Fig. 16 (p. 215).

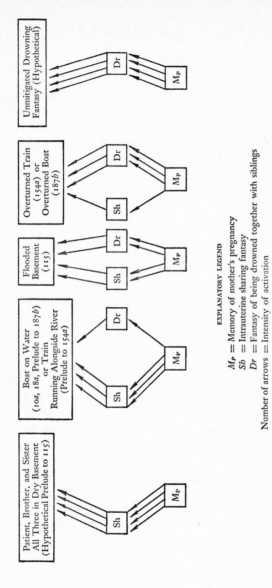

EXPLANATORY LEGEND

M_p = Memory of mother's pregnancy
Sh = Intrauterine sharing fantasy
Dr = Fantasy of being drowned together with siblings

Number of arrows = Intensity of activation

FIG. 17.—Intrauterine sharing and drowning fantasies in the water dreams

CHAPTER XXXVIII
Drinking or Drowning

Oral Cravings in the Water Symbolism.—We have interpreted the patient's fantasies of being drowned as a reaction formation against his impulses to attack the mother's pregnancies. He longs to solve his conflict in relation to the mother's pregnancies by sharing the brother's and sister's place in the mother's affections, but his jealous hostility toward brother and sister threatens to make this solution impossible by estranging him from the mother. He accordingly inhibits and disavows his hostile impulses and, turning these impulses back against himself, pictures them as a force from outside that threatens himself as well as brother and sister. Rather than be estranged from the mother's love, he shares with brother and sister the danger that threatens from hostile impulses which he refuses to recognize as his own.

Yet our functional interpretation of the water symbolism has led us to suspect that water is significant not only as urine and as something to choke over or drown in but also as something to drink. In accord with this expectation, this patient's water dreams are closely associated with a craving for drink and for liquid food. Even in the whiskey dream (116*b*) whiskey is something to be enjoyed as well as feared. In this dream "everyone had drinks," and "the other men drank it and smacked their lips." Evidently the others, at least, were drinking for pleasure. Only for the patient was whiskey a suffocating drink which he resisted having forced upon him.

In other dreams, too, we find an association between enjoying drinking and being suffocated. For example, we may compare the beer dream (162*a*) and the hot stove dream (162*b*) of the 162d hour. In the beer dream (162*a*) the patient first drinks beer with another man, then treats one woman to whiskey and another to candy. In this dream drinking and eating candy are gratifications; but in the hot stove dream (162*b*) he is taking delight in gagging two inspectors in a boxcar by urinating upon a hot stove.

From their close juxtaposition it is evident that the two dreams (162*a*, 162*b*) are erotized and unerotized derivatives of the same unconscious fantasy. In the beer dream (162*a*) the patient is able to share drinks and is proud of his ability to treat the two women; in the hot stove dream (162*b*) his hostility has transformed this fantasy of giving drinks into one of gagging or suffocating the two inspectors by the odor of his urine.

In the bridge dream (10*a*) we have a similar juxtaposition. The scene of the girl on the bridge, with which this dream (10*a*) begins, is an allusion to the drowning fantasies; but the dream ends with his sharing the mother's love with brother and sister and receiving from the mother a glass of "cool, refreshing milk." A similar close association of milk and water is hinted at in the milk can that has been filled with water in the fireplug dream (19*a*).

Effect of Frustration on Drinking Fantasies.—When we compare the situations that provoked these dreams, we find that as the degree of frustration increases, drinking tends to be replaced by drowning in the fantasies underlying these water dreams.

For example, in reaction to the thought that he might leave home, the trainwreck dream (154*a*) puts the patient out in the open country, far away from the train that symbolizes the mother. Inside the train are soldiers, symbolizing her children. In this dream (154*a*), the meaning of the water symbolism is hostile; the dreamer wishes to drown the children. Yet in the flood dream (115) he has found another solution. This dream is in reaction to the analyst's indulgence of his talk about sex. According to the dream symbolism, he is sharing with the young woman and the child his position inside the "basement," as though they were brother and sister. At least in terms of the symbolism, he has the mother's love, though sharing it with brother and sister. Under these circumstances his hostility is diminished. The hostile meaning of the water symbolism has been mitigated into an erotic one. Instead of destroying the sister-figure, he is only soiling her erotically, and both he and the girl can wash their faces in the "dirty water."

Comparison of flood dream (115) and whiskey dream (116*b*) suggests a similar quantitative relationship. Evidently the patient cannot long be satisfied with the fantasy of sharing with sister and brother their place in the "basement." As the sense of frustration emerges, this fantasy takes on a hostile character. In the whiskey dream (116*b*) in the next hour, the drink that is being forced upon him is a "suffocating" drink that threatens to knock him out.

When we compare the bridge dream (10*a*) with the flood dream (115), we find evidence of further mitigation of this patient's drowning fantasies. In the flood dream (115), in which the patient symbolically shares the mother with sister and brother, drowning has been mitigated into drinking dirty water. In the final episode of the bridge dream (10*a*), when he is really able to share the mother with brother and sister, the drink offered by the mother is described in terms of unmixed pleasure, as "cool, refreshing milk."

The dirty food dream (39), in which a gypsy woman offers him "some kind of milk" which he rejects as dirty, sounds like a condensation of receiving milk from the mother, as in the bridge dream (10*a*), with the fantasy of taking dirty water into his mouth, that is suggested by the flood dream (115). As in the bridge dream, receiving milk from the mother is associated with willingness to share the mother's love, for he tells us that there was "food enough for a regiment"; but his rejection of the food as dirty corresponds to his depreciation of the analyst's indulgence[1] of his sexual talk in the flood dream (115).

This ambivalence toward the "food" that the "gypsy" mother is offering in the dirty food dream (39) is explained by the two conflicting trends in his reaction to the analyst's encouragement at this time. This dream (39) follows a long flight reaction from the seductive implications of the analyst's indulgent attitude toward his "dirty" thoughts; but the dreamer has again begun to entertain the hope of regaining a mother's approval by willingness to share her with his rivals. In the dream text (39) these two conflicting trends find expression in his rejection of the food as dirty, even though there is "enough for a regiment."

Physiological Absorption by Hopes of Maternal Approval and by Oral Gratification.—Thus we can arrange this patient's drinking fantasies in a series corresponding to progressive increase in the unneutralized pressure of his conflict. When his willingness to

---

[1]. See chap. x of this volume, pp. 73–74.

share his food and drink with brother and sister makes him sure of the mother's approval, he can dream of receiving "cool, refreshing milk" from the mother (dream 10*a*) or of drinking beer with another man and treating girls to drinks and candy (dream 162*a*). When his rivalrous impulses can be partially, but not entirely, neutralized by hopes of the analyst's indulgence, they can still be mitigated into erotic fantasies of taking dirty water (urine) into his mouth. When the rivalrous hostility becomes excessive, he must dream of having a suffocating drink forced upon him (dream 116*b*), or of drowning, together with his rivals (dream 154*a*).

The quantitative relationships just illustrated can best be accounted for by the hypothesis that the integrative capacity of the patient's hopes of a mother's approval or indulgence is supplemented by a mechanism of physiological absorption of sexual and hostile impulses by oral gratification. When hope of a mother's approval can neutralize a large part of the disturbing pressure, then oral satisfaction is adequate to absorb the disturbing pressures, and the dreamer's enjoyment of his drink is frank and not mixed with discomfort; but when unneutralized pressure increases and can no longer be completely absorbed by enjoyment of the drink, feelings of distaste (such as are implied by dirty water) begin to appear; and, finally, if unneutralized pressure becomes excessive, it gives rise to sensations of suffocation and fantasies of drowning.

In Figure 18 we have schematically represented these relations in terms of our working concept of more or less complete replacement of one alternative, being drowned or suffocated (O_D), by another, enjoying drinks (O_E).

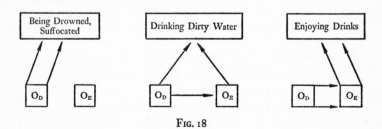

Fig. 18

CHAPTER XXXIX
Active Mastery of Drowning Fears

In the light of later dreams it is evident that the detail in the bridge dream (10a) of the girl on the bridge looking at boats in the river is an allusion to the sexual wish to urinate on the girl that appears in the flood dream (115), to the hostile wish to drown the girl that comes to view in the train wreck dream (154a) and the capsized boat dream (187b), and to the fear of being suffocated or drowned in retribution, that is suggested in the whiskey dream (116b). A fear of being drowned or of having a suffocating fluid forced upon him appears to be at the root of all this patient's water dreams.

To illustrate these relations, we shall first reconstruct the organizational pattern of the detail of the girl on the bridge looking at boats (dream 10a): Not only the water but also the boats in the earlier dream (10a) remind us of the girl tipped out of the boat and in danger of drowning in the later dream (187b). Making use of the later dream (187b) to throw light on the boat symbolism of the earlier one (10a), we infer that the dream detail of the girl leaning on the bridge looking at boats (10a) must have arisen as a defense against the deeper fear of her drowning that becomes manifest in the later dream (187b). The earlier dream (10a) has been able to project this fear and also to reassure the dreamer by substituting a beautiful peaceful scene for the dangerous one. In the earlier dream the girl is merely looking at boats. She herself is on a bridge, well up above the water. There is no suggestion of danger, of boats tipping over, or of anyone's drowning. By interpolating between the two dream fragments we can reconstruct this bit of dream work as in Figure 19a.

In the bridge dream (10a) the girl is not the only one on the bridge; the patient also walks over it. From the flood dream (115) and the whiskey dream (116b) we have learned that the patient, too, needs protection against the fear of drowning. Expanding our diagram to include the fantasy that the patient, too, is in danger of drowning, we arrive at a reconstruction something like Figure 19b.

If this reconstruction is correct, we might expect to find in the interim a dream in which the bridge defense can be abandoned and in which the patient dreams of himself in a boat on the river. The rowing dream (18a) corresponds roughly to this expectation.

This dream (18a) is motivated by a desire to flee from the analyst to a father, to be cared for by a father instead of by a mother. As the clinic dream (18b) shows, the sick old man who wants to be rowed upstream by a father-figure is the patient himself. We have not yet explained why the dream chooses to symbolize life-struggles in terms of rowing a boat upstream; but now that we have reconstructed the patient's unconscious drowning fantasies, the symbol of rowing on a river acquires a new meaning. The patient is struggling to overcome all that is symbolized in later dreams by the threatening river or flood. He is fleeing not only from the temptation to urinate on the mother but also from the fear of punishment by being urinated upon, drowned, by the father. The river is a symbol of both these dangers. The boat is a symbol of protection from the threatening flood. Similarly, rowing is a symbol of active protest against the fantasy of being drowned.

In real life the patient's father was a threatening, rather than a protecting, figure. In the fantasy of being rowed upstream the patient has substituted a good father to protect him from the punishing father, whom he fears. The best basis for such a hope of a protective father-figure is his experience with doctors and others who have treated him with special indulgence when he is ill. In the clinic dream (18b) he reverts to such a wish to be ill and treated in a clinic; but before giving up to this submissive fantasy, he entertains for a moment the compensatory impulse to imagine himself again in a protective rather than a dependent role, by inverting the fantasy and rowing the sick old man upstream.

We summarize this reconstruction diagrammatically in Figure 19c.

In later dreams, these defenses break down. This finds symbolic expression in the idea of water penetrating into the protecting inclosed space, in the flooding of the basement in the flood dream (115), in the tipping-over of the train into the river in the train wreck dream (154*a*), in the tipping-over of the boat in the capsized boat dream (187*b*).

We shall now attempt briefly to reconstruct the patterns of organization of these later dreams.

The flood dream (115) needs little further discussion. In the dream text the flood has already entered the basement room, but the dreamer's sense of the analyst's indulgence of his erotic wishes has made possible a series of attempts at active mastery of the fears of being drowned. These attempts take the form of (1) walking in the dirty water, (2) reminding himself that he is a father by referring to his own son, and (3) washing his face in the dirty water (see Fig. 19*d*).

In the train wreck dream (154*a*) the patient's defense is projection of his drowning fantasy, supplemented by a double attempt at active mastery. The patient himself is on a hillside far above the train and the river, and even the train is at first not in the river but presumably running along beside it. The train's later tipping over (into the river, we suspect) indicates that this latter attempt at active mastery has failed (see Fig. 19*e*).

Like the train in the train wreck dream (154*a*), the boat in the capsized boat dream (187*b*) is a symbol of an attempt at active mastery that fails. We reconstruct the process of organization of this dream (187*b*) somewhat as follows: The original fantasy was one of urinating upon the mother and drowning the child. Reacting against this wish, the patient next disavowed the urinary impulse, giving it only projected recognition as a "little lake." In this version the mother as a person has disappeared, being represented now only as an impersonal symbol, the boat, in which the sister rides protected on the top of the water. But under the sexual stimulation of the last hour (186) the patient's sadistic sexual wishes are intensified, so that they now override the defenses. The boat is tipped over, and the sister is again in danger of drowning (see Fig. 19*f*).

Fig. 19.—Historical background of the water symbolism in five dreams

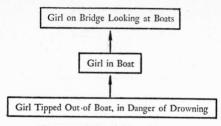

Fig. 19a.—The bridge dream

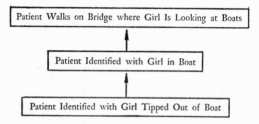

Fig. 19b.—Expanded diagram of bridge dream

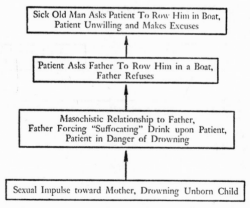

Fig. 19c.—The rowing dream

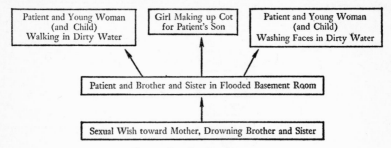

Fig. 19d.—The flood dream

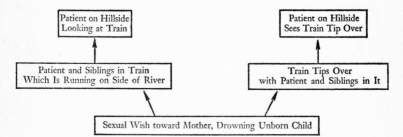

Fig. 19e.—The train wreck dream

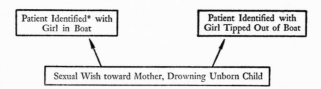

Fig. 19f.—The capsized boat dream

* See chap. xxxvii of this volume.

CHAPTER XL

Erotizing Effects of the Analyst's Encouragement

In the last two chapters we have traced two different trends of reaction to this patient's fantasies of being drowned: (1) fantasies that seek mastery of the fear of drowning by walking above or climbing on top of the threatening water and (2) fantasies in which the water itself has become less threatening, so that the patient is able of his own will to drink it or bring it near to his mouth.

We have not yet accounted adequately for the choice between these alternative reactions, but we have found that hopes of a mother's approval or indulgence tend to make the water a less dangerous fluid and thus favor the alternative of taking the fluid into or near his mouth. In this chapter we shall study more systematically the effects of such hopes of a mother's indulgence.

Erotized and Unerotized Water Dreams.—In some of this patient's water dreams (e.g., 18a, 116b, 154a, 187b) the need to master fears of drowning is dominant; in others (e.g., 10a, 19a, 115, 205) a conflict arising out of his erotic impulses is the presenting problem. Yet these two groups of dreams are closely interrelated; the same fantasies that are of central importance in the drowning dreams have also played significant roles in shaping the dreams that are struggling with an erotic problem. In other words, we are dealing with unerotized and erotized versions of the same basic patterns.

In all four of the erotized water dreams, hopes of the mother's approval (dream 10a) or indulgence (dreams 19a, 115, 205) have served as the immediate precipitating stimulus. The bridge dream (10a) was in response to the hope of pleasing the analyst by bringing her a dream; the fireplug dream (19a), to an interpretation that the patient felt to be a hint that he should play a more masculine role. His first spontaneous confession of sexual attraction to the analyst precipitated the flood dream (115); and in the dirty hole dream (205) a number of interpretations by the analyst of the patient's unconscious reactions toward her are being accepted by the patient as a sexual invitation.

Effects of Hopes of a Mother's Indulgence.—By comparing these erotized water dreams with the underlying unerotized patterns we can reconstruct the effects of the analyst's encouragement. In a number of respects these effects run parallel in the four dreams (10*a*, 19*a*, 115, 205).

We have already discussed two of these effects, which are closely associated with each other:

1. Rivalrous hostility replaced by sharing. Hope of winning a mother has made it possible to forestall or diminish activation of hostile impulses toward rivals for the mother's love by substituting fantasies of sharing the mother with brothers and sisters. The sharing fantasies in these dreams take two forms: (*a*) fantasies of sharing drinks and (*b*) symbolism suggestive of intrauterine sharing fantasies.

2. Drowning mitigated into drinking. The intrauterine sharing fantasies in these dreams have not been successful in forestalling activation of hostile impulses toward brothers and sisters; but hopes of the analyst's approval or indulgence have succeeded in mitigating fantasies of drowning and being drowned into fantasies of drinking dirty water and sometimes even into fantasies of sharing in the enjoyment of drinks.

The erotizing influence of the analyst's encouragement does not stop with the forestalling of rivalrous impulses by sharing fantasies or with mitigation of drowning into drinking fantasies.

3. Erotization of hostile impulses. In all four of these dreams, emerging hostile impulses toward brother and sister have been replaced by erotic interest in a sister-figure. In the bridge dream (10*a*) the patient pinches the girl playfully in the back; in the fireplug dream (19*a*) he embraces and kisses her. The flood dream (115) is organized about a memory of erotic advances to a young woman in the mother's home; and in the dirty hole dream (205) he embraces the woman in the hole, rubs his cheek against hers, and feels her breasts.

4. Hostile impulses replaced by protective attitudes and impregnation fantasies. In all four of these dreams the patient's

erotic advances stop short of a genital sexual relationship but are either preceded or followed by behavior and symbolism suggestive of paternal protective attitudes and of an underlying fantasy of giving the mother a child. In the bridge dream (10a) the patient returns a daughter to her mother. In the fireplug dream (19a) the girl's growing into a woman and the patient's helping her carry a five-gallon can suggest an adolescent fantasy of their growing up and sharing adult responsibility; and the number five is probably an allusion to the number of the mother's pregnancies after the patient was born. In the flood dream (115) he watches the young woman make up a cot for the girl's much younger brother, who also reminds him of his own son and thus of the fact that he is a father; and the symbolisms of both flood dream (115) and dirty hole dream (205) suggest a fantasy of giving the mother a child by urinating upon her.

Protective Attitudes in the Unerotized Dreams, Too.—We have until now confined this discussion to this patient's erotized water dreams. Yet even in the unerotized dreams we find less successful attempts to compensate for the drowning impulses by impulses to protect or rescue the brother- and sister-figures who are threatened by them.

Thus in the rowing dream (18a) the suggestion that the patient row the sick old man upstream should probably be regarded as a parallel to the protective or paternal role of escorting the girl home in the bridge dream (10a). In the train wreck dream (154a) the patient is impelled to rush to the scene of the accident. In the dancing girl dream (187a), which is so closely associated with the capsized boat dream (187b), the patient's reassuring the anxious girl with a kiss parallels his embracing the "sister" in the "hole" in the dirty hole dream (205); and even in the capsized boat dream (187b) he is sympathetically identified with the girl's anxious struggle to escape drowning.

Conflicting Effects of a Traumatic Memory and Present Encouragement.—During the course of this patient's treatment he has not once been in danger of drowning. Indeed, there is no report or evidence of his ever having been really in danger of drowning. Yet a fear of being drowned has played a significant part in shaping every one of his water dreams.

Our analysis shows that his fear of drowning is in reaction to a conflict between hostile impulses toward the mother's pregnancies and fear of offending the mother. Yet there is no report of any mother-figure having been pregnant during the course of his treatment. Evidently, disturbing events long since past are continuing to exert an influence of some importance in patterning these dreams.

A past event that continues to exert such a disturbing effect on present behavior we call a "traumatic memory." We explain its persisting disturbing effect as follows: Present behavior is patterned on past experience. In order to solve a present problem, one reactivates patterns that were successful in the past; but if the present problem is one that has never been really solved, then one reactivates and must struggle to overcome the disturbing effects of past failures.

When once a traumatic memory pattern has been reactivated, the integrative mechanism has the task of mastering it, of struggling against being overwhelmed by the excessive pressures that arise from it. When the reactivated pressures are excessive, the integrative mechanism is actually overwhelmed. When integrative capacity is just adequate, the integrative mechanism becomes completely preoccupied with the task of mastering the disturbing pressures. If the traumatic memory pattern has been less intensely reactivated, a residue of integrative capacity may still be available to continue efforts to find a solution for the present problem.

In this way we can now account for the differences between our patient's unerotized and his erotized water dreams. In the unerotized water dreams he is dominated by the need to master the fears of drowning arising out of the traumatic memory of his conflict about his mother's pregnancies. In the erotized dreams there is still integrative capacity available to deal with the present problem arising out of his sexual impulses toward the analyst, even though he is still handicapped by the task of having to mitigate and master the hostile impulses persisting from his childhood conflict.

CHAPTER XLI

A Frozen Version of the Water Dreams

Before discussing further the effects of erotization on the water dreams, we shall illustrate another kind of variation upon their underlying pattern.

Frozen Gutter Dream and Flood Dream.—In the first dream (67) after the long summer interruption of the first year of our patient's analysis we encounter a symbol whose functional significance is not immediately clear. This frozen gutter dream (67) was a reaction to the sexual temptation resulting from resuming the analysis. The patient, who has been suffering from asthma as well as indigestion, constipation, and chills since the first day after resuming treatment, has been conscious of sexual attraction to a married woman who has been his partner at pinochle; but the house in the dream text (67), that has been empty all summer and has just been redecorated, is a reference to the analyst's house—which indicates that the patient's attraction is not to his card partner alone but also to the analyst. In this dream he is turning away from heterosexual temptation to a man who is speaking in derogatory terms of the frozen gutter. As the analyst points out, the frozen gutter is a symbol of the inhibition or "freezing-up" of the patient's sexual wishes; and the man, by speaking in derogatory terms of this frozen gutter, is encouraging the dreamer to turn away his interest both from his sexual wishes and from the woman (house) who is the object of them.

But why has this dream chosen a frozen gutter as symbol of the dreamer's inhibited sexual wishes? Let us reason about this symbol in functional terms: We recognize freezing as a symbol of sexual inhibition. If the water in the gutter were not frozen, it would presumably be flowing off the roof. Perhaps the frozen gutter in this dream is another variant of the flowing-water symbolism.

To test this hypothesis, we inquire whether the pattern of

233

organization of this dream is recognizable as a variant upon the pattern that underlies the other water dreams. If flowing water is to be interpreted literally as a symbol of the patient's sexual wishes toward the analyst, then the water should flow into the house. Following this clue, we compare this dream (67) with the flood dream (115): In the flood dream water has entered the basement of a house; in this frozen gutter dream the water, if it were not frozen, would flow off the roof of the house. If the frozen gutter dream is homologous with the flood dream, we must postulate that the fantasy of water entering the basement has undergone three reversals in the earlier dream (67): (1) The water is flowing *off* the house *instead of into* it; (2) the water is flowing off the *roof instead of* into the *basement;* and (3) the water is *frozen instead of flowing.*

These reversals all make good sense in the psychological context of the frozen gutter dream (67), since each one is a repudiation of the underlying sexual fantasy. We are encouraged, therefore, to make a more detailed comparison of the patterns of the two dreams:

1. *Motivation of Reversal of Flow.*—From the symbolism of the flood dream (115) it is evident[1] that the patient is not reacting directly to his sexual wish toward the analyst. The dirty water in the basement has come in from outside and is wetting not only the girl but the patient as well. From this detail we have concluded[1] that in the process of organization of the flood dream the patient has turned away from his fantasy of urinating on the girl and has substituted a fantasy of both himself and the girl being urinated upon by a father-figure. In the dream text (115) his walking with the girl in the dirty water and their washing their faces in it are masculine protest reactions against this underlying fantasy of being urinated upon.

In the frozen gutter dream (67) the patient is quite frankly turning away from heterosexual temptation, to a man. Our present hypothesis is that in the frozen gutter dream (67), as in the flood dream (115), he first turned to a fantasy of being urinated upon by a father-figure; and that this fantasy (of himself and the woman being urinated upon) is the one that is

1. See chap. xiii of this volume.

being reversed and repudiated in the frozen gutter dream, too.

If this hypothesis is correct, then the frozen gutter dream has rejected this submissive fantasy, not by walking in the dirty water, but by reversing the direction of flow of the water: In the underlying cognitive structure he has substituted a fantasy of urinating for one of being urinated upon.

2. *Reversal of Flow and Displacement Upward in Pump Dream.*—If this reconstruction is correct, we should expect to find other dreams in which there has been a similar reversal of the direction of flow of water, so as to make it flow away from the patient instead of toward him. We might also expect to find details in other dreams whose significance is comparable to the substitution of roof for basement.

In the pump dream (41) there is water in a hole dug for the basement of a house, corresponding to the water in the basement in the flood dream (115), but the direction of flow is reversed, as in the frozen gutter dream (67); the water is being pumped out instead of flowing in. The substitution of roof for basement, which we postulate in the frozen gutter dream (67), has no parallel in the manifest content of the pump dream (41); but in the associations to this dream the patient tells us that the hole is his empty head and that the dirty water is the "dirt of my life," which the analyst is pumping out of him. Thus our comparison suggests that the substitution of roof for basement in the frozen gutter dream (67) is a "displacement upward" from pelvis to head; in the latent content of the pump dream (41) it is dirty thoughts that are symbolized by the water and that should be pumped out of the patient's empty head.

3. *Reversal of Flow, Displacement Upward, and Inhibition of Flow in Vomiting and Dirty Hole Dreams.*—For a mechanism homologous to the freezing of the water, we turn to the vomiting dream (190) and to the dirty hole dream (205). In the vomiting dream (190) we must suspect that the large amount of dirty water that the patient is vomiting up is water that he has swallowed. Thus this dream, too, repeats the mechanism of reversal of direction of flow of the water that we have postulated for the frozen gutter dream (67), but the vomiting dream is no longer interposing the house symbolism to mask the fantasy of

swallowing dirty water. Accentuating still further the parallelism between the two dreams (67 and 190), we find in the vomiting dream (190), too, a "displacement upward" from pelvis to head. Paralleling the dirty thoughts that are being pumped out of his head in the pump dream (41), the little stream of dirty water that is coming out of his mouth in the vomiting dream probably represents his somewhat halting stream of associations in the therapeutic sessions.

In the frozen gutter dream (67) the water is frozen; in the vomiting dream (190), too, the flow of water out of the patient is inhibited, though only partially—it is "only a little stream." This detail of a partially inhibited flow of water away from the patient is repeated in the dirty hole dream (205), in which the "water ran" only "slowly" out of the dreamer's hose and with "no pressure behind it."

In Figure 20, the relations between these dreams (67, 115, 41, 190, 205) are plotted in a four-dimensional "map," with dimensions representing mechanisms as follows: (a) substitution of house for the dreamer (plotted horizontally); (b) reversal of flow (plotted vertically); (c) displacement from pelvis to head (plotted diagonally; up and to right); (d) inhibition of flow (plotted diagonally, up and to left). In order not to complicate the diagram unduly, reference has been omitted to the fact that the house represents not only the patient himself but also the woman (analyst) who is object of the patient's sexual wishes.

In Table 1 the same relations between these dreams have been summarized in a series of equations.

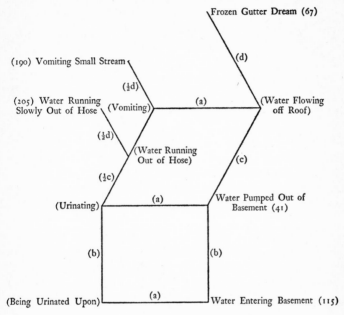

Fig. 20.—Relations between frozen gutter dream and a number of water dreams.

TABLE 1

RELATIONS BETWEEN FROZEN GUTTER DREAM
AND A NUMBER OF WATER DREAMS

Being Urinated Upon $+ a \longrightarrow$ Water Entering Basement (115)

Being Urinated Upon $+ a + b \longrightarrow$ Water Pumped Out of Basement (41)

Being Urinated Upon $+ a + b + c \longrightarrow$ Water Flowing Off Roof

Being Urinated Upon $+ a + b + c + d \longrightarrow$ Frozen Gutter (67)

Being Urinated Upon $+ b \longrightarrow$ Urinating

Being Urinated Upon $+ b + \frac{2}{3}c \longrightarrow$ Filling Hole with Water from Hose

Being Urinated Upon $+ b + \frac{2}{3}c + \frac{2}{3}d \longrightarrow$ Water Running Slowly from Hose, Half-filling Hole (205)

Being Urinated Upon $+ b + c \longrightarrow$ Vomiting

Being Urinated Upon $+ b + c + \frac{2}{3}d \longrightarrow$ Vomiting Small Stream (190)

CHAPTER XLII

Interaction between Two Reactivated Memories

In our study of these water dreams so far, we have usually been one-sidedly preoccupied with this patient's hostile reactions to his mother's pregnancies. To correct this one-sided emphasis, we shall next study how these water dreams deal with his erotic conflict and then return to the question of how his erotic conflict and his conflict about his mother's pregnancies are related.

The Erotic Conflict in the Water Dreams.–In a large proportion of these water dreams there are two women; often the two women are identified as a mother and her daughter. For example, in the bridge dream (10a) the patient is returning a girl to her mother; in the fireplug dream (19a) the young woman breaks away from his embrace to answer her mother's call. Although there is only one woman in the text of the flood dream (115), the dream thoughts are organized about a memory of his mother's rebuke for sexual advances to a younger woman. In the beer dream (162a) he is buying treats for two women. In the capsized boat dream (187b) one woman is in danger of drowning; but the associations of this hour tell of a girl and her mother. In the vomiting dream (190) both the analyst and her maid are there; and in the dirty hole dream (205) the woman who gets into the hole is again one of two.

However, the conflict that motivates these dreams involves only one woman. Sexual impulses toward the analyst are in conflict with a need to be loved by her as a mother. In the dream texts two women have been substituted for the one; the dream work has substituted a younger woman as object of the patient's sexual wishes. It is not difficult to reconstruct the motive for this substitution. We assume that in the patient's childhood his mother was less likely to be offended by sexual wishes toward a sister-figure than by sexual impulses toward herself.

We have already discussed reasons[1] for believing that this pa-

1. See chap. xiii of this volume.

tient's sexual wishes toward mother and sister are inhibited not so much by fear of the father as by fear of offending the mother. There is remarkably little evidence in these water dreams of competition with the father for the mother. Evidently, fear of offending the mother inhibits his sexual impulses too soon to permit competition with the father to develop. The father finds his way into these dreams not as a rival but as a more punitive mother-substitute. Turning away from his conflict with the mother, the patient seeks in fantasies of sexual submission to the father a way of reconciling his need for sexual gratification with his dependent need for parental love.

Substituting sister for mother does not long protect the patient from fear of rebuff from the mother. To escape from this conflict, he must next turn from his dependence as well as from his sexual interest in the mother to a feminine submissive fantasy toward the father. Such a need to turn away from mother and sister to father appears after each of the erotized water dreams: The bridge dream (10a) is followed by the patient's turning to a male physician in the first clinic dream (10c) and by the fantasy of his being beaten by the father that underlies the anvil dream (12). After the fireplug dream (19a) he is rebuked by men in the brake dream (19b) and in the pencil-stealing dream (25). In the whiskey dream (116b), as sequel to the flood dream (115), he is having a suffocating drink forced upon him by a number of men. And the dirty hole dream (205) ends with the woman's husband approaching while the patient is embracing her.

Complementary Relationship between Two Conflicts.—In this, our patient's own particular variant of the Oedipus conflict, we evidently see the influence of his earlier fear of offending the mother by his hostility toward her pregnancies. Since his sexual fantasies are still burdened with the task of erotizing his hostility toward brother and sister, they carry with them a much greater fear of rebuff from the mother than might otherwise be the case. The influence of the earlier conflict is also betrayed by the symbolism suggestive of intrauterine sharing fantasies. Such symbolism is a setting peculiarly inappropriate for masculine competition for the mother.

The erotic conflict in these dreams is not only an erotized derivative of the earlier conflict arising out of hostility toward brother and sister. In our earlier discussions we oversimplified the relationship between these two conflicts. We have been interpreting this patient's erotic impulses as attempts to give mitigated outlet to his hostility. Yet both now and in the past his erotic impulses also involved him in conflict on their own account; and our analysis of the water symbolism shows that his rivalry with brother and sister had as its background an attachment to the mother that was sexual as well as dependent. We picture him as reacting to memories of his mother's pregnancies, first, with sexual excitement and impregnation fantasies and only later with resentment of the expected child. In other words, we must now recognize that his hostile impulses did not antedate his erotic interest in the mother but that hostile and sexual impulses run along side by side in the motivation of his behavior, although sometimes one and sometimes the other predominates.

However, although we were in error to speak of this patient's erotic impulses as derivatives of his hostile impulses, we were correct in postulating that they serve as mitigated substitutes for these hostile impulses.[2] Although, in the erotized dreams, both sexual and hostile wishes threaten to estrange him from the mother, his attempts to solve the two conflicts complement each other.

In the first phase of his conflict, by transferring his erotic interest from mother to sister, he not only diminishes the intensity of his erotic conflict, but *utilizes the erotic interest* thus *transferred to the sister to neutralize* some of the pressure of *his hostility toward her* and thus to diminish the intensity of his hostile impulses, too. And similarly when later, turning away from mother and sister, he transfers his erotic interest to the father, the *erotic interest* thus *transferred to the father* can again be *used to mitigate his fantasy of the three siblings being drowned* into a fantasy of their all drinking dirty water or washing their faces in it.

Another Incomplete Replacement of One Alternative by

2. For further theoretical discussion of the "erotization" of hostile impulses we refer the reader back to our thesis of the neutralization of the pressure of needs by pleasure in functional activity for its own sake (see Vol. I, chaps. xx and xxvii, and also Vol. IV).

Another.—Differences in the extent of erotization of hostile impulses in these water dreams can now be understood in terms of our concept of more or less complete replacement of one alternative reaction by another (see Fig. 21). In dreams like the capsized boat dream (187b) hostile impulses have been only slightly mitigated by condensation with erotic ones. On the other hand, if our patient's sexual interest in the analyst had completely replaced his hostile reactions to his memories of his mother's pregnancies, we should expect that traces of these hostile impulses would have disappeared from his erotized water dreams and that these dreams would have been preoccupied solely with his conflict between sexual impulses and fear of loss of a mother's love. Actually, in all these dreams we find the effects of these two conflicts complexly intertwined.

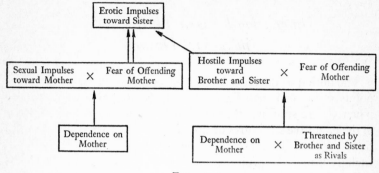

FIG. 21a

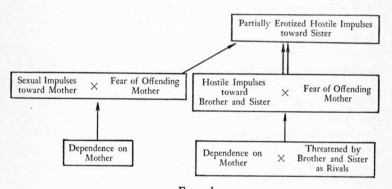

FIG. 21b

FIG. 21.—Schematic diagrams of interaction between hostile and erotic impulses in water dreams.

CHAPTER XLIII

Interaction between Three Conflicts in Several Dreams

The notion of different kinds of distribution of traffic at choice points on a road map has proved to be a very useful analogy when we are studying the relations between elementary fantasies in the cognitive structures of dreams; but when we study the relations between more complex constellations of fantasies, another analogy is more helpful:

Freud often compared his study of neurotic symptoms and dreams to a historian's study of manuscripts. Often textual analysis of a historical document finds fragments of a tale of ancient days more or less successfully remodeled to fit the much altered realities of a later time. While utilizing characters and incidents from the ancient legend, the more recent story has rearranged the roles of the characters and reorganized the plot.

Something closely analogous to this has occurred in the process of organization of the erotized water dreams. In these dreams we find dynamic patterns from at least three phases in this patient's development: reactions (1) to his mother's pregnancies, (2) to his Oedipus conflict, and (3) to his present situation in the therapy.

As a concrete illustration of how these three "manuscripts" are interrelated, we shall now study the dirty hole dream (205).

The Therapeutic Situation and the Oedipus Conflict.—As related to the therapeutic situation, the underlying argument of this dream is that the analyst, by insisting that she is the object of his sexual wishes, is trying to get him to make sexual advances to her and that he, somewhat reluctantly, is yielding to her urging. The dream text starts with a plea of innocence: He is merely filling a hole with water from a hose. In this harmless symbolism the dream is representing his somewhat halting stream of talk in the therapeutic sessions as an entirely impersonal act which has nothing to do with the analyst. Yet in the next statement in the dream text, "Two women are mixed up in it." In other words, he must admit that his wishes are not so impersonal after all. Next comes his excuse, putting the blame on the analyst: "One woman got into the hole after it was half-filled with water and dirt." Thus justified for the moment, he embraces her, though he still needs to protest that he does so reluctantly: He "felt little joy in holding the woman." Finally, his guilt emerges more plainly in his "fear and embarrassment" about her husband, who is approaching.

Thus in this dream the patient pictures himself yielding reluctantly to a woman's seductive pressure and then being compelled, with "fear and embarrassment," to give her up to her husband, a father-figure. This dream's solution for the dreamer's Oedipus conflict is to let sexual gratification be urged upon him half against his will by a sister-figure and then to yield to her husband as a father-figure.

A Reluctant Masculine Protest.—It is only a short step from yielding to a mother's or sister's seductive urging to the simpler fantasy of having a father (or brother) force "raw food" upon him (dream 207). Yielding to mother's or sister's urging still requires some initiative on his own part; the cognitive pattern is simplified when he resigns himself to a submissive role and lets sexual gratification be forced upon him by a father.

It is significant that the patient's "fear and embarrassment" in the dirty hole dream (205) and the asthmatic wheezing with which he awakens are so slight. This confirms the impression that we get from the rest of the dream text that he had committed himself only reluctantly to his heterosexual impulses. Since the water only ran slowly without pressure behind it and since he "felt little joy in holding the woman," it is probable that the husband's appearing did not surprise him too much, that he had unconsciously expected and half-hoped to be interrupted.[1] We get the impression that this dream (205), from beginning to end, is only a half-hearted masculine protest against an underlying fantasy of having dirty water forced upon him by a father-figure.

Relations between the Oedipus Conflict and Memories of the Mother's Pregnancies.—This dream (205) is so well erotized that

1. Similarly, in the fireplug dream (19a) he had been reassured all along by the knowledge, repressed only for the moment, that the girl was still subject to her mother's call (see Vol. I, chap. xxxvii).

we may not at first recognize the influence of the earlier conflict centering about resentment of the mother's pregnancies. However, traces of this earlier conflict are still discernible. The intrauterine sharing fantasy implied by his getting into the hole with his "sister" is evidently a detail taken out of the earlier "manuscript"; and even more significant is the fact that he needs so much urging from the woman. This need for urging is a sign of a deep underlying fear of offending her, persisting from the earlier conflict.

In this dream (205), as in these water dreams in general, the patient's attempts to find solutions for his two conflicts supplement each other. From the symbolism it is evident that the woman who gets into the hole is a sister-figure; when the patient gets into the hole and embraces her, he is transferring his erotic interest from the mother to a sister-figure. As in the other water dreams, the erotic interest thus transferred from mother to sister serves also to neutralize some of the hostility toward the sister that stems from his sibling rivalry conflict (see Fig. 21).

The half-heartedness of this dream's (205) erotic response, symbolized by *the slow flow of the water from the patient's hose*, has significance for both the underlying conflicts. It *is a sign that the dreamer has succeeded only imperfectly in erotizing the underlying hostility* toward a sister-figure: this underlying hostility is still finding expression in his reluctance to embrace her. *And the grudging character of his erotic response* to mother and sister *also serves to protect him from becoming too much involved in his Oedipus conflict.*

The impregnation fantasy depicted in the dream symbolism is a boast of sexual prowess; he would like to imagine that his "water" gave the mother her child; his sexually tinged pride in this boast neutralizes some of his hostility toward the child and makes it possible for him to substitute such an impregnation fantasy for his desire to harm the child. Yet the fact that the water runs only slowly shows that he is half-hearted about giving the mother a child who will be another rival; and his reluctance serves also to protect him from committing himself too much to sexual wishes that the mother disapproves.

In the chronological succession of episodes in the dream text

(205) we can now recognize, behind the erotic version of this dream, a series of attempts to utilize the patient's erotic interest in mother and sister to mitigate a progressively emerging underlying hostility toward the mother's pregnancy:[2]

The first attempt is the reluctant impregnation fantasy just discussed; but this attempt must have failed, since it is followed by another device for mitigating hostility.

In the next dream episode he is trying to forestall emergence of his rivalrous hostility by sharing the "hole" with his "sister."

Then comes another half-hearted attempt to erotize his hostility by embracing her.

And, finally, his hostility, again emerging, is turned back against the dreamer himself, as evidenced by his fear of the approaching husband at the end of the dream.

Some Homologies with Other Water Dreams.—The pattern of this dream (205) as a whole has significant homologies with the patterns of other water dreams. To illustrate this fact, we shall compare it with the vomiting dream (190) and shall then compare the two sequences: (1) dirty hole dream (205), raw food dream (207); and (2) flood dream (115), whiskey dream (116*b*).

In the vomiting dream (190) the underlying fantasy of being drowned is easier to recognize than in the dirty hole dream (205). Vomiting up five gallons of dirty water implies a preceding fantasy of having swallowed it. The little stream of water in the vomiting dream (190) is also similar to the water running slowly

2. In other words, we suspect that in the dirty hole dream (205), as in the other water dreams of this patient, a fantasy of drowning the sister underlies the more obvious sexual fantasy of the dream text. If so, the impregnation fantasy implied by the dream symbolism makes good sense as part of the self-justifying argument of this dream (205). "It is not my fault if my sister gets drowned," the dream is protesting, "I was already filling the hole with water before she got into it." In other words, the patient can argue with some reason that he had a prior claim on the mother before his sister came, that he was already sexually interested in the mother before she became pregnant.

Thus this dream's use of pregnancy symbolism for its self-justifying argument leads us to the same conclusion that we arrived at in our discussion of the water dreams in general: This patient's rivalry with brother and sister and hostility to his mother's pregnancies had as its background a sexual as well as a dependent interest in his mother. His sexual and his sibling rivalry conflicts, continuing side by side, interact; and the reactions to the two conflicts complement each other.

and without pressure from the patient's hose in the dirty hole dream (205). Thus in the vomiting dream (190) it is more directly evident than in the dirty hole dream (205) that the little stream of water is a half-hearted masculine protest against a feminine submissive fantasy of swallowing dirty water.

If the five-gallon can, as we suspect, is an allusion to the mother's pregnancies with the patient's five younger siblings, then filling this can with dirty water (in the vomiting dream, 190) probably symbolizes an impregnation fantasy homologous with the one suggested by the symbolism of the dirty hole dream (205).

Analysis of the symbolism of the flood dream (115) has suggested that in this dream, too, the dream text gives expression to a masculine protest against an underlying fantasy of having dirty water forced into the dreamer's mouth by a father-figure. By allowing for the fact that masculine protest takes different forms in the two dreams (115 and 205), we can now recognize that walking in the dirty water in the flood dream (115) is homologous with half-filling the hole with water in the dirty hole dream (205).

In the sequence of flood dream (115) and whiskey dream (116b) we found a progressive emergence of the feminine submissive fantasy, just as we do in the sequence of dirty hole dream (205) and raw food dream (207). In the flood dream (115) walking in the dirty water is followed by the dreamer's washing his face in the dirty water and then, in the whiskey dream (116b), by his having a suffocating drink forced upon him. Similarly, in the dirty hole dream (205), half-filling the hole with water from his hose is followed by getting into the hole with the water in it, then by the appearance of the woman's husband, and, finally, in the next dream (207), by having "raw food" urged upon him.

CHAPTER XLIV

A Check on Our Method of Reconstruction

In our interpretations of the water, room, and boat symbolism we have assumed that a series of similar dreams, dreamed at different times during a period of over two years, may all be interpreted as parts of a single emotional context. We made this assumption as a working hypothesis but promised ourselves to reexamine it after we had determined where our comparisons would lead us. Starting with this assumption, we have reconstructed and compared the processes of organization of nine dreams in which water symbolism plays a prominent part. Now, in addition to the recurring details in manifest content that first suggested that these dreams are all parts of one context, we have found extended parallels in structure, suggesting that they are all variants of a single cognitive structure, based probably on a common set of reactions to the same early memories. The validity of our working assumption seems to be confirmed.

Yet there is a possible source of error. Are we sure that we are not just finding again the parallelisms that we assumed in the first place? Have we found parallels in organizational pattern other than those that we assumed when we treated these dreams as belonging to a single context?

In this chapter, to reassure ourselves on this point, we shall select the bridge dream (10*a*) and the flood dream (115) as a sample and review critically the reasoning that leads us to the conclusion that they are variants of a single organizational pattern, that they really are parts of a single context.

Do Bridge Dream and Flood Dream Belong to One Context?— Both these dreams are struggling with the same dynamic problem. In each of them the patient is trying to reconcile his sexual impulses toward the analyst with his need for a mother's love. In each he tries to diminish this conflict by substituting a younger woman as the object of his sexual interest. Yet the two dreams differ: In the bridge dream (10*a*), the erotic impulse is expressed

249

by pinching the girl in the back; in the flood dream (115), it is an impulse to wet the bed, accompanied probably by a fantasy of urinating on the girl.

Another parallel is significant. In the bridge dream (10*a*), the patient is returning a child to her mother; in the flood dream (115) he is watching the young woman take care of his child. Thus both dreams deal with a mother-child relationship, and both put the patient in a protective or paternal role toward the child. Yet once more the two dreams fail to run parallel: In the bridge dream (10*a*) the girl is the child whom the patient is returning to her mother, whereas in the flood dream (115) the young woman is playing a mother-role in caring for the child.

Thus, although the similarities between the two dreams (10*a* and 115) are suggestive, there are important differences. There is still room for some doubt whether these dreams really do belong to the same context, whether we are warranted in using our interpretation of the symbolism of the flood dream (115) to supplement our interpretation of obscure points in the bridge dream (10*a*).

However, we make this assumption as a working hypothesis, which we hope to check later: We assume that the river in the bridge dream (10*a*), like the flood in the flood dream (115), is a projected symbol of the patient's wish to urinate upon the young woman.

This assumption fits the bridge as well as the river into the interpretation suggested by the context of the bridge dream (10*a*). The river has become a symbol of the sexual wishes that threaten to estrange the dreamer from a mother-figure; and the bridge, by lifting him up above the river, symbolizes his mastery of the disturbing wishes. This implied capacity for mastery of his sexual and hostile wishes fits well with the fact that later in the dream text (10*a*) he is able to renounce these wishes and escort the girl home to her mother.

Still, the discrepancy between the mother-child relationships in the two dreams (10*a* and 115) remains unaccounted for: In the bridge dream (10*a*) the girl is the child whom the patient is returning to her mother; in the flood dream (115) the young woman is playing the role of mother in caring for his child.

Comparison of Their Patterns of Organization.—This discrepancy can be accounted for if the two forms of this fantasy are an earlier and a later version, respectively, of the text of one of the dreams.

Actually, our reconstruction of the process of organization of the flood dream (115) suggests just this conclusion. In the flood dream (115), as in the bridge dream (10a), a younger woman has been substituted for the mother as object of the patient's sexual wishes. The intrauterine sharing fantasy suggested by the symbolism of the flood dream (115) implies an early version of this dream, in which the younger woman was a sister-figure just as she is in the text of the bridge dream (10a). In the text of the flood dream (115) this sister-figure is playing mother to a child who is identified first with the girl's brother and then with the patient's son. This suggests a later version of the dream text (115) in which the patient and the young woman are playing father and mother to a child who was originally a brother-figure. *Thus in this flood dream (115) we find evidence first of an early version in which the young woman and the child are brother and sister, as in the bridge dream (10a), and then of a later version in which the patient and his "sister" are playing father and mother to the "brother."*

According to our interpretations, both these dreams (10a and 115) have substituted a sister-figure for the mother as object of the dreamer's sexual wishes. We now suspect that the fantasy of playing father and mother with a sister-figure has resulted from a similar substitution from an earlier fantasy of giving the mother a child. Literal interpretation of the dream symbolism has already suggested that this fantasy was an early version of the flood dream: The flood has entered the basement, and the patient's child is there. Since the basement is a symbol of the mother and the flood represents the patient's own urine, literal interpretation of this symbolism implies a fantasy of giving the mother a child by urinating upon her.

In these interpretations we are recapitulating reconstructions of the flood dream (115) that were originally made without reference to the bridge dream (10a). And now, utilizing these reconstructions, we can account adequately for the difference between the mother-child relationships in the manifest contents of the two dreams. In an early version of both dreams, we postulate, a sexual impulse toward the mother culminated in a fantasy of giving her a child by urinating upon her; and in a later version of both dreams the sister replaced the mother as object of his sexual impulse. However, at this point the organizational patterns of the two dreams begin to diverge. In the bridge dream, on account of his greater fear of the mother, he quickly renounces his sexual impulses toward the young woman; then, by relinquishing her as a child to her mother, he lives out in an acceptable symbolic way his earlier fantasy of impregnating the mother (giving her a child). On the other hand, in the flood dream (115) he has not only made the young woman the object of his sexual wishes but has followed out this fantasy by transferring to her the role of mother of his child.

This is what occurs in the dream text. However, in the symbolism of the flood dream (115), as in the text of the bridge dream (10a), he continues to share the mother (basement room in 115; milk and house in 10a) with both the young woman (sister) and her brother.

We have represented these relations diagrammatically in Figure 22.

Thus, by independent reconstruction of the flood dream (115), we have confirmed our working hypothesis that bridge dream (10a) and flood dream (115) are variations upon the same underlying pattern of organization.

Comparison with Two More Water Dreams.—By bringing two more dreams into the comparison, we find further confirmation for our working hypothesis that all four of the erotized water dreams are variations upon the pattern of organization that we have just reconstructed.

We have already[1] pointed out how the dirty hole dream (205) repeats in more transparent symbolism the chief steps in our reconstructed pattern of organization of the flood dream (115): first, a fantasy of impregnating the mother, then an intrauterine sharing fantasy and transfer of erotic interest from mother to

1. See chap. xv of this volume.

sister. In this dream (205), apparently, the role of mother to the patient's child has not been transferred to the sister.[2]

In the fireplug dream (19a) the transition from a brother-sister relationship to playing father and mother, that we have postulated, is dramatically portrayed in the manifest content: In the dream text (19a) the little girl grows into a mature woman before our eyes.

And the dream symbolism gives further evidence of the importance of this transition for the shaping of this dream (19a): The can which the patient and the little girl share between them was originally a milk can, symbolic of their common dependence on the mother; but in the dream text it has become a five-gallon water can, a symbolic allusion to the fact that the mother was five times pregnant after the patient was born. The fact that the patient and the girl are carrying this can between them suggests again that a boy and girl who originally shared the mother's love as brother and sister are now playing father and mother by symbolically assuming responsibility for children.[3]

2. Unless possibly such a fantasy is hidden behind the appearance of the woman's husband at the end of the dream. In an earlier version of the text the husband may have been a brother-figure who gets into the hole and plays a role similar to that of the child in the flood dream (115).

3. In chap. viii (p. 58) we compared the fireplug dream (19a) with the bridge dream (10a) in two different ways:

a) In the fireplug dream (19a) the patient wins the girl's thanks and a kiss by helping her carry the water can, just as in the bridge dream (10a) he wins the mother's thanks and a glass of milk by returning the girl to her mother.

b) In the fireplug dream (19a) he lets his embrace of the girl be interrupted by her responding to her mother's call, just as in the bridge dream (10a), after the pinching episode, he returns the girl to her mother.

Thus the kiss in the fireplug dream (10a) corresponds in one comparison to the pinching episode of the bridge dream (10a) and in the other comparison to the glass of milk in the bridge dream (10a) (see Fig. 23).

This double homology implies that pinching the girl and receiving the glass of milk in the bridge dream (10a) are themselves variations on the same underlying pattern.

We now know what this underlying pattern is: a fantasy of erotic approach to the mother, culminating in giving her a child. In the pinching incident he has transferred his erotic interest to a sister-figure, but his erotic advance is interrupted by fear of offending the mother; in the next dream episode the underlying fantasy of giving the mother a child is acted out in harmless symbolism by returning the girl to her mother.

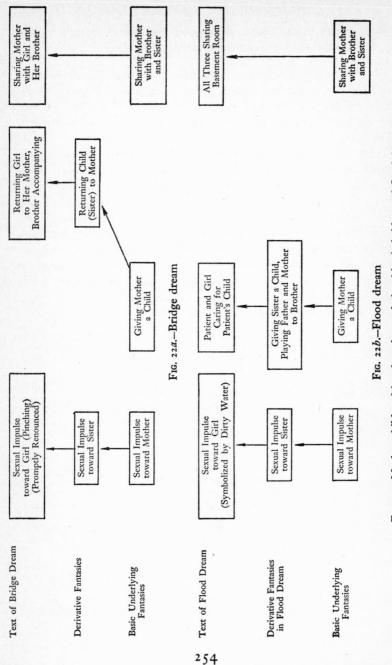

FIG. 22*a*.—Bridge dream

FIG. 22*b*.—Flood dream

FIG. 22.—Mother-child and brother-sister relationships in bridge and flood dreams

254

FIG. 23.—Bridge dream and fireplug dream superimposed in two different ways

10*a* Pinches Girl | Returns Girl to Her Mother | Receives Thanks and Glass of Milk from Mother

19*a* | Helps Girl Carry Water Can | Receives Thanks and Kiss from Girl | Embrace Interrupted by Girl Answering Mother's Call | Receives Thanks and Glass of Milk from Mother

10a | | Pinches Girl | Returns Girl to Her Mother | Receives Thanks and Glass of Milk from Mother

255

SECTION VIII

Attempts at Internal Mastery

CHAPTER XLV

Internal Mastery of Pressure

The fantasies underlying the water dreams deal chiefly with problems of adapting to other people in the external world: Either (1) hostile and sexual aggressive impulses directed toward other people involve real external consequences, such as the danger of losing a mother's love; or (2) the turning-back of the patient's aggression against himself results in fantasies of sexual or hostile aggression from other people.

Problems of another kind arise when the integrative mechanism is able to elaborate disturbing impulses internally by mechanisms of physiological absorption that involve no consequences in the external world. In this way a problem of external adaption is transformed into one of internal mastery of disturbing pressures; and as long as a person is successful in such attempts at internal mastery, he acquires a certain self-sufficiency in relation to the external world.

The psychoanalytic literature[1] has long recognized a relationship between these attempts at internal mastery of pressure and anal erotism. Tonic contraction of the anal sphincters (and perhaps of the whole lower bowel as well) is a mechanism of physiological absorption of pressure that involves relatively few consequences in the external world. For this reason the anal erotic gratification associated with retention of the stools often serves the purpose of making a person independent of others for the satisfaction of his needs and thus of relieving him of the necessity of adapting to other people. The psychoanalytic literature on the "anal character" has also emphasized the fact that money and other possessions can be utilized to make a person independent of other people.

Another way to achieve independence is to develop a conscience of one's own. Freud (1923) has shown how the "Superego," or conscience, arises by internalization of a person's fear

1. See especially S. Freud, 1908*b*; E. Jones, 1919; and K. Abraham, 1923.

of offending one of the parents. By identifying with the parent and incorporating the parent's standards as his own, a person begins to build his own independent conscience, which judges and may even inflict punishment upon him, regardless of whether the parents know or approve. In this way one acquires moral independence, attitudes of responsibility guided by standards that have become one's own and are independent of the approval or disapproval of others.

In the next few chapters we shall study our patient's attempts to convert his external problems into internal ones and observe how his external problems re-emerge when his attempts at internal mastery fail.

CHAPTER XLVI

A Vain Search for Self-Sufficiency

Need for Justification Contrasted with Fear of Loss of Love.—
The borrowed book dream (27) is the first in our patient's
material that was motivated by a need for self-justification. "You
are only returning a borrowed book; therefore I owe you nothing," so begins the argument of this dream (27). "Besides," the
argument continues, "the stocks that you give me are mistreated
and worthless anyhow."

The first statement of this argument finds its justification in
the fact that the analyst must base her interpretations on the
patient's own associations. He gives the analyst his associations—
so runs the dream argument—and the analyst gives them back to
him as interpretations.

The second part of the argument is based on a projection
mechanism. The patient had hoped that the analyst would make
a man of him, but he is being disillusioned. She has only brought
closer to consciousness his hostile wishes toward children. Projecting responsibility for these hostile wishes onto the analyst,
who is encouraging the patient to become aware of them, the
borrowed book dream (27) represents these wishes as "mistreated" stocks that the analyst is giving him and thus makes
use of his disillusionment to rid himself of his sense of guilt and
obligation by depreciating the value of the analyst's help.

Let us compare this borrowed book dream (27) with two
earlier dreams (10a and 12). The bridge dream (10a) was motivated by the hope of winning the mother's love by returning
her daughter safely to her; and lurking behind this hope we
could sense a fear of losing the mother's love on account of
hostile (as well as erotic) impulses toward sister and brother.
Similarly, the anvil dream (12) was motivated by a need for
punishment, lest his hostile (as well as erotic) impulses might
lose him the love of the mother. Thus both of these earlier
dreams (10a and 12) were concerned with the mother's reac-

tions as a person, with the fear of offending her and the hope of pleasing her. In contrast to this direct concern with the mother as a person, the borrowed book dream (27) is concerned with the derivative problem of justifying the dreamer in terms of more generalized social standards. He is distressed because he feels he does not deserve the help that the analyst is actually offering him. This dream (27) is an argument whose aim is to satisfy his conscience in terms of an impersonal standard. Instead of trying to please the mother, this dream (27) is trying to satisfy an impersonal ethical standard that is binding for both him and the mother.

An Intermediate Stage in Development of the Conscience.—The conscience arises by identification with one or both parents. The child takes over and imposes on himself the ideals and prohibitions that the parents once imposed on him. Freud (1923) explains this identification with a parent's standards by postulating that the child transfers to his own conscience part of the dependence and affection that he feels toward the parent. The child's own conscience is substituted for the parent as a love object. We see this mechanism particularly clearly during a transitional phase in childhood[1] before development of the conscience is completed and in neurotic patients in whom the development of the conscience was never completed.[2] Children often use the parents' own words to pass judgment on brothers and sisters or even on the parents themselves. This is a first step in the child's struggle to achieve moral independence of the parents. By transferring to generalized ethical principles part of the authority that the parent has in his eyes, the child struggles to make himself independent of the parent's authority.

The borrowed book dream (27) illustrates this intermediate stage in the development of the conscience. It is characteristic of this patient that he is very insecure in his attempts at self-justification. His capacity for moral self-sufficiency is meager. For this reason his self-justifying thoughts must be put back into the mouth of a mother-figure. Instead of himself defending his rationalizations, he must appeal again to the analyst's in-

1. See T. Reik, 1924.
2. See S. Freud, 1918.

dulgence. In the last hour she remarked that he felt inferior in relation to women. The dream work chooses to interpret this statement as an indulgent admission that he owes her nothing: "Yes, what I am giving you is really worthless; you do not need to feel guilty about accepting it from me."

Self-sufficiency by Means of Possessions.—Comparison with the bridge dream (10a) throws into relief another way in which the borrowed book dream (27) is struggling to achieve self-sufficiency. In the bridge dream the patient received from the mother thanks and a glass of milk, gratifications of real needs and real evidence of her favor. In the borrowed book dream he receives a book, a symbol of the instruction he desires to receive from the analyst. He has now become aware of the inadequacy of his efforts to please a mother, and he wishes that the analyst would teach him how; but the text of the dream has gone one step further. In the dream text he is receiving not instruction but a material object that symbolizes instruction. This substitution of a material object, of a book, for personal instruction is another device to free him from his dependence on mother and analyst. If one has a book, he will perhaps not need personal instruction. Possession of a book could make him self-sufficient in relation to his desire for instruction.

Another detail of the dream (27) makes clear the central significance of this substitution of a material possession for the instruction that he needs. It is not only a book that he is receiving. The book contains two stocks. Stocks, as a kind of money, are a nonspecific symbol of possession. A book has a specific use, one can learn something from it; but money cannot be used except as a medium of exchange, as something that one can hold onto, as a potential power that might later be exchanged for many unspecified things that might be desired in the future. The patient has wished to be taught how to play a man's role; but the power of money can compensate for many deficiencies. If a man has money, he can please a woman with gifts. If he has money, he will not need to be taught or even to learn from a book. The possession of money will make him self-sufficient. This idea of pleasing the mother or discharging an obligation by giving a gift evidently played an important role in the dream work. That the analyst is not giving him anything but only returning something that she has borrowed is one of the dream's most important self-justifying thoughts.

Failure To Achieve Self-sufficiency.—We have already called attention to this patient's compulsion to throw away his money. On account of this need to lose money, he is as incapable of financial self-sufficiency as he is of moral self-sufficiency. In this field also he is thrown back on his dependence on a mother. If he is to have money to compensate for his inadequacies, he must receive it as a gift.

Thus both this patient's devices for achieving self-sufficiency meet with prompt failure. His capacity for moral self-sufficiency is so inadequate that he must immediately appeal to the hope for the analyst's indulgent reassurance that he really owes her nothing; and the longing for the self-sufficiency that money brings leads him back immediately to the wish for a gift.

Substitution of a More Impersonal Conflict.—Yet it would be a mistake to conclude that nothing has been changed by this brief and unsuccessful attempt to withdraw into a self-sufficient attitude toward his problem. The patient is not merely returning to the same conflict between hostile impulses and the need for a mother's love with which he started in the bridge dream (10a). On the contrary, in the course of his abortive attempt to achieve self-sufficiency the character of his conflict has undergone a significant reorganization.

Involved in conflict between his wish to "mistreat" the mother's (analyst's, wife's) children and the need to please her, he has first turned to the analyst for instruction. He has wished to be taught what to do about this conflict; but the analyst has only made him more acutely aware of his hostile wishes. Instead of helping him find a solution, her attempts to help have only increased the guilt he feels at receiving help from one whom he wishes to hurt. Against this acute conflict, this dream (27) has found a most welcome defense. This consists in substituting a task of meeting social obligations of an impersonal character for the problem of trying to solve a conflict between the need to please and the desire to hurt persons. Instead of hostile impulses toward a child, there appear in this dream (27) crumpled-up stocks. Instead of the human problem of reconciling his hostility toward the analyst's child with his need to be helped by the child's mother, there is substituted an impersonal problem in accounting, that of discharging an obligation by returning a borrowed possession.

CHAPTER XLVII

Persistent Traumatic Effect of a Childhood Conflict

Why are this patient's efforts to make himself self-sufficient so unsuccessful? To find an answer to this question, we return to our comparison of the borrowed book dream (27) and the bridge dream (10*a*).

Equivalence of Pattern in Bridge Dream and Borrowed Book Dream.—When we allow for this patient's two ways of trying to achieve self-sufficiency, we find a close equivalence in the patterns of the bridge dream (10*a*) and the borrowed book dream (27). In the bridge dream (10*a*) he returned a child to her mother and received the mother's thanks and a glass of milk. In the borrowed book dream (27), instead of returning the child, he has given (loaned) the mother a book; and, instead of her thanks and a glass of milk, she is returning the book to him. Thus, again comparing the two dreams, the borrowed book dream has substituted a material object in place of both the child and the mother's love. When we allow for this substitution of a material object for both the child and the mother's love and when we also allow for the attempt at internalization of the conflict, then the two dreams (10*a* and 27) become practically identical.

Continuing with our comparison, in the bridge dream (10*a*) we sensed a latent ambivalence toward the girl on the bridge. In the dream text the patient is assuming a protective attitude toward her, taking her home to her mother; but back of this protective attitude, we sense hostile wishes toward her. The protective attitude toward her was a reaction formation against these hostile wishes. In the borrowed book dream (27) there is a similar ambivalence toward money. The "mistreated" stocks in the borrowed book dream correspond to the latent hostile wishes in the bridge dream (10*a*), and his protective attitude toward the young girl in the bridge dream is paralleled by holding onto money in the borrowed book dream. We infer, accordingly, that, just as the protective impulses toward the girl in the bridge dream are a reaction formation against hostile impulses toward her, so also in the borrowed book dream holding onto money and possessions is a reaction formation against his impulses to destroy children and money.

In other words, if we can trust our deductions from the equivalence of pattern in these two dreams (10a and 27), the urge to hold onto possessions in the borrowed book dream (27) must have arisen as a device for mastering the pressure of the patient's impulses to "mistreat" or get rid of a child, by giving these impulses a harmless substitute outlet in the antagonistic tonic impulse to hold onto something.

Why Must This Patient Lose His Money?—Thus the capacity of the integrative mechanism to master these disturbing pressures resolves itself into a physiological capacity to bind or absorb disturbing pressure in the tonic activity of holding onto possessions. Why is this mechanism so unsuccessful in this patient's case?

Evidently, the pressure of this patient's impulses to get rid of a child cannot be successfully diverted into the contrary impulse to hold onto possessions. We have already learned[1] that guilt on account of his hostile impulses toward children compels him to destroy or lose his money. When this dream (27) pictures the analyst as giving him "mistreated" stocks, it is referring to this compulsion to lose his money that the analysis is beginning to mobilize.

The Same Problem in Another Form.—Yet this interpretation only presents us with the same problem in a new form. If the pressure of the patient's destructive impulses could be bound in the tonic activity of holding onto possessions, he would not need to feel guilty about them or to punish himself for them. Our comparison with the bridge dream (10a) suggested that in the borrowed book dream (27) the patient is trying to substitute possession of a material object not only for the child that he was returning to the mother in the earlier dream (10a) but also for his need for a mother's love. This is a mechanism that plays a very important role in the character formation of some in-

1. See chap. xxi of this volume.

dividuals. Miserly characters often succeed in high degree in finding in the love of money a substitute for human ties. If this patient could avail himself of a similar mechanism and substitute the love of money for his craving for a mother's love, then he might find relief from much of his conflict. Freed by his miserly love of money from his too intense dependence on a mother, he would need no longer to hate brother and sister as rivals for the mother and could perhaps then be free of the guilt that has arisen from these impulses. This is an adjustment that some misers are able to make. Why was this patient unable to solve his problem according to the same pattern?

Effects of Fixation on a Traumatic Memory.—The answer to this question is to be sought in the principle of commitment[2] to subsidiary goals that we discussed in relation to the anvil dream (12). In discussing this dream, we sensed that a large part of the pressure of the patient's craving for a mother's love had been concentrated on an impulse to attack the rivals that threatened to come between him and the mother. Even after he realized that these impulses could only estrange him from the mother, he was unable to withdraw the pressure that had been concentrated on them. Instead of finding some better way to satisfy his dependent needs, he was still under compulsion to put into execution these impulses that threatened only to defeat their original purpose. He was already committed to these impulses, unable to withdraw from them and to focus their pressure elsewhere. The need to retain the mother's love could no longer alter the content of the disturbing impulses. Somebody or something must be beaten. The fear of estranging the mother could succeed only in maintaining a precarious control over the dangerous impulses by turning them back against himself as a punishment.

We must assume a similar commitment to account for his compulsive need to destroy or lose his money. In the case of the miser who is successful in substituting the love of money for human ties, we infer that the substitution of love of money for the need for a mother must have taken place before, and instead

2. See Vol. I, chap. xxvi.

of, commitment to destructive impulses toward rivals. In this patient's case the attempt to substitute money for love must have come after he was already committed to destructive impulses toward the pregnant mother. Consequently, he deals with money not as money but as a symbol of the child who is his rival. Just as he plays a protective role toward the child sometimes, so he also sometimes holds onto his money; but he must also pay for his destructive impulses toward the child by a compulsion to lose his money.

Since this pattern of reacting too late to his hostile impulse toward siblings is one that recurs often in this patient's dreams, we assume that it is based on a traumatic memory. This memory is presumably the same one that we reconstructed as underlying the grasping-hand symbolism, a memory in which hostility toward the mother's pregnancy found real or symbolic expression in an impulse to reach out a grasping hand toward her and was followed by signs of the mother's displeasure. According to our reconstruction, the fear of offending the mother that results from beginning reactivation of this memory does not exert its inhibitory effect until after the integrative mechanism has already committed itself to the reactivated hostile impulse. In the anvil dream (12), unable to renounce the disturbing impulse, the patient must fantasy being beaten for it. In the borrowed book dream (27), he attempts to forestall further reactivation of the disturbing memory by substituting inanimate "stocks" for the mother upon whose love he is so dependent; but the already reactivated hostile impulses persist as a need to "mistreat" his possessions. In the next chapter we shall discuss the effects of this memory on two more of this patient's grasping-hand dreams.

Before concluding this chapter, however, we wish to point out that this patient's lack of moral self-sufficiency, too, can best be understood as a consequence of this same traumatic memory. His attempt to substitute his own conscience for his need to please the mother has come too late. Since he is already committed to impulses that are in conflict with his conscience, his self-justifying arguments can be nothing more than specious rationalizations. Therefore, the borrowed book dream (27) must put his self-justifying argument into the analyst's mouth, appealing to her indulgence to overlook the flaws in his argument. If he is to achieve real moral independence, his conscience must become an integrative pattern guiding his behavior instead of being called upon, too late, to pass judgments on impulses to which he is already committed.

CHAPTER XLVIII
Some Reorganizations of Motor Pattern

Underlying this patient's grasping-hand symbolism we have postulated a memory in which hostility toward the mother's pregnancy found real or symbolic expression in an impulse to reach out a grasping hand toward her and was followed by signs of the mother's displeasure. In the last chapter we found evidence that fixation on this same memory was responsible for his need to "mistreat" his stocks and lose his money. In this chapter we shall study other ways in which this memory has been elaborated in his dreams.

Two Forms of the Same Motor Pattern.—The symbolism of arm and grasping hand is duplicated in both the Mexican woman dream (44) and the anvil dream (12). In the Mexican woman dream the organ that administers the scrubbing and the organ that receives it are the same. A scrubbing is administered with arms and hands; and it is the boy's arm that receives the scrubbing. Similarly, in the anvil dream the iron bar with a hook on the end of it symbolizes an arm and a grasping hand, and it is beaten by a hammer wielded by arms and hands. These facts suggest the possibility that the acts of scrubbing and beating are modified forms of the impulse for which the dreamer is being scrubbed or beaten.

This suggestion takes on increased significance in the context of our interpretation of the grasping-hand symbolism. The impulse for which the patient is being punished is a hostile impulse against a child (the unborn child of the pregnant mother); but in each dream (44 and 12) punishment is inflicted not on the patient himself but on a substitute object. In the associations to the Mexican woman dream (44) the child who receives the scrubbing is identified, first, with the patient's son and only later with the patient himself; and in the anvil dream (12), too, the iron bar probably represents not only the patient himself but also a brother-figure. In each case the patient is inflicting upon a brother-figure the punishment that he himself deserves; behind the mask of inflicting punishment on a substitute object, he is giving outlet in modified form to the very same hostile impulse for which he needs punishment. In other words, in the anvil dream (12) the act of beating the iron bar is discharging in modified form the pressure of the impulse symbolized by removing clinkers from a furnace; and scrubbing the little boy in the Mexican woman dream (44) is giving substitute outlet to the hostile impulse toward the mother's pregnancy for which the patient needs punishment.

The broom dream (26) now fills in a gap in this hypothesis. In the process of organization of the anvil dream (12), according to our reconstruction, the patient substituted beating an iron bar for an act symbolic of getting rid of a child. In the broom dream the desire to make a similar substitution becomes manifest in the dream text: he is "supposed" to hit a squirrel but aspires to hit a golf ball. In the broom dream, as in the anvil dream (12), an act of hitting an inanimate object, idealized as a masculine achievement, is contemplated as a substitute for an act symbolic of hostility toward a child; the substitution that we reconstructed as one step in the process of organization of the anvil dream (12) is consciously wished for in the text of the broom dream (26).

Adaptation by Lowering the Level of Aspiration.—In the Mexican woman dream (44) the patient has modified his aspiration. Instead of beating a bar on the anvil or hitting a golf ball, he is scrubbing a child, identifying with the mother's rather than with the father's role as a parent. A curious detail of the broom dream (26) permits us to observe this transition in process. In the broom dream a broom is to be used, not to sweep, but to hit something. Evidently the dreamer wishes to use it as a golf stick. He still aspires to a masculine achievement, hitting a golf ball, but he has only a woman's tool, a broom, to hit with.

Shaping an iron bar on the anvil and hitting a golf ball are activities requiring skill. In the anvil dream (12) the dreamer is much impressed with the mother's good workmanship. Working as a blacksmith, she is not just discharging motor pressure, beating something; she is using her blacksmith's hammer to make something, to shape a hook on the end of the iron bar. Her muscular activity is co-ordinated, guided by a cognitive pattern to achieve a goal. Similarly, one hits a golf ball, not just for the sake of hitting it, but in order to drive it as far as possible in the direction of a goal. Like a blacksmith's work on the anvil, a good golf stroke is a highly co-ordinated act, requiring subordination of more elementary motor impulses to a learned pattern.

To understand either the anvil dream (12) or the broom dream (26), we must distinguish between the dreamer's ideal of motor achievement, which we call his "cognitive pattern," and his actual pattern of motor excitation. In the anvil dream (12) his ideal of motor achievement is based on the memory of his father working at the anvil; his actual pattern of motor excitation is not easy to reconstruct with certainty, but the symbol of the iron bar to remove clinkers from a furnace suggests that an aggressive impulse corresponding to a fantasy of attacking the mother's pregnancy has been frozen into a pattern of stiffening up in anticipation of being beaten. To achieve his ideal of good workmanship at the anvil, the dreamer would have to co-ordinate his antagonistic aggressive and tonic impulses into a well-integrated skilled performance. In the anvil dream (12) he does not attempt this difficult integration but, by picturing his mother's skill at the anvil, contents himself with the reassurance that a woman can do a man's work.

Thus in the anvil dream (12) he has set his ideal high but has not put himself to the test by trying to achieve it. In the broom dream (26) he is awaking to the fact that he is not capable of so much subordination of his cruder and more destructive motor impulses. In this dream he is struggling against readjusting to his inability to achieve his higher masculine deal of performance; he is repudiating the notion of lowering his level of aspiration: He realizes that he does not have a golf stick but resents the suggestion that he might use a broom.

Yet, several months later, in the Mexican woman dream (44), he does succeed in making the readjustment that he repudiated in the broom dream (26). In the later dream (44) he has adjusted his ideal of achievement to his capacity for sublimation; desiring to think of himself as a parent, he is content in this dream (44) to share with a mother her task of scrubbing a child, instead of aspiring in vain to a more masculine role. Scrubbing a child does not require so much skill as a blacksmith's work and involves much less modification of his underlying wish to get rid of a brother-figure. Accordingly, in the Mexican woman dream (44) he is no longer in the role of observer but is able to imagine himself actively co-operating in the mother's task of caring for her child.

Attempts To Co-ordinate Two Antagonistic Motor Patterns.— We shall now bring the borrowed book dream (27) into our comparison. The borrowed book dream, too, is struggling with the problem of mastering destructive impulses toward a child by deflecting their pressure into other channels. In this dream the patient tries to divert the pressure of his hostile impulses into the tonic muscular activity of holding onto possessions; but the disturbing pressure cannot long be bound in this way and soon re-emerges in the notion of "mistreating" the stocks and throwing them into the waste basket.

In the borrowed book dream (27) tonic binding of pressure and motor discharge of pressure are in conflict; holding onto possessions and throwing them away are two antagonistic patterns. The three dreams (12, 26, 44) that we have just been studying are attempts to resolve this conflict by integrating motor discharge and tonic muscular absorption of pressure into single co-ordinated acts. In each of the motor patterns in these three dreams, the patient is manipulating a tool. Tools must be held firmly while they are being manipulated. Holding onto the tool corresponds to our concept of tonic absorption of motor pressure, whereas manipulation involves a co-ordinated pattern in which both motor discharge and tonic absorption are involved.

In the borrowed book dream (27) an attempt to hold onto possessions is in conflict with an impulse to grasp and throw them away. In the manipulative acts in the three other dreams (12, 26, 44) we find several intermediate steps between holding onto something and grasping and throwing it away. *Holding onto a possession implies suppression of the more active impulse in favor of the tonic function of holding onto something;* but, in the use of a tool, holding onto it is subordinate to the activity involved in manipulating it. *The use of a tool involves a less complete inhibition of activity and movement in favor of the tonic act of holding.*

From this point of view the different tools mentioned in these dreams may be graded, both according to their function and the physiological activity that they symbolize and also according to the kind of activity involved in their use. The iron bar used to remove clinkers in the anvil dream (12) and the broom and the brush in the broom (26) and Mexican woman (44) dreams are tools for getting rid of something. We think of the iron bar used to remove clinkers as symbolic of a hand that grasps and throws away and the broom as symbolic of a hand that brushes something away. On the other hand, the hammer corresponds perhaps to a clenched fist, and a clenched first involves tonic muscular contractions not so different from those involved in holding onto something.

We find similar relations when we compare the muscular pattern involved in using the hammer with that of throwing something away. The activity of arms and hands in wielding a hammer is not so different from that involved in throwing a heavy object. The chief difference between the two activities is the fact that, in throwing, one lets go of the object, whereas, in beating with a hammer, one must retain his grip on the hammer. We conclude that the substitution of hitting for grasping and throwing away corresponds to a modification of muscular pattern in which the closed fist or tonic contraction of the gripping hand is substituted for the hand that relaxes to throw something away.

CHAPTER XLIX
A Temporarily Interrupted Transition

We have reconstructed[1] the process of organization of the fire-tending dream (45a) in two steps:

Reacting to the analysis as a sexually seductive situation, the first step registers a protest by substituting a hotel lobby, where an American Legion post meeting had brought prostitutes for entertainment.

A second step, by making the situation respectable again, permits the patient to remain in it. For the sexual temptation, the dream text has substituted the symbol of stove, ashes, and fire, and a "lady" who is merely requesting the dreamer to clean out the ashes and get the fire burning.

In the first of these steps, substitution of the hotel lobby not only emphasizes the mixed feelings of fascination and repudiation with which he is reacting to the temptation but also hints at his desire to turn away from the analyst to the company of men. In the dreams (46a and b) reported in the next hour, this transition is completed: he has turned away from the analyst, as a dangerous temptation, to the desire for a father to give him sexual instruction. In the burning logs dream (46a) this wish finds inverted expression in the advice that he gives his son. This dream does not even mention the tempting woman directly but substitutes for her a bonfire of railroad ties and logs; and he warns his son not to touch them but to wait until they burn themselves out.

The symbolism of these dreams gives evidence of the same transition, temporarily interrupted, from heterosexual to homosexual fantasies. The stove in the fire-tending dream (45a) is not only a symbol of the woman who is object of the patient's sexual desires; the fire clogged with ashes is also a symbol of his own ambivalence toward the temptation. The fire is going

1. See chap. vii (pp. 54 and 57) of this volume.

out, the ash pit is full of ashes mixed with coal, and the "lady" is asking the patient to clean out the ashes and get the fire burning. Evidently, the dream is accusing the lady of trying to stir up his passion; in the dream thoughts it is not the lady who is reluctant. It is the "fire" of his own sexual excitement that is clogged up by his resistance.

Thus the symbols of the stove and of stirring up the fire have two different meanings corresponding to two versions of the dream text. *In one version the stove represents the "lady,"* and stirring up the fire is symbolic of the patient's sexual impulses toward her; *in the other version* the fire clogged with ashes is a symbol of his own resistance, which would imply that *the stove represents the patient himself.* In this version, since the stove is the patient, stirring up the fire must be symbolic of a feminine submissive fantasy. This interpretation is quite consistent with the patient's attitude toward the therapy, since he evidently has little urge to stir up anyone else but comes to the analyst rather with the expectation that she will stir him up.

The hypothesis of an underlying feminine sexual fantasy is also in harmony with our first reconstruction of the process of organization of this dream. Our inference that the patient had imagined himself in the feminine role in a sexual fantasy is only an extension of our previous conclusion that he wished to turn away from the analyst to the company of men.

The dreams of the next hour confirm this reconstruction also. Not only does the urge to turn to a father-figure come to franker expression in these dreams (46a and b), but in the symbolism of the burning logs dream (46a) and in the actual text of the penis envy dream (46b) the sexual content of this interest in a father-figure is indicated much more directly. In the burning logs dream (46a), as in the fire-tending dream (45a), the sexual excitement symbolized by the fire is projected into the burning logs; and in the dream text, back of both the patient and his son, are two snakes, half-coiled, half-erect, symbolic of the homosexual impulses that threaten them both. We have already recognized that this dream (46a) about the patient and his son is really an inverted picture of his own wish for a father; and when he next dreams (46b) of his son's admiring his (the patient's) own penis, he is really preoccupied with his own childhood admiration of his father's penis.

Thus the feminine fantasies implied in a literal interpretation of the symbolism of the fire-tending dream (45a) are premonitory of the much more openly expressed feminine fantasies in the symbolism of the burning logs dream (46a) and in the text of the penis envy dream (46b). In the fire-tending dream (45a) this transition to a feminine submissive relationship to a father was temporarily interrupted by hopes based on the analyst's encouragement.

CHAPTER L

Ice, Ashes, and Fire

Transition from Water Symbolism to Constipation.—We interpreted the ice clogging the gutter in the frozen gutter dream (67) as a symbol of the inhibition of our patient's sexual impulses;[1] but we did not inquire what happened to his sexual pressures when his sexual impulses toward his card partner and toward the analyst were inhibited. It is our thesis[2] that *an impulse cannot be inhibited without finding some substitute to take its place.* In this case, since we have no report of any symptomatic acting to account for a displaced discharge of the pressure of the inhibited impulses, we must suspect that this pressure has been physiologically absorbed in some other way.

Actually the symbol of the frozen gutter suggests just such a mechanism of physiological absorption. A gutter full of ice instead of flowing water suggests some tonic sphincter action obstructing excretion. In fact, the patient has been telling us for a number of days that he is constipated. Probably the pressure of his sexual impulses is being absorbed by tonic contraction of urethral or anal sphincters.

The events of the next two hours confirm this hypothesis: The analyst interpreted the patient's desire to "freeze up" his sexual interest in her and repeated her interpretation of the sexual transference in the next hour (68). At the end of this 68th hour the patient reported that he felt better, that his bowels had moved, and that his appetite was better. Then followed the stable dream (69), in which he reacted to the analyst's interpretations of his sexual interest in her, first, by representing childbirth as taking place in a stable with horses and cows, and then by picturing the analyst as a woman who was all slopped

1. See chap. xli of this volume.

2. This thesis is really a special case of the principle of complementary substitutes discussed in Vol. I, chap. xlvi.

up after stepping right into cow manure. The frank reference to cow manure in this dream (69), as well as the implied identification of childbirth with defecation, contrast sharply with the frozen gutter in the preceding dream (67). We correlate this contrast with the fact that the patient's constipation has finally loosened up in the interval between the two dreams (67 and 69).

Thus in the frozen gutter we have another symbol of transition. In this case the transition is from an impulse to urinate (implied by the water symbolism) to absorption of the pressure of this impulse by constipation: In the process of organization of this dream (67) the patient was evidently preoccupied with flowing water. Then came the need to inhibit the urinary impulses symbolized by flowing water and to absorb their pressure in some form of tonic innervation; but in this dream we do not have a frank symbol of constipation, as we did, for example, in the stove clogged with ashes in the fire-tending dream (45a). Rather, the symbol of flowing water is still retained in a modified form. Instead of being replaced by another and solid waste product, the water itself has been frozen and is now clogging the gutter. The frozen gutter is thus a symbol of transition from the impulse to urinate, symbolized by the flowing water, to physiological absorption of the pressure of this impulse by constipation.

In the stable dream (69) we have evidence of relaxation of this need to absorb sexual pressure by tonic innervations, but we also have evidence that before this relaxation took place the transition to constipation had been completed—for relaxation of inhibition releases not flowing water or impulses to urinate but references to defecation.

Transition from Constipation to Re-emerging Sexual Excitation.—The ashes and fire symbolism of the fire-tending and burning logs dreams (45a and 46a) suggests a transition in the opposite direction, from constipation to re-emergence of sexual excitation.

The momentarily interrupted transition from heterosexual to submissive homosexual fantasies is not the only significant transition in these dreams (45a and 46a); their central preoccupation is rather one as to whether the patient's sexual urges shall be stirred into life, as the "lady" is urging in the fire-tending dream (45*a*), or whether they shall be allowed to burn out, as the patient advises his son in the burning logs dream (46*a*).

The repeated identification of children with ashes and waste in this patient's material has reminded us of the familiar depreciatory identification of a child with a stool; and we have recognized that the stove clogged with ashes is a symbol of constipation, which has been regressively substituted for pregnancy. The symbol of the stove and fire clogged with ashes has a significance very similar to that of the frozen gutter in the frozen gutter dream (67). It is a symbol of inhibition of sexual wishes made possible by a mechanism of physiological absorption. The associations to this dream stress the fact that ashes are waste. Yet the ashes have not been removed from the stove; they are still clogging the fire. In the dream text the patient is being asked to clean them out. Interpreted physiologically, this symbolism suggests tonic sphincter reaction obstructing excretion; and we suspect that much of the pressure of the patient's sexual impulses is being absorbed by such tonic contraction of the anal sphincter.

On the other hand, since the fire has not entirely gone out, it is evident that the sexual excitation has not been entirely absorbed in this way, that the patient is threatened with a re-emergence of the underlying sexual excitation.

Physiological Interpretation of Fire and Ashes Symbolism.— We have referred to fire and ashes as a deanimated symbolism. Yet a fire in a stove has a dynamic quality that contrasts sharply with such symbols as pencils and pads in a boxcar or a book with stocks in it. Fire does not impress us as really inanimate. This suggests, again, that fire is a symbol with a transitional significance. In the fire-tending and burning logs dreams (45*a* and 46*a*), we are observing in actual process the deanimation or reanimation of living persons that we have seen as an already accomplished fact in the manifest content of other dreams.

For ages it has been customary to speak of the "fire of life," to think of life itself as a fire. In modern times chemistry teaches us that this age-old identification of life and fire has a scientific justification: Since both are processes of oxidation, life is really a very slow fire. Yet, even without this scientific knowledge, it is evident that fire is closely analogous to life itself. Both have a dynamic rather than a material continuity of existence, constantly consuming new matter and giving rise to waste products that must be gotten rid of if life is to continue or if the fire is to continue to burn. In particular, the relation of a fire to inanimate matter is very similar to that of a living organism. A fire must be fed with fuel, just as a living organism must have food; and life, like fire, is continually converting living or burning matter into inanimate matter which we call excrement or ashes.

When we examine the text and associations of these two dreams (45a and 46a), it is evident that this analogy is more than an accidental one. In the fire-tending dream (45a) the dream action centers about letting the fire go out or getting it to burn again; and the associations to this dream explicitly mention feeding the fire with coal and characterize ashes as refuse and waste. Then again, in the burning logs dream (46a) the patient's advice to his son is to let the fire burn down. In this context the analogy of the fire's going out with its dying, and of getting it to burn with its reviving, is very clear.

We spoke earlier of physiological absorption of sexual excitation by tonic contraction of the lower bowel—by constipation. In this formulation we were thinking in terms of anatomical displacement of pressure. Just now we have been discussing this same mechanism of physiological absorption in quite different terms. The symbolism of these two fire dreams gives us a much more dynamic picture of this mechanism—as the burning-down of a fire into ashes. Is this merely an analogy, or is there a physiological pattern corresponding also to this dynamic symbolism?

By bringing the central integrative mechanism into our picture, we can reconstruct the functional significance of this symbolism and the physiological pattern that underlies it. Sexual excitation is often perceived by the central integrative mechanism as a sense of warmth or heat. If the sexual excitation can be partially or wholly absorbed by tonic innervations corresponding to constipation, then the sense of heat will diminish or disappear. A similar diminution in the sensations of irradiated warmth occurs when one is standing near a fire and the fire burns down into ashes. Because of this similarity, fire has become a symbol of sexual excitation; and the burning-down of fire into ashes, in this patient's material, has become associated with the physiological absorption of sexual excitation by constipation.

Functional Significance of Fire Symbolism.—Thus our analysis suggests that *fire is a symbol of sexual excitation emerging from physiological absorption by tonic innervation of the musculature* of the lower bowel or from some other form of tonic motor absorption, as by holding onto possessions. This formulation fits not only these two dreams ($45a$ and $46a$)[3] but also Dora's dream in Freud's case history. In Dora's dream we recognized[4] the substitution of jewels for sexual wetness as a reaction formation based on her infantile training in cleanliness; and the contrasting symbols, fire and jewel case, point to an unsuccessful attempt to bind sexual excitation by holding onto a prized possession.

According to our proposed formulation, fire is a symbol of emerging sexual excitation, which we should contrast with an active sexual impulse. Such sexual excitation corresponds to a feminine sexual wish to receive sexual stimulation from someone else rather than to a masculine sexual impulse to do something to someone else; and we must expect, accordingly, that the fire symbolism will be associated with the emergence of feminine rather than masculine sexual wishes. All our examples fulfil this expectation. In the fire-tending dream ($45a$) the fire in the stove corresponds to a desire to be "stirred up." In the burning logs dream ($46a$) the patient and his son are being threatened from behind by two snakes. In the anvil dream (12), even a phallic symbol, the iron bar, is not active but is submitting to a beating, after having been (presumably) heated in a fire. Dora's dream was quite frankly in reaction to feminine sexual wishes; and the fire dream which I reported in an earlier paper[5] was also in reaction to emerging and threatening masochistic homosexual wishes in the father transference.

3. The same formula fits equally well a fire dream which I have reported in an earlier paper (see French, 1936).

4. See chap. iii of this volume.

5. See n. 3.

SECTION IX

Survey of Relations between Dream Patterns

CHAPTER LI

An Intercommunicating System of Fantasy Patterns

Symbolism that is repeated in a number of dreams of the same person is usually a sign of an underlying constellation of fantasy patterns common to them all. We have already mapped out in detail one such constellation of dynamically interrelated fantasies, by superimposing the cognitive structures of our patient's water dreams; and we have found indications of a similar constellation underlying the grasping-hand symbolism and of another constellation common to the two money dreams.

There are also interrelations between constellations corresponding to different symbolisms. In many dreams we find more than one kind of symbolism. For example, in the bridge dream (10a) the pinching incident takes place on a bridge over a river. Sometimes, also, we find close parallels between dreams with different symbolisms—as, for example, between bridge dream (10a) and borrowed book dream (27).

In other words, we suspect that the constellations of fantasy patterns underlying this patient's dreams are all parts of a single intercommunicating system. Under the activating influence of different present situations, sometimes one and sometimes another part of this system is brought into focus, while other parts fade into the background.

Of course, it is not only a person's external situation that determines at a given moment what he will do. The motivational patterns and cognitive structures that guide behavior are continuous from one moment to the next, or even from one hour or day to the next. What we do now has consequences for the future. In purposive behavior the achievement of one subsidiary goal is followed by efforts to achieve the next objective in a more comprehensive plan. Similarly, in neurotic behavior and even in sequences of dreams extending over a number of days there is continuity of integrative pattern.[1]

1. See Vol. I, Secs. III and IV.

287

We have already suspected that constellations common to considerable numbers of dreams are parts of a "cataloguing system" or "road map" whose function is to guide the integrative mechanism in its selection of appropriate patterns from the past to be utilized in seeking solutions for present problems. This concept implies that the patterns underlying different groups of dreams intercommunicate, just as road maps of different sections of a country are continuous with the maps of adjoining sections. Since patterns of motivation do not usually change abruptly and completely, the integrative mechanism must have at its disposal a comprehensive system of intercommunicating "road maps" which make available the whole range of latent reaction patterns from the past and can be used in seeking solutions for a wide range of present problems.

The notion of a road map is, of course, only an analogy;[2] it is one possible way of visualizing the cognitive structure of the personality as a whole. We are trying to get some concept of the logical and dynamic relations that determine how one cognitive field that has been activated tends to activate successively other cognitive fields. We get a picture of some of the most elementary of these relations when we superimpose the cognitive structures of different dreams of the same person. By extending comparisons of this kind, we get a more and more comprehensive understanding of how the fantasy patterns of a particular patient are related both to one another and also to significant events in his past. And then, when we have reconstructed how single cognitive fields are re-

2. To understand our map analogy we must keep in mind that "points" on our "map" represent not points but patterns (cognitive fields) and that the dimensions in our diagrams represent not different directions but different kinds of possible transformations of cognitive pattern.

Since there are evidently many more than two independent kinds of possible transformations of cognitive pattern, our map will, of course, be multidimensional; but the most serious difficulty with our map analogy is the fact (see chap. xxxvi of this volume) that it does not give us any good way to represent condensations of cognitive fields. It is possible that this defect could be corrected by the use of some kind of non-Euclidean geometry (with condensation mechanisms represented by the meeting of parallel lines, like the great circles on a spherical surface). I have not made such an attempt, however, because I do not wish to overemphasize the artificial geometrical features of this analogy.

lated, we can begin to understand or even to predict how more complex cognitive structures (i.e., constellations of cognitive fields) succeed one another in actual behavior or in sequences of consecutive dreams.

In the next few chapters we shall continue with the program that we have just sketched out. By reconstructing parts of the cognitive structures of single dreams and by superimposing the cognitive structures of different dreams, we shall continue to map out the relations between different constellations of this patient's fantasy patterns. And then we shall use our reconstructions of these relationships in order to improve our understanding of this patient's dream sequences.

CHAPTER LII

A Recurring Sequence in the Water Dreams

Another Question about the Historical Pattern of the Water Dreams.—We have recognized from the beginning that in his water dreams our patient is struggling with two conflicts at the same time; but we are now no longer satisfied[1] with our earlier explanation that treated his erotic conflict as only a derivative of the conflict arising out of his hostile impulses. We know now that his erotic conflict was persisting side by side with, and to some degree independent of, his sibling rivalry conflict and that attempts to find solutions for the two conflicts complemented each other. Can we still reconcile this interpretation with our concept of the problem-solving function of the dream work, with our notion that when the dream work struggles with two problems at the same time they are always intimately and intelligibly related to each other?

Fortunately in another connection we have already found the answer to this question.

Dynamic Consequences of Infantile Sexual Discoveries.—We were impressed[2] by the fact that interpretations of this patient's sexual impulses toward the analyst have twice served as the stimulus for a dream of repudiation of the mother's pregnancies. The explanation was obvious enough, since the patient knows that a sex relationship is likely to result in the woman's pregnancy. Yet we were surprised that he is still reacting with strong emotion to this fact instead of adapting to it; that his disgust and resentment are still sufficient to "freeze up" his sexual interest in women, as in the frozen gutter dream (67), to inhibit his sexual curiosity, and to make him dream (in dream 69) of being advised by a man in a clean white suit that such things are not for his eyes. Why, we inquired, is his curiosity not yet satisfied? After so many years why must he still be dreaming about the problem of where children come from?

1. See chaps. xlii and xliii of this volume.
2. See chap. xxii of this volume.

Our answer to these questions was as follows: This patient's sexual investigations ended with a discovery whose emotional consequences he could not accept. This discovery established an associative linkage between his own sexual impulses and his still unsolved conflict about sharing the mother's love with other children. In order to avoid reactivating this conflict, he was compelled, in the frozen gutter dream (67), to freeze up his sexual impulses; and in the stable dream (69) he was still struggling to restrain his curiosity, to accept the advice of the man in the clean white uniform that it was not for him to look at such things.

The very fact that the patient could not accept the emotional consequences of this discovery made its effect on his subsequent behavior profound; for it so linked together his sexual conflict with his conflict over hostility toward babies that these two traumatic conflicts tend now to be condensed into one and to augment each other. As a result of this associative linkage the disturbing memories of his rivalry with brother and sister tend to be reactivated not only by actual rivalry situations in the present but also by his own heterosexual impulses.

Reactivation of the Water Fantasies, a Theoretical Reconstruction.—By means of this historical reconstruction we can now round out our picture[3] of how this patient's water fantasies are successively reactivated.

We know that the erotized water dreams occur in reaction to reawakened hopes of the analyst's approval or indulgence. Encouraged by such hopes, we postulate, infantile sexual impulses to urinate upon the mother emerge; and these sexual impulses then reactivate the memories of the mother's pregnancies and confront the patient once more with the problem of sharing the mother with other children. Under the mitigating influence of hope of the analyst's indulgence, the threat of rivalry from brother and sister is not fully appreciated at first. While integrative capacity is still adequate, the patient can accept the anticipated child and take pride in the fantasy that his "water" had impregnated the mother; but the danger of rivals for the mother's love soon becomes real and, reactivating his hostility and his fear of estrangement from the mother, destroys once more his present hope of indulgent

3. See our earlier reconstructions in chaps. xvi and xxxiii of this volume.

response. Then the impregnation fantasies are replaced by impulses to use his "water" to drown the child inside the mother and by fears of being drowned in retribution.

An Unsuccessful First Attempt To Check This Reconstruction.—If this reconstruction is correct, we should expect impregnation fantasies to come first in the texts of the water dreams and to be followed by derivatives of the drowning fantasies. This expectation is confirmed by only one of the four erotized water dreams: The dirty hole dream (205) does start with symbolism suggestive of an impregnation fantasy and then continues with the woman and the patient in the hole half-filled with dirty water. However, in two of the other three erotized water dreams attempts to master the underlying drowning fears come first and are followed by protective and paternal attitudes toward sister- and brother-figures: In the bridge dream (10a) the patient first walks over the bridge, then escorts the girl home to her mother; and similarly in the flood dream (115) playing father and mother to the child follows rather than precedes his walking in the dirty water.

Another Attempt.—We shall inquire later whether this discrepancy can be accounted for; but first we shall examine how this patient's water dreams fit into the sequence of his other dreams. When we do so, we find these water dreams closely associated in pairs or in short sequences separated by much longer intervals. If, instead of single dreams, we now study these short dream sequences, we find that the order of succession of events does correspond to what we should expect from our hypothesis. The first dream in each sequence is in response to the patient's reawakened hope of approval or indulgence from the analyst and is followed by one or more dreams in which the fear of a suffocating drink emerges more plainly.

This succession of events is clearest in three sequences in which an erotized water dream comes first and is followed by an unerotized water dream.[4] Thus the bridge dream (10a) is followed by the railroad station dream (10b), a dream of flight with

4. In only one case is the order reversed: the fireplug dream (19a) follows, instead of preceding, the rowing dream (18a). The reason for this apparent exception will appear in a moment (see discussion of two waves of hope).

water in the background. The flood dream (115) is followed by the whiskey dream (116b). The capsized boat dream (187b) and the vomiting dream (190) follow the seductive bathtub dream (185) and a memory of enuresis (186) in the home of a motherly landlady.

It is true that a few sequences begin with unerotized water dreams, but even these sequences are no exception to the general rule that the first appearance of water symbolism is in each case in response to hopes inspired by the analyst's tolerance or encouragement: The bridge dream (10a) was inspired by the hope of pleasing the analyst with a dream. The rowing dream (18a) followed closely on the kindly policeman dream (17). The dirty food dream (39) and the pump dream (41) were in response to reawakening hopes of the analyst's tolerance of forbidden wishes. The flood dream (115) was stimulated by discussion of sexual impulses toward analyst and mother. The train wreck dream (154a) followed permissive discussion of the possibility of an extramarital affair. The dirty hole dream (205) was partly in protest against, but even more in positive response to, interpretations from the analyst which the patient felt to be seductive.

Two Waves of Hope, Each Followed by Fear.—When we now study these sequences in greater detail, we can distinguish, in each, two successive waves of hope, each followed by reactivation of fears arising out of the underlying traumatic memories. In each sequence, we postulate, *the first of these waves of hope is responsible for* the emergence of enuretic impulses and for *the first appearance of* the *water symbolism.* This emergence of enuretic impulses, according to our reconstruction, next reactivates the underlying traumatic memories and the fears of drowning that arise out of them, and the dreams try to master these fears by fantasies of climbing or walking above the water. Then *the second wave of hope* begins to exert its facilitating effect. This time the dreamer hopes no longer for indulgence of his genital and urinary impulses but dreams rather *of oral gratification* from mother or sister. Yet this second wave of hope, too, is only temporary. After a time these hopes of oral gratification, in their turn, give way to dreams in which fear of punishment emerges even more frankly.

This more detailed reconstruction accounts more adequately than our first one for the details of these dream sequences. In all the water dreams except the dirty hole dream (205) the first wave of hope has spent itself in the process of dream organization; we assume that genital impulses and impulses to urinate have been activated, even though they do not become manifest; in the dream texts attempts to climb or walk above the water are evidence that the associated drowning fears have already been reactivated. This explains the fact that puzzled us earlier in this chapter,[5] that the first episodes in the texts of the bridge dream (10a) and the flood dream (115) are not erotic impulses but symbolic attempts to master the drowning fear.

Then follow the fantasies of oral gratification resulting from the second wave of hope. In the bridge dream (10a) the dreamer receives a glass of milk. In the fireplug dream (19a) the girl offers him a kiss. Even in the dirty food dream (39) there is enough milk for a regiment. In the flood dream (115) he washes his face in the dirty water. In the vomiting dream (190) the analyst's and her husband's indulgence takes the slightly variant form of good-naturedly mopping up the water that the patient vomits. In the dirty hole dream (205) he embraces the girl and feels her breasts.

Finally, when this second wave of hope wanes, fantasies with a punitive significance appear, usually in a succeeding dream.[6] After receiving a glass of milk in the bridge dream (10a) he is fantasying himself being beaten in the anvil dream (12). After kissing the girl in the fireplug dream (19a) he is rebuked in the brake dream (19b). After he and the young woman have washed their faces in the dirty water in the flood dream (115) he is having a suffocating drink forced upon him in the whiskey dream (116b). At the end of the dirty hole dream (205) the woman's husband appears while the patient is embracing and kissing her; and in the next dream (207) a man is expecting him to eat a lot of "raw stuff."

5. See p. 292.
6. These punitive dreams are often not water dreams. See discussion in next chapter of transition to grasping-hand symbolism.

CHAPTER LIII

The Symbolisms of Water and of the Grasping Hand

In one set of our patient's dreams water is the most conspicuous symbol; in another group of dreams the grasping-hand symbols play a central role. Are these two symbols dynamically interrelated? For an answer to this question, we turn first to dreams in which both symbols appear.

In real life the hand can be turned to many different uses. To what uses have arm and hand been put in these water dreams?

End Goals and Subsidiary Goals.—At the end of the bridge dream (10a) the patient's hand is stretched out to receive a glass of milk from the mother. Here the hand is subordinate to the mouth. Its function is to receive the milk to convey it to the mouth. Receiving the milk with the hand is subordinate to the end-goal of drinking it.

Similarly, pinching the girl in the bridge dream (10a) is a sexual gesture, an act subsidiary to the genital sexual impulses symbolized by the river.

In purposive behavior in waking life, incentive pressure is transferred temporarily from the desire to achieve an end-goal to efforts to achieve subsidiary goals. After the subsidiary goals have been achieved, the incentive pressure reverts to the desire for the end-goal. In the same way in the bridge dream (10a) incentive pressure has been transferred from the desire for milk to the act of reaching for it and has then reverted back to the end-goal of drinking it.

Similarly, we picture the pressure of the impulses symbolized by the river as being transferred to activate the pinching gesture; but in this case the activating pressure does not revert to the end-goal, since fear of offending the mother promptly inhibits the underlying sexual impulses.

In the fireplug dream (19a) we have a more dramatic example of a sexual approach interrupted and inhibited before its end-goal is achieved. Walking, seeing the girl at the fireplug, helping her carry the water can, embracing and kissing her are successive steps in a sexual approach that is brought to a sudden end when the mother calls.

Aggressive Protest and Mastery of Pressure.—Thus in the bridge dream (10a) we can recognize walking toward the girl and pinching her as first steps in sexual approach; but in the rowing dream (18a) rowing is no longer a sexual approach. It is rather a symbolic substitute for the masculine sexual urges that the dreamer has renounced, and an attempt at active mastery of his fears of being drowned. This dream is one of those in which the patient is using his hands to manipulate tools, as a substitute for the masculinity that he cannot assert in real life.

The hand and tool symbolism is similarly motivated also in dreams in which there is no water symbolism. In the anvil dream (12) the patient is protesting against the fantasy of being beaten by identifying himself also with the woman who is wielding the blacksmith's hammer. In the broom dream (26) he is able only to hit a squirrel with a broom but aspires to hit a golf ball with a golf stick. In the fire-tending dream (45a) stirring up the fire is a symbolic substitute for the male role in coitus. In these dreams arm and hand and tool play the role of a phallic symbol.

When Masculine Aspirations Fail, the Hand Becomes a Destructive Organ.—In the examples that we have just discussed, arm and hand sometimes serve goals that are subsidiary to the oral and genital end-goals of the water symbolism, sometimes they are used as a symbolic substitute for a masculinity that the patient is unable to achieve. Finally, as pressure increases, the patient's masculine aspirations begin to lose their dominance, and arm and hand increasingly take on a significance hostile to the mother's pregnancies.

In this patient's dreams, impulses to use the hand to take and get rid of the mother's unborn child occur usually in condensation with use of the arm as a phallic symbol. We have already analyzed many examples of this condensation: the gesture of pinching the girl in the bridge dream (10a), the iron bar used to remove clinkers from a furnace in the anvil dream (12), stealing pencils from a boxcar in the pencil-stealing dream (25), the choice between playing golf and hitting a squirrel in the broom dream (26), stirring up the fire and removing the ashes in the fire-tending dream (45a). In all of these examples we have a condensation in varying degree of the use of arm and tool as a phallic symbol, with hostile impulses toward the mother's pregnancies.

Aggressive Discharge of Pressure by the Bodily Musculature. —The fact that in the water dreams arm and hand are used for purposes of active mastery suggests that the enuretic fantasies underlying the water symbolism are functionally not so well suited to give aggressive outlet to large amounts of pressure as the arm and hand are and that a mechanism exists for transfer of excessive pressure to these and other large muscle groups. In this patient's water dreams, we may add, not only impulses involving arm and hand but also the muscular activity of walking appear as ways of discharging the pressure of the conflict underlying the water symbolism when it becomes excessive.

Another fact gives some confirmation to this hypothesis. In this patient's dreams both sexual and hostile impulses undergo very different fates, depending on whether their physiological pattern involves genitals and mouth, as in the water symbolism, or arm and hand, as in the grasping-hand symbolism. In the water symbolism impulses to urinate upon a woman are most energetically inhibited and replaced by drinking fantasies or fantasies of being drowned; but the impulses that make use of arm and hand have often retained their aggressive form (pinching girl, stealing pencils, hitting squirrel, removing ashes from furnace) instead of being turned back against the dreamer.

We arrive thus at the following reconstruction:

In this patient's dreams, fear arising out of traumatic memories of having offended the mother leads to energetic inhibition of genital and urinary impulses and resultant increase of pressure in the form of fantasies of having a suffocating drink forced upon him; but then the excessive pressure is displaced to the musculature of arm and hand to seek discharge in aggressive behavior.

When once activated, these motor impulses can sometimes be

utilized as means toward the oral and genital end goals represented by the water symbolism; sometimes they serve the purpose of active mastery of the patient's fear of drowning; and sometimes, escaping still further from the control of these endgoals, they give symbolic expression to his hostile wishes toward the mother's pregnancies.

CHAPTER LIV

Transitions from Water Symbolism to Grasping-Hand Symbolism

As a check on our formulation of the relations between the water and the grasping-hand symbolisms, we turn next to a study of the dream sequences in which these two symbolisms occur.

Dream Cycles.—The short sequences of water dreams discussed in chapter lii are only parts of more extended recurring dream sequences. We can recognize these most easily as an alternation of periods of positive response and periods of withdrawal from, or resistance to, the analyst's therapeutic encouragement. In the period beginning with the bridge dream (10*a*) and continuing through the $20.00 bill dream (60*c*) we recognize three periods of positive response, each followed by a period of resistance or withdrawal.

The bridge dream (10*a*) is one of positive response. It is followed by a phase of flight or withdrawal in the railroad station (10*b*), clinic (10*c*), anvil (12), and snake (14) dreams.

A second cycle of contrasting periods is much longer in both its phases: The positive phase begins with the kindly policeman dream (17) and ends with the pencil-stealing dream (25). The phase of resistance, this time much more intense, begins with the patient's inability to confess in the pencil-stealing dream (25) and continues up to the dirty food dream (39).

However, the reference to "food enough for a regiment" in this dream (39) gives advance notice of another phase of positive response. The new positive response phase becomes manifest in the patient's relief in admitting the truth of the analyst's interpretation of the sexual transference in the 41st hour, and continues through the penis envy dream (46*b*). Yet the patient's turning away from the analyst to a male substitute in the burning logs (46*a*) and penis envy (46*b*) dreams is already premonitory of another resistance phase. This resistance phase starts with a mood of resignation and feelings of inferiority and dependence (hours 47–49), after which the patient withdraws into a role of detached observer in the crooked wagon dream (50*a*) and later betrays his desire to run away from his responsibilities as a parent by reactivating his memory of leaving his brother in the rye field (61st hour). The vacation interruption of the analysis at this point prevents our knowing how much longer this resistance phase might have continued.

Water Symbolism and Grasping-Hand Symbolism in the Dream Cycles.—If we leave out of account one dream (17), which will be mentioned shortly,[1] each of the three dream cycles that we have studied begins with the water symbolism. Afterward in each there is a transition to the grasping-hand symbolism. After this transition, in each cycle, with again one exception (dream 45*b*), the grasping-hand symbolism continues to be the dominant symbolism until the end of the cycle.

To test these statements we review the dreams of each cycle.

Cycle 1 starts with the bridge dream (10*a*), a water dream, and continues with the railroad station dream (10*b*), in which the railroad station is close to the lake front. In the clinic dream (10*c*), the anvil dream (12), and the snake dream (14) there is no reference to the water symbolism but the dream action in each case implies use of the grasping hand: taking a culture in the clinic dream (10*c*); the bar with a hook on the end of it and wielding a hammer in the anvil dream (12); the child's grasping the snake to pull it back in the snake dream (14).

In the kindly policeman dream (17), with which cycle 2 begins, there is no water symbolism, and the references to the real estate man who cheated the patient are related to the grasping-hand (stealing) theme. This is the one exception to which we referred earlier; but the rowing dream (18*a*), which is the second dream in this cycle, is a water dream; and after the second clinic dream (18*b*) the fireplug dream (19*a*) again involves prominently the symbolism of flowing water. After this there is no recurrence of the water symbolism in this cycle; but the grasping hand plays a central role in the pencil-stealing dream

1. See n. 3, p. 302.

(25), in the broom dream (26) (i.e., grasping a tool), in the dream of the borrowed book (27) (giving and receiving with the hand and holding onto possessions), and in the memories of stealing which are reported later.

Cycle 3 begins again with the milk and dirty water symbolism of the dirty food dream (39) and the dirty water symbolism of the pump dream (41). In the pig dream (43) the dream action centers about talking and contains no clear reference either to the water symbolism or to the grasping hand. In the Mexican woman dream (44) the woman is pouring a solution, but the main dream action involves arm and hand. After this, with the single exception of the tub-flushing dream (45b), there is no recurrence of water symbolism; but we have the symbolism of the grasping hand in the fire-tending dream (45a) (stirring up fire and removing ashes), in the burning logs dream (46a) (picking up ashes), in the crooked wagon dream (50a) (pushing baby carriage down terrace), in the weeding dream (55) (pulling up weeds), in the elephant dream (60a) (picking up stones with the elephant's trunk), and in the references to stealing in the $20.00 bill dream (60c).

An effect of Increasing Pressure.—Since we know that this patient's water dreams tend to appear at points when hopes of the analyst's indulgent approval can mitigate somewhat his fears of offending a mother-figure, it should not surprise us that his dream cycles begin their positive phase with the positive response type of water dream.

The transition to grasping-hand symbolism occurs when fears of offending the mother, beginning to emerge again, increase the intensity of conflict. In the bridge dream (10a) we have a pretty example of this in the transient emergence of the grasping-hand symbolism in the incident of pinching the young girl. In our analysis of the chronological order of the episodes in this dream[2] we concluded that pressure reached its height in this pinching incident just before it was mitigated in the pseudo-awakening induced by hopes of pleasing the analyst. At this point of maximum pressure the grasping-hand symbolism appears. The relaxation of pressure that follows is associated with, and

2. See Vol. I, chap. xlii.

is a result of, the patient's gratification from the cool, refreshing milk that the mother offers him. In other words, associated with rise of pressure, there is a transition to the grasping-hand symbolism, but the return to the milk and water symbolism is accompanied by a relaxation of pressure.

The transition to grasping-hand symbolism in the clinic and anvil dreams (10c and 12) corresponds to the progressive increase of pressure that results from the waning of the hopes that inspired the bridge dream (10a).

In the kindly policeman dream (17), with which cycle 2 begins, it is significant that references to the real estate man's cheating occur before and not after[3] the policeman shows the patient that the analyst's purpose is therapeutic rather than punitive.

In the rowing dream (18a) and the fireplug dream (19a) we have both water symbolism and grasping-hand symbolism, but the grasping hand in each case plays a subsidiary or subordinate role. The definite transition to grasping-hand symbolism in cycle 2 occurs after the fireplug dream (19a), in which the dreamer so abruptly failed to maintain his hope of the analyst's indulgence for his erotic wishes. This transition to the grasping-hand symbolism in the pencil-stealing dream (25) and in the two dreams (26 and 27) that follow is again correlated with an increase in the pressure of the patient's conflict.

In cycle 3, the arm and hand symbolism first becomes dominant in the Mexican woman dream (44). (In this case the woman's role in pouring the solution is subsidiary to the patient's scrubbing of the boy's arm.) This is immediately after the failure of his hopes of winning reconciliation with the analyst by means of confession, of which we find evidence in the pig dream (43). Thus again we find transition to the grasping-hand symbolism correlated with an increase in intensity of conflict. In this case, however, the increase in intensity of conflict is not so great, as is evidenced by the fact that he is still able to obtain relief

3. To maintain our hypothesis that each cycle begins with water symbolism, we might perhaps reckon the first part of the kindly policeman dream (17) to cycle 1, and begin cycle 2 with the policeman's showing the patient his clothes.

by accepting the analyst's interpretations. This fact will perhaps help us to account for another recurrence of the water symbolism that occurs apparently after transition to the grasping-hand symbolism.

In cycle 3 the most difficult detail to account for in terms of our hypothesis is the re-emergence of the water symbolism in the tub-flushing dream (45b). This dream was reported immediately after the fire-tending dream (45a) in the same hour. The patient did not tell us whether it was dreamed before or after the fire-tending dream (45a) but in either case the water symbolism plays a more important role in this dream (45b) than in the Mexican woman dream (44) reported in the preceding hour. If we wish to bring the re-emergence of water symbolism into harmony with our thesis that transition to the grasping-hand symbolism is correlated with increase of pressure, then we may note that both the tub-flushing dream (45b) and the fire-tending dream (45a) are again reacting to what the patient feels to be seduction on the analyst's part. Such a seductive situation tends to encourage hopes similar to those that elicit water dreams; but the sense of the analyst's seductiveness comes this time at a moment when the patient is already reacting with energetic defenses against his erotic wishes. In the fire-tending dream (45a) the patient's ambivalence toward the temptation finds expression in the symbol of the fire clogged with ashes, which the lady is encouraging him to stir into life. In the tub-flushing dream (45b) he is protesting with vigorous sarcasm against the analyst's throwing dirt into the tub and her then telling him to flush it down the drain. Yet it is evident that he is unconsciously responding positively to the temptation, or it would not be necessary for the dream to protest so vigorously against it. To his unconscious positive response, we correlate the re-emergence of the water symbolism in this dream; while the already awakened defenses account for the fact that the dreamer's manifest response is one not of positive response but of sarcastic protest.

We have spent a disproportionate amount of time in attempting to account for this one exception, but, if we leave this one dream out of account, it is clear enough that a transition from water symbolism to grasping-hand symbolism in each of the three dream cycles occurs at a point where pressure is rising because of beginning frustration of the patient's positive response to the analyst's encouragement.

This is evidently in accord with our formulation in the last chapter—that arm and hand are functionally better suited than urination to give outlet to large amounts of pressure and that when the pressure that is being elaborated in the water symbolism becomes excessive, it is transferred to the musculature of arm and hand to seek discharge in aggressive behavior.

CHAPTER LV

Two Different Physiological Patterns of Internal Absorption of Pressure

We have studied three dreams in which more or less success-ful absorption by tonic motor innervations has played an im-portant role in the process of dream organization.

In the frozen gutter dream (67) there is a transition from the physiological pattern underlying the water symbolism to the symptom of constipation. A similar tonic innervation of the lower bowel is suggested by the ashes symbolism of the fire-tending dream (45a). In the borrowed book dream (27) we find evidence of an attempt to bind pressure not by constipation but by holding onto possessions.

As an afterthought to the borrowed book dream (27) the patient recalls that he threw the stocks in the waste basket. The sequence of holding onto possessions and throwing them away in the borrowed book dream (27) is paralleled by similar se-quences in both fire-tending (45a) and frozen gutter (67) dreams. In the fire-tending dream (45a) the stove clogged with ashes seems to be a projected symbol of constipation, but it is also suggested that the patient get rid of the ashes. Similarly, the frozen gutter dream (67), which symbolizes and is accom-panied by constipation, is followed by loosening up of his con-stipation and by the stable dream (69), with its frank refer-ences to defecation. Thus in all three cases there is absorption of pressure by tonic innervation, followed by getting rid of the retained object.

These parallels suggest a question about the physiological pat-tern of the borrowed book dream (27). At the time of the frozen gutter dream (67) we know that the patient was actually con-stipated; and constipation seems to be directly represented in the symbolism of the fire-tending dream (45a). Must we con-clude that tonic innervation of the lower bowel has played a part in the process of organization of the borrowed book dream (27), too?

Since Freud published his *Character and Anal Erotism*,[1] psychoanalytic literature has been full of clinical reports showing that both holding onto possessions and getting rid of waste products are intimately related to anal erotism. There are two possible explanations of this relationship. Some of the neurotic patterns reported suggest that the patient is clinging to money or other possessions as a substitute for holding onto his stool or is symbolically defecating by throwing things away. Abraham (1923), for example, tells of a woman who was very reluctant to throw anything away and whose only way of getting rid of something useless was by tucking it behind her back under her apron string and then "losing" it while she walked in the woods. This behavior suggests very plainly that the woman fantasied that she was getting rid of the useless object by defecating.

However, the rectum and anus are not the only parts of the body that have retentive or expulsive functions or both. Alexander (1935) has taken account of this fact in his vector concept, which designates the function (vector) of retention or expulsion without specifying the organ involved. In terms of his vector concept, constipation and holding onto possessions with one's hands are two different forms of the same retentive vector; and urination, ejaculation, defecation, spitting, vomiting, and throwing something away are all different forms of the same expulsive vector.

In these studies we take account of the fact that similar functions may be performed by different organs by distinguishing[2] between motivational pattern (functional significance) and physiological pattern. Thus in our patient's dreams, both giving the mother a child and destroying her child are expressed sometimes in terms of urinating upon her, at other times in terms of an outstretched giving or grasping hand. And, similarly, tonic absorption of the pressure of disturbing sexual and hostile wishes has been achieved in the frozen gutter and fire-tending dreams

1. S. Freud, 1908*b*.
2. See chap. xxiii of this volume.

(67 and 45a) by constipation and in the borrowed book dream by holding onto possessions.

Our procedure is in each particular case to interpolate between the situation to which the patient is reacting and the dream or other behavior that we are trying to understand. In the case of the borrowed book dream (27) the patient is reacting to guilt because he wishes to mistreat the child of a woman from whom he is receiving help. The dream work has tried to mitigate this conflict by substituting stocks for the child whom he wishes to mistreat; and in this context we can recognize holding onto possessions as an attempt to bind the pressure of his destructive impulses toward the child. Since there is nothing in the dream text or associations that makes it necessary to interpolate a fantasy of tonic innervation of the lower bowel, we conclude that in this case the pattern of holding onto possessions, involving tonic innervation of arm and hand, has been directly activated, without interposition of an anal erotic fantasy.

CHAPTER LVI

Tonic Motor Absorption of Pressure in the Dream Cycles

We shall examine next how the mechanism of tonic motor absorption of pressure is fitted into our patient's dream cycles. In the first three cycles of this patient's material we have found that transition from water symbolism to grasping-hand symbolism occurs at the point where re-emerging fears of offending the mother increase the intensity of conflict. The function of this transition is to facilitate aggressive motor discharge of the pressure resulting from inhibition of the genital heterosexual impulses underlying the water symbolism. We wish now to know whether the mechanism of tonic motor absorption of pressure occurs in any consistent relation to the transition from water symbolism to grasping-hand symbolism.

An Intermediate Step between Water and Grasping-Hand Symbolism.—In the frozen gutter (67) and stable (69) dreams there is a transition from the water symbolism, not to the grasping-hand symbolism, but to the symptom of constipation. Transition to the grasping-hand symbolism does not occur until the next dream (72),[1] which we have not yet reported.

The fire-tending dream (45*a*) follows the Mexican woman dream (44), in which the woman is pouring a solution but the main dream action involves arm and hand; and it is followed by the tub-flushing dream (45*b*). Thus this fire-tending dream (45*a*) occurs during the period of transition from water symbolism to grasping-hand symbolism in cycle 3.

In our reconstruction[2] of the process of organization of this dream (45*a*) we concluded that an initial attempt to bind sexual pressure in the symptom of constipation had been followed by re-emergence of sexual excitation, symbolized by the fire and

1. This dream will be reported and discussed in Vol. III.
2. See chap. 1 of this volume.

resulting in a desire to be "stirred up." In the text of the fire-tending dream (45*a*) the suggestion that the patient stir up the fire serves as a masculine protest reaction to his own desire to be "stirred up." Stirring up a fire implies use of arm and hand to manipulate a tool. Thus *in this dream (45a)* we find evidence that *tonic innervation of the lower bowel has occurred as an intermediate step between the water symbolism of preceding dreams and the transfer of energy to an impulse to utilize arm, hand, and tool as a phallic symbol.* It is only when the attempt at internal mastery of pressure fails that the aggressive act of stirring up the fire is suggested.

Such attempts to bind pressure internally have occurred also as transitional steps in the organization of the bridge dream (10*a*) and of the anvil dream (12) of cycle 1. In the anvil dream (12) the bar used to remove clinkers from a furnace indicates that a stove clogged with ashes has played a part in the process of organization of this dream (12), also. In some of the fantasies underlying the bridge dream (10*a*), too, the patient is probably identified with the girl who is pinched in the back, just as in the later fire-tending dream (45*a*) he is identified with the fire clogged with ashes that has to be "stirred up."

Thus we conclude that in cycle 1, as in cycle 3, tonic innervation of the lower bowel has occurred as an intermediate step in the transition from water symbolism to grasping-hand symbolism.

Tonic Motor Absorption of Pressure in Three Sequences.— In cycle 2 the need for internal mastery of pressure gives rise not to tonic innervation of the lower bowel but to the fleeting attempt to hold onto possessions in the borrowed book dream (27).

We have already pointed out that the sequence of holding onto possessions and then throwing them into the waste basket in the borrowed book dream (27) parallels the sequence of constipation followed by discharge of pressure by defecation in frozen gutter dream (67) and stable (69) dream. In both cases there is an absorption of pressure by tonic innervation followed by getting rid of the retained object.

However, the two sequences differ in the physiological system involved: In the earlier dream (27) the pattern involves the hands and money; whereas in the later dream sequence (67 and 69) the lower bowel and its content are involved.

The sequence of patterns in the fire-tending dream (45a) differs from that in the borrowed book dream (27) in another way: In the fire-tending dream (45a) the attempt to bind pressure internally by tonic innervation of the lower bowel precedes the transition to the grasping-hand impulse; in the borrowed book dream (27) the transition to the grasping hand has occurred first and has been followed by tonic motor absorption of pressure.

This difference in the timing of tonic motor absorption of pressure now suggests the probable reason why two different methods of binding pressure have been employed in the two sequences. In the borrowed book dream (27) the attempt to bind pressure by tonic innervation involves the already activated hand and arm, whereas in the fire-tending dream (45a) the attempt to bind pressure, occurring before pressure has been transferred to arm and hand, involves tonic innervation of an organ (the lower bowel) in the anatomical neighborhood of the sexual impulse (urination) whose energy is being absorbed.

When we bring the sequence of frozen gutter dream (67) and stable dream (69) into our comparison, the effects of timing on the dream symbolism can be still more clearly seen: The attempt to bind pressure by tonic innervations occurs in the borrowed book dream (27) after completion of the transition to grasping-hand symbolism; in the fire-tending dream (45a), while this transition is still in process; in the frozen gutter dream (67), before there is any hint of transition from water symbolism to grasping-hand symbolism. Thus tonic motor absorption of pressure, occurring earlier and earlier in the cycle, results in the symbolism of holding onto possessions in cycle 2, of a stove clogged with ashes in cycle 3, and of a frozen gutter at the beginning of cycle 4.

Effect of Differences in the Phase of Elaboration of the Patient's Problem.—The fact that tonic motor absorption of pressure occurs later in cycle 2 than in cycle 3 is reflected not only in the physiological patterns but also in differences between the total cognitive structures of the borrowed book and fire-tending dreams (27 and 45a). In the fire-tending dream the attempt to bind pressure by tonic innervations occurs while the patient is trying to modify the nature of his disturbing impulse so as to make it more acceptable to the analyst. In the borrowed book dream (27), holding onto possessions is utilized to change the character of the total conflict situation, to transform a personal conflict into an impersonal one.

The pencil-stealing dream (25) is the dream in cycle 2 that most closely parallels the fire-tending dream (45a), since the pencil-stealing dream, too, has modified the disturbing impulse in order to diminish the danger of offending the analyst. The borrowed book dream (27) occurs after the disturbing impulse has already been repudiated (at the end of the pencil-stealing dream [25] and in the broom dream [26]); and, with this attempt at repudiation, the nature of the patient's problem has changed. The problem in the borrowed book dream (27) is one of self-justification, of rationalizing away the patient's sense of guilt for accepting the analyst's help while he still wishes to "mistreat" her child. *Instead of finding a compromise impulse* to act upon, *this dream (27)*, having repudiated action, *has confronted cognitively his two conflicting wishes.* This dream is trying to argue away the sense of guilt that results from confronting a need for help with a hostile wish toward the mother-figure who is helping him.

In the fire-tending dream (45a) tonic innervation of the lower bowel is used to bind the pressure of the disturbing impulse. In the borrowed book dream (27) holding onto possessions is employed to absorb the pressure not only of one but of both sides of the patient's conflict. By holding onto possessions, the dreamer is seeking a substitute for his need for a mother's love as well as for his compensatory impulse to return a child to her mother; and this double substitution has succeeded in transforming his very disturbing personal conflict in relation to a mother-figure into the much less disturbing impersonal problem of returning a borrowed possession. In brief: The internal absorption mechanisms in these two dreams differ not only in timing and in physiological pattern but also in function, which is one of *mitigating a disturbing impulse in the fire-tending dream (45)*, one of *mitigating both sides of a guilt conflict in the borrowed book dream (27)*.

Another Money Dream in Cycle 3.—Our comparison of the borrowed book dream (27) and the fire-tending dream (45*a*) suggests the notion of a succession of phases in each of the two cycles to which these two dreams (27, 45*a*) respectively belong and of phases in each cycle corresponding to each of the phases of the other. We suspect that the phasic position of the borrowed book dream (27) in cycle 2 is later than that of the fire-tending dream (45*a*) in cycle 3 and that the dream in cycle 2 which corresponds in phasic position to the fire-tending dream (45*a*) is the pencil-stealing dream (25). If this reasoning is correct, we should expect to encounter later in cycle 3 a dream whose dynamic and physiological pattern is similar to that of the borrowed book dream (27).

This expectation is fulfilled by the $20.00 bill dream (60*c*). The $20.00 bill dream (60*c*) is again an attempt to justify the patient against his sense of guilt on account of his hostile impulses toward the child of a mother from whom he wishes to receive. Again, as in the borrowed book dream (27), money has been substituted for the mother's love that he craves, as well as for the child for whose care he is responsible; and again, as in the earlier dream (27), he must reject the gift because he wishes to get rid of the child.

Evidently, in the interval between fire-tending dream (45*a*) and $20.00 bill dream (60*c*) there has again been a transition from an attempt to bind the pressure of the disturbing impulse, to an attempt to transform the whole interpersonal situation into a much less personal one.

CHAPTER LVII

Functional Significance of the Boxcar Dreams

We have been studying the relations between our patient's water dreams, his possessive impulses, and his grasping-hand patterns. Now in order to bring talking and the boxcar symbolism into the comparison we shall first compare the two boxcar dreams (25 and 43) with the two money dreams (27 and 60c), and then study the functional transitions in the series of consecutive dreams that begins with the fireplug dream (19a) and ends with the borrowed book dream (27).

Two Boxcar Dreams and Two Money Dreams.—In the pencil-stealing dream (25) the objects in the boxcar that the patient is tempted to steal are characterized as "merchandise." This suggests a physiological pattern similar to that of the borrowed book dream (27) in which possessions are being held onto, loaned and returned, taken and thrown away. In the pencil-stealing dream (25) the role of the mother, as symbolized by the boxcar, is one of holding onto these possessions. The switchman may be thought of as offering them to the patient, the patient as taking them.

However, in the pencil-stealing dream (25) most of the pressure of the patient's conflict is channeled into trying to answer the watchman's question; and, with pressure thus deflected from the mother's role, she can be replaced by a deanimated symbol, the boxcar.

Similarly, in the other boxcar dream, the pig dream (43), the "lady" is one who owes the patient money. This shows that in this dream (43), too, there are traces of a tendency for the patient to seek to justify himself, as in the borrowed book and $20.00 bill dreams (27 and 60c), by substituting money for children. Yet in the pig dream (43), even more than in the pencil-stealing dream (25), the pressure of the patient's conflict has been channeled into talk, into an attempt to achieve reconciliation with the analyst by means of mutual understanding and confession. In this

313

dream (43), emphasis has shifted completely from action to talking.

Transition from Fireplug Dream to Borrowed Book Dream.— To elucidate the relations between the pencil-stealing dream (25) and the dreams that precede and follow it, we shall next study the functional transitions that lead from the fireplug dream (19*a*) to the borrowed book dream (27).

The fireplug dream (19*a*) is a dream of action in response to the analyst's encouragement. In the borrowed book dream (27), instead of acting, the patient is repudiating the analyst's encouragement and attempting to bind the pressure of his disturbing impulses by holding onto possessions. The pencil-stealing dream (25) occurs at the turning point in this transition. In the first part of this dream he responds positively, even though hesitantly, to the switchman's temptation, by taking the pencils; but after the watchman appears, he closes the door of the boxcar as a token of renouncing the temptation.

This transition from action to inhibition occurs in several steps. (1) As a first step we recognize, even in the first part of the pencil-stealing dream (25), that the patient's response to the analyst's encouragement has become more cautious. In the fireplug dream (19*a*) he embraced and kissed the young girl, but in the pencil-stealing dream (25) he only very timidly and hesitantly performs a trivial symbolic act. (2) A second step in this transition begins when the watchman appears. Now for a short time the dream action centers no longer on doing something, but on thinking and talking, on trying to explain the situation in answer to the watchman's question. This phase ends when he closes the door of the boxcar. (3) A third phase is his struggle to repudiate the analyst's encouragement, which starts with his closing the door of the boxcar in the pencil-stealing dream (25) and then comes to clear expression in the broom dream (26); (4) in a fourth phase this repudiation of the analyst's seductive encouragement is supplemented by the attempt in the borrowed book dream (27) to bind the disturbing pressures by holding onto possessions.

We shall now study this transitional process in greater detail. *First and Second Transitional Phases: Motor Inhibition, then*

Substitution of Talking for Acting.—In the fireplug dream (19*a*) the patient's erotic response to the analyst's encouragement was followed by abrupt inhibition; but the wave of inhibition was short lived. Even in the brake dream (19*b*) he is being reproved not for his forbidden impulses but for putting on the brakes too energetically; and in the first part of the pencil-stealing dream (25) he is again responding positively to the analyst's encouragement.

However, the pencil-stealing dream soon gives evidence of the beginning of a much more prolonged wave of inhibition. It is this beginning of a longer wave of inhibition that we are interested in studying now.

The substitution of a trivial symbolic act and then of talking in the pencil-stealing dream (25) implies a partial inhibition of the underlying disturbing impulses.[1] Yet talking is entirely inadequate as an outlet for his violently aggressive impulses and must, therefore, undergo physiological disintegration and discharge in the acute asthmatic attack with which the dreamer awakens. All the characteristic features[1] of this dream are consequences of its attempt to permit only a limited and cautious discharge of the pressure of the underlying disturbing impulses during the period while the patient is testing out the analyst's attitude toward these impulses.

However, this testing-out of the analyst is a transitional phenomenon. In the first part of the fireplug dream (19*a*) his hopes of the analyst's indulgence were dominant, and he acted on them. In the broom dream (26) and borrowed book dream (27) his fears are dominant, and he struggles to repudiate the analyst's encouragement. In the pencil-stealing dream (25), hope and fear are nearly in equilibrium; and at this point a judicial process of

1. We have already discussed (see chap. xxvii of this volume) how other important features of this dream have resulted from the need to hold in restraint the patient's underlying aggressive impulses against the mother's pregnancy. To this end the analyst's role in the patient's life must be divided into three parts. In order to avoid sensing how she must react to his agressive impulses toward her, an inanimate symbol, the boxcar, has been substituted for her in so far as she is the object of these disturbing impulses. Only in her real role as someone to whom he can talk and on whose approval he is dependent, can she be represented by two persons, the switchman and the watchman.

weighing his hope and his fear against each other begins. First, he tests the analyst by a trivial symbolic act; then for a moment he considers and discusses the question of whether her attitude is really as permissive as he hoped.

During the brief conversation with the watchman the problem with which the dreamer is struggling is one of regaining rapport with the analyst (watchman) by means of speech. He has just acted on the assumption that she is permissive, like the switchman. The open door of the boxcar is a symbol of this permissive attitude. Now there arises a doubt as to whether she has really given him permission to take those pencils. Perhaps the door should have been closed all the time. The watchman appears to represent her in this presumably prohibitive role. During the brief conversation with the watchman the patient is debating whether or not the analyst really intended to "leave the door open." He does not wish to offend her by taking for granted a permission that she is not willing to give.

Then the still undischarged pressure of the disturbing aggressive impulses stirs up his fears more intensely and destroys the momentary equilibrium that made it possible for him to balance and discuss alternatives. Now comes a wave of inhibition so strong that it promptly blocks thought and speech as well as action and permits him to utter only one word "No." The urge to speak more at length undergoes physiological disintegration and is discharged in a severe attack of asthma.

Third Phase: Repudiation of Analyst's Encouragement.—However, in the broom dream (26), reported in the next hour, he must struggle to justify himself. We can best understand the significance of this broom dream by comparing it with the earlier railroad station dream (10*b*). In the earlier dream (10*b*) he blamed and turned away from his wife as a symbol of temptation, to seek approval from the analyst as a mother-figure. In the broom dream (26) he is blaming and turning away from the analyst's encouragement, but he is seeking approval not from a mother-figure but from his own conscience or from some kind of "public opinion" symbolized by a "bunch of men."

Interpreting the analyst's tolerance for his forbidden impulses as a seduction, the broom dream tries to justify the dreamer by attributing to her encouragement his impulse to hit a child (squirrel). "I wanted you to teach me how to be a man," the argument of the dream (26) runs, "but you tell me to kill a child."

Social standards that are well-nigh universal regard it as cowardly for a man to attack a helpless chlid and condemn especially severely hostile impulses toward anyone from whom one has received help. The projection mechanism in the broom dream (26) succeeds temporarily in protecting the patient against these standards by attributing responsibility for his hostile impulse to suggestion from someone else and by obliterating the relationship between his hostile impulses and the person vitally affected by these impulses from whom he is receiving help. When stripped of the projection by means of which the dreamer is trying to justify himself, the argument of the broom dream (26) reduces to the following: "I want you to help me but I also want to destroy your child." However, in the dream text (26) he wishes to be taught the masculine sport of golf, and someone else is expecting him to hit the squirrel. By keeping these two wishes from being brought into relation with each other the dream forestalls the reactivation of the social sanctions against wishing ill to someone from whom he has received help.

But what if these two wishes should be seen in relation to each other as part of a single cognitive field? In that case we must expect that he will either become aware of guilt feelings or attempt some sort of self-justification against the charge of wishing to hurt someone from whom he is receiving help. From our analysis of the borrowed book dream (27) we know that the second of these alternatives corresponds to what actually occurred.

Fourth and Last Phase: Attempt To Absorb Excess Pressure by Holding onto Possessions.—When the watchman first confronted the patient with the task of justifying himself in the pencil-stealing dream (25), the patient was able to utter only the single word "No"; then his need to make an explanation underwent physiological disintegration into an attack of asthma. Yet in the borrowed book dream (27) a few days later he has been able to respond to the same need for an explanation by elaborating a self-justifying argument. This contrast between the two dreams (25 and 27) suggests a question. What has happened in the interval between the two dreams to make it possible for him to elaborate in the borrowed book dream (27) the self-justifying explanation that he could only choke over in the pencil-stealing dream (25)?

The explanation is to be found in the borrowed book dream's (27) attempt to bind the pressure of the disturbing wishes by holding onto possessions. In the pencil-stealing dream (25) the re-emergence of his fear of offending the mother suddenly confronted him with a conflict too intense to be spanned by his unstable hope of permissive indulgence from the analyst. In the borrowed book dream (27) much of the disturbing pressure is being channeled into tonic impulses to hold onto possessions. This has diminished the integrative task and brought it within the span of his hope for the analyst's indulgence for his self-justifying argument.

This relief of the integrative mechanism by the pressure-absorbing effect of holding onto possessions is the last step in the transition from fireplug dream (19a) to borrowed book dream (27).

Transitional Position of the Two Boxcar Dreams.—In both the boxcar dreams (25 and 43) that we have studied, the dream action, at least for a moment, centers on talking. This suggests that there may be a complementary relationship[2] between the boxcar symbolism and trying to regain rapport with the analyst by means of speech. A boxcar is a devaluated symbol of pregnancy, a mere container rather than an evidence of the mother's encompassing love. We suspect that the notion of being encompassed by the mother's love can be deprived of its tenderness just because the patient's longing for the mother is being channeled elsewhere, into talk.

In the pencil-stealing dream (25), this attempt to channel the pressure of his conflict into speech occurs at the moment of transition from acting to inhibition. The centering of dream action on speech in the pig dream (43) occurs at a similar point of transition, although this time it is a transition in the opposite direction—from inhibition to action. The pig dream (43) follows the dirty food dream (39) and the pump dream (41), in which the patient is repudiating the analyst's encouragement and trying

2. See chap. xxvii of this volume.

to get rid of his dirty thoughts, and is followed by the Mexican woman dream (44), in which he is actively co-operating with the analyst in her therapeutic task. Thus in the pig dream (43), as in the pencil-stealing dream (25), centering of the dream action on talk occurs at a moment when hope of the analyst's encouragement and fear of rebuff are nearly in equilibrium and a judicial process of weighing his hope against his fear is thus made possible. In later chapters[3] we shall inquire whether this formula is applicable also to other boxcar dreams of this patient.

3. See Vol. IV.

CHAPTER LVIII

A Survey of Interrelations between Physiological Patterns

We shall now summarize the preceding chapters from another point of view by sketching out some of the relations between elementary physiological patterns that serve as a common background for all of this patient's dreams. The schematic outline to be discussed in this chapter will be elaborated more thoroughly in Volume IV.

The integration of goal-directed behavior involves three different kinds of physiological absorption[1] of the pressure of the motivating need. These are: discharge or temporary absorption of pressure by motor activity, temporary absorption of pressure by fantasy, temporary absorption of pressure by interest in external stimuli. As a starting point for our analysis of the relations

---

1. See Vol. I, chap. xl; and for explanation of the concept of physiological absorption, see Vol. I, chaps. xxvii, xxviii, and xxix, p. 140, and also chap. xxiii of this volume.

To follow the argument of this chapter, it is important not to confuse physiological absorption of pressure with ultimate satisfaction of the need or wish whose pressure is being absorbed. Physiological absorption is a temporary event. In its striving toward final satisfaction, a goal-directed effort usually activates successively many different patterns of physiological activity, each of which, we postulate, temporarily absorbs the activating pressure.

Neither the motivating pressures that we postulate nor the physiological activities that are activated by them should be confused with the vector tendencies postulated by Alexander (1935). A motivating pressure (as we define the term) does not have a direction of its own but acquires direction only after it has been channeled through an integrative field. As we stated in Volume I (p. 60), "motivating pressure toward a goal is motivating pressure that has been rechanneled through a guiding integrative field by the hope of achieving a positive goal." And the physiological activities activated by a particular goal-directed effort usually do not all have the same vector tendency in Alexander's sense. My end-goal may be to get food and eat it (receptive vector), but getting the food may require energetic muscular activity (eliminatory vector), and preparing it may require considerable planning (retentive vector, according to Alexander) and keeping materials in readiness (retentive vector) until the proper time to use them.

between different kinds of behavior, we shall first consider behavior in which one or another of these physiological absorption mechanisms is predominant and shall inquire under what circumstances emphasis shifts from one kind of physiological absorption to another.

Aggressive Behavior.—Behavior in which motor discharge is predominant we shall call "active" or "aggressive"[2] behavior.

In the simplest active behavior, motor discharge is supplemented by channeling small amounts of pressure through a guiding integrative field. We can distinguish different kinds of active behavior according to the nature of the relationship between motor discharge and the guiding integrative field. When the motor mechanisms are in a state of functional readiness and the pressure of underlying needs is not high, activity takes on a playful character, with perhaps greater discharge of motor energy than is necessary to achieve the goal, or even with a tendency to easy shifting of goals. In such a case we may speak of "playful activity." When the pressure of the underlying need is higher, obstacles in the way of achieving the goal stimulate energetic efforts to overcome them. Such behavior we shall call "aggressive effort." On the other hand, excessive pressure resulting from frustration may result in disintegration of the guiding integrative mechanism and in more or less goal-less discharge of the accumulated energy. This is the mechanism of an attack of rage or a temper tantrum.

Motor Discharge in Flight.—When aggressive behavior encounters serious obstacles or involves one in danger, fear of disturbing consequences may considerably modify its pattern of motor discharge.

In the simplest case, overt aggression merely gives place to flight: The predominant physiological pattern continues to be motor discharge, but its goal changes. For example, when a fleeing cat turns to snarl, the dog that is chasing it may turn tail and

2. The word "aggressive" in ordinary speech usually implies hostile or destructive behavior or at least energetic overriding of obstacles. Behavior in which motor discharge is predominant may or may not be "aggressive" in this sense. When it is particularly important to avoid the hostile or destructive implications of the word "aggressive," we shall use the word "active" instead.

run away. Similarly, in our patient's kindly policeman dream (17), his desire to show up the real estate man gives way to precipitate flight.

Preoccupation with Anticipated Consequences.—When flight is impossible for some reason, pressure is next focused on the anticipated consequences. For example, in the anvil dream (12), the pressure of the patient's aggressive impulses (both sexual and hostile) has been deflected into a fantasy of being beaten. In the most extreme cases the anticipated consequences may be experienced as a hallucination.

Preoccupation with external stimulation, anticipated, received from, or inflicted by the external world, we shall call "sensory" or "receptive" absorption of pressure. In the mechanism just described, fear of consequences results in *replacement of a pattern of motor discharge by one of receptive absorption.*

A special case of preoccupation with anticipated consequences is the mechanism known in the psychoanalytic literature as *turning back aggression against one's self,*[3] or as punishment according to the talion principle: An aggressive wish is inhibited and then gives rise to the fear or wish that someone else will do to the aggressor what he wishes to do to his victim.

Such turning-back of an aggressive impulse against one's self is usually a sign that the inhibiting motive was fear of hurting or offending a loved person or someone on whom one is dependent. We can deduce this mechanism from our reconstruction[4] of how we understand the motives of another person: To understand another person, I must identify with him, we postulate; my being deterred from beating someone by reluctance to hurt him implies that a physiological pattern has been activated in me, similar to the pattern that would be activated if I were myself being beaten. However, cognitive grasp of the notion of hurting someone else requires that I distinguish my own role as the one who is doing the beating from the role of the other person who is being beaten; a superordinated interpersonal field must keep separate the patterns of hurting and being hurt, ascribing the latter to the other person. Yet the interpersonal field may be inadequate for this

3. See S. Freud, 1919.
4. See chap. xxv of this volume.

task. If the physiological pattern corresponding to the role of being beaten is too intensely activated, I may no longer be able to ascribe this role to the other person and will then imagine myself being beaten. This, we postulate, is what occurs when reluctance to hurt another person energetically inhibits my too intense aggressive impulse toward him: The pressure of my impulse to beat him is diverted from motor discharge and concentrated on the already activated pattern corresponding to the role of being beaten. And this too intensely activated pattern, which can no longer be projected as the role of another person, now emerges as a fear or expectation of myself being beaten.

Pain as a Sign of Excessive Absorption of Pressure.—The capacity of the sensory functions to absorb pressure is not great. Excessive external stimulation is painful and interferes with sensory discrimination and perception; and the sensory functions have also a low threshold for absorbing internal pressure; excessive pressure is experienced as unpleasant or painful.

The oral fantasies in our patient's water dreams illustrate these principles. In these dreams, as pressure increases, satisfying oral fantasies are replaced by unpleasant fantasies of being forced to drink dirty water and then by sensations of suffocation and choking.[5] Similarly after the anvil dream (12) the patient's pains in muscles and joints are signs of the excessive pressure of his fantasy of being beaten.

Cognitive Elaboration of Pressure in Visual Projection.—Instead of picturing the patient as either beating or being beaten, the anvil dream (12) has absorbed the pressure of both these fantasies in a visual image of the mother beating an iron bar. Thus in the anvil dream patterns of motor discharge and of sensory absorption have been replaced by a visual pattern.

On first thought we should perhaps classify visual elaboration as a form of sensory absorption of pressure. Yet the function of vision in this dream is predominantly one of cognitive grasp rather than a purely sensory one. A dream of a flash of light might appropriately be classified as an example of sensory absorption of pressure comparable to the satisfaction in drinking a glass of milk or to the sensations of suffocation associated with the

5. See chap. xxxviii of this volume.

water symbolism or to the pains in muscles and joints that followed the anvil dream (12); but vision more than other senses is able to show us objects in relation to one another. In the anvil dream it serves the function of integrating the physiological patterns corresponding to beating and being beaten, so as to permit them to be grasped or understood as two roles in a single act. Such understanding of objects or of physiological patterns in relation to one another is what we mean by "cognitive grasp." A visual field is a prototype of the cognitive and integrative fields by means of which behavior is guided to its goals. We prefer, therefore, to classify *absorption by visual imagery* as *one form of cognitive elaboration of pressure*.

Cognitive Elaboration of Pressure by Talking and by Understanding Speech.—Another form of cognitive elaboration of pressure is the understanding of speech. The understanding of speech differs from just hearing a noise in the same way that the visual perception of relations between objects differs from seeing a flash of light.

As examples of attempts at cognitive elaboration of pressure by means of speech, we select the patient's attempts to understand the analyst's attitude toward his forbidden wishes and to explain or justify his own impulses toward her, that begins with the brake dream (19b). In this brake dream his confusion about whether he is being encouraged or rebuked is evidence of failure of this cognitive effort. In the pencil-stealing dream (25) his attempt to make explanations to the watchman disintegrates into an attack of asthma. In the borrowed book dream (27), in response to the same need to make explanations, he has found a self-justifying argument.

Thus in the brake dream (19b) and in the pencil-stealing dream (25) we have unsuccessful attempts at cognitive elaboration of the pressure of his conflict by means of speech. In the borrowed book dream (27) his attempt to absorb the pressure of his conflict by problem-solving intellectual activity has been temporarily successful.

Tonic Motor Absorption of Pressure and Its Supplementary Relationship to the Cognitive Functions.—In the pencil-stealing dream (25) the attempt to find an explanation failed because the cognitive mechanism necessary for speech did not have sufficient integrative capacity to bind the pressure of the patient's emerging conflict. We have already discussed[6] why the borrowed book dream (27) was able to carry the search for an explanation further. In this dream the tonic muscular activity of holding onto possessions was able temporarily to relieve the pressure on the cognitive mechanism underlying thought and speech.

Thus these two dreams (25 and 27) illustrate dynamic relations between two kinds of internal elaboration of pressure. These we shall call "cognitive elaboration" and "tonic motor absorption." Cognitive elaboration of pressure is of central importance in the integrative process; but tonic motor innervations are also important because their capacity to absorb pressure is quantitatively much greater than that of the cognitive functions. Like sensory discrimination and perception, cognitive grasp is much impaired by excessive pressure. Tonic motor absorption of pressure has a function that is supplementary to the cognitive process. The function of tonic motor absorption is to spare the cognitive apparatus by relieving pressure upon it and thus to make possible an increase in the integrative capacity available for the problem-solving cognitive process.

In the dreams of our patient, two patterns of tonic motor absorption play prominent roles. In the borrowed book dream (27) the pattern is one of holding onto possessions, involving tonic innervations of arm and hand. Closely associated with the frozen gutter dream (67) we have evidence of another mechanism of tonic absorption of pressure—in the symptom of constipation, involving tonic innervation of the lower bowel.

A Way of Classifying Substitution Mechanisms.—Until now we have discussed shifts of emphasis from patterns of motor discharge to patterns of sensory absorption and then to cognitive elaboration, which may be supplemented by tonic motor absorption of pressure. Such designation of shifts of emphasis from one physiological pattern to another offers us a convenient way of classifying the mechanisms of substitution that we find in the process of dream organization. As we have already pointed out,

6. See preceding chapter, p. 318.

turning back aggression against one's self usually involves replacement of a pattern of motor discharge by one of sensory absorption. Projection often involves visual or other cognitive elaboration of a pattern of motor discharge or of sensory absorption. Many of the mechanisms included under the concept of anal erotic regression in the psychoanalytic literature involve a shift from motor discharge or sensory absorption to tonic motor absorption.

There are also possible shifts that we have not yet considered. A shift from sensory absorption to motor discharge we shall call *reactive aggression*. When tonic motor absorption gives place to motor discharge or sensory absorption we shall speak of the *emergence of motor discharge or of sensory excitation from tonic motor absorption.*[7]

We shall postpone more extended discussion of these mechanisms and of more complex physiological patterns until Volume IV.

Summary.—Summarizing our discussion in this chapter, we picture as follows some of the dynamic relationships between physiological patterns that are basic for the integration of both normal and neurotic behavior and of dreams:

In the absence of distracting influences or inhibitory factors such as sleep or the fear of consequences, we infer that any considerable amounts of pressure will tend predominantly to seek motor discharge, supplemented by diversion of small amounts of pressure to a guiding integrative field and to orienting interest in external stimuli. Active or aggressive behavior is behavior in which relatively uninhibited motor discharge of pressure is more or less successfully subordinated to the task of overcoming obstacles in the way of achieving a positive goal.

When motor discharge is inhibited by fear of consequences, the displaced pressure tends first to be focused on anticipation of consequences in accordance with past experiences. If loss of the love of another person is the consequence that is most feared, the pressure will then tend to be focused on fantasies of suffering from someone else the same pain that one had originally wished to inflict upon the other person. Physiologically, both these

7. See our discussion of the fire symbolism in chap. l of this volume.

mechanisms consist in the substitution of sensory or receptive absorption for motor discharge of pressure.

If a certain threshold is exceeded, sensory absorption of pressures becomes painful, increasingly so with increase of pressure. As this threshold is approached or exceeded, pressure tends to be diverted elsewhere.

If the threshold of sensory absorption has been exceeded and motor discharge continues to be inhibited, mechanisms of internal elaboration of pressure tend to be activated.

There are two main classes of internal elaboration of pressure. These are cognitive elaboration and tonic motor absorption. Of these, tonic motor absorption is the mechanism that is capable of absorbing much the larger amount of pressure. The cognitive functions are increasingly impaired with increase of pressure if their rather low threshold is exceeded.

The principles governing the distribution of pressure between tonic motor absorption and cognitive elaboration have not yet been satisfactorily worked out in our material, but for the present we shall assume as a working hypothesis that pressure tends, first, to be diverted to cognitive elaboration and, after that, to tonic motor absorption when the threshold for cognitive elaboration is exceeded. This hypothesis accords well with the sequence of the pencil-stealing dream (25) and borrowed book dream (27) and is also illustrated by the frozen gutter dream (67) in which visual projection (one form of cognitive elaboration) is supplemented by the freezing-up (tonic motor absorption) of the symbol of flowing water.[8]

8. See chap. xli of this volume.

CHAPTER LIX
Recapitulation and Preview

As we pointed out at the beginning of these studies,[1] we habitually assume that a person's behavior is determined by two sets of factors: (1) a relatively permanent constellation of reaction patterns, which we call his "personality," and (2) the situation to which he is reacting at a particular time. Starting with this preliminary formulation, we proposed an empirical method for reconstructing the pattern of a patient's personality. By exploring and comparing his dreams, we hoped to find a constellation of underlying reaction patterns common to them all. And while we were isolating factors common to a number of dreams, we hoped also to split off the factors in which these dreams differ and to learn in this way how different situations activate different parts of the dreamer's personality.

We have now completed our preliminary survey of the interrelations between our patient's dreams. In the historical backgrounds of all the dreams that we have studied, we have found evidence of reactions to his mother's many pregnancies. Sometimes the patient reacted to these memories erotically with fantasies of impregnating the mother. In other dreams the patient's resentment of the mother's pregnancies was more in evidence, giving rise to impulses to do violence to the expected child, to fears of losing the mother's love as a consequence, and to attempts to avoid estranging the mother by turning back his aggressive impulses against himself, by substituting trivial or harmless symbolic acts for these violent impulses, or by reacting with self-justifying fantasies.

Thus the historical backgrounds of all these dreams are centered about the same constellations of childhood conflicts. The dreams differ chiefly in their symbolism and in their physiological patterns. In the water dreams impulses to urinate and fantasies of drinking or of being suffocated play a central role. Another

1. See I, 5.

group of dreams centers about impulses to reach out arm and hand to grasp something or to give or throw something away. In the two boxcar dreams talking plays a significant role, and in several other dreams there is preoccupation with constipation or with holding onto possessions.

In the last few chapters we have found these different physiological patterns related to one another in two different ways. Sometimes one pattern replaces another in successive steps in the process of organization of a single dream. At other times there is a transition from one to the other of the same two patterns in successive dreams. In our last chapter we tried to work out some of the principles on which transitions from one physiological pattern to another are based.

Thus we have found confirmation for the hypothesis with which we started—that the constellations of fantasy patterns underlying this patient's dreams are all parts of a single intercommunicating system and that, under the activating influence of different present situations, sometimes one and sometimes another part of this system is brought into focus, while other parts fade into the background.

Having mapped out some of the main features of this underlying system of reaction paterns, we are now ready for the task which we have reserved for our third volume: to trace the successive emergence of different constellations during the course of our patient's treatment. Our account of the patient's first three dream cycles[2] was already a first step toward this goal.

In order to understand the recurring, but ever varying, sequences in our patient's dreams and other behavior, it will be necessary to separate out some of the factors responsible for different kinds of transformations of cognitive pattern. This will lead us over into our task for Volume IV, which will be to analyze our patient's behavior into some of its component factors. We have already presented a few samples[3] of this kind of analysis.

2. See chap. liv of this volume.
3. See especially chaps. xli, lvi, and lviii of this volume.

APPENDIX

Appendix

CASE REPORT AND INTERPRETIVE COMMENT[1]

The patient, a forty-six-year-old married man, worked in a railroad yard. He was referred by a well-recognized allergist for analysis because of asthma, for which he had been under treatment at an out-patient clinic for a number of years.

He was the oldest of six children. His father, a blacksmith in a small village in Poland, was strict and severe with the children, did not allow them to talk in his presence except when spoken to, and punished them severely for any infraction of discipline. The patient was very much afraid of him.

According to the patient, he got along well with his mother, who used to help him out in arguments with his father. When asked about real upsets in his life, he mentioned only his mother's death, which occurred when he was thirty-nine.

One of his earliest memories was being kicked by a horse, when he was seven. Afraid that his father would demand to know why he was in the blacksmith shop, he started to run away rather than tell him; but a neighbor took him home. Afterward, his father "raised hell" about paying the hospital bill. His nose was "broken and caved in" as a result of the accident, which left a permanent scar.

He also recalled vividly being frightened by a dog in an open space at the age of ten or twelve.

He wanted to be a blacksmith like his father, but his father said, "That is no life." He had a very difficult time in school and was sent away from home at eleven to attend school. At fifteen he was beaten by his father for flunking his examinations, and he ran away to live with his mother's people. It was then arranged that he take a mechanic's training for three years, also away from home. His father always rejected him after this.

The patient never got along well with the brother, who was two years younger, but his relationship with his four other younger siblings (two brothers and two sisters) was always very pleasant.

He came to America when he was twenty and at first had a difficult time. But after two years of skipping from one job to another, he held one job for thirteen years and then changed to the job which he still held at the time of the treatment, eleven years later.

According to his report, his first attack of asthma occurred around Christmas time when he was nine or ten years old. His second attack,

1. Reprinted from Vol. I, chaps. xvii and xxxiii, and xviii and xxxiv.

333

at the age of twelve, was on Christmas Eve. The family thought he had a cold, but he remembered distinctly that he wheezed. At six, when he was supposed to start in school, he had an itching eczema like a rash all over his face. This kept him home from school and isolated from other children. When he was twenty-six, he developed what seemed like hay fever, with much coughing and sneezing and sinus trouble. This lasted for four years. His skin, always very sensitive, felt raw and itchy and burned after shaving. During this time he was in the army for four months. He was discharged, chiefly because of illness associated with his hay fever and cough. He felt that his stay in the army had made this condition worse. Then, at the age of thirty, asthma developed; his first attack was severe. At that time he already was interested in the girl he later married, but was also going around with other girls.

At the age of thirty-three he married. He said that he was happy with his wife for a little over a year. The time of their increasing unhappiness coincided with their buying a school-supply shop, which she ran and which occasioned arguments; this was also the year of her first pregnancy. He insisted that he wanted children. He was still very unhappy with his wife when he started therapy. He complained that she was very critical; that she quarreled with him so that the neighbors could hear; that she didn't give sufficient attention to his diet; that she was careless of her own personal appearance and had doubled her weight since he married her; and that she neglected the children. She was a good housekeeper and kept the house clean. His attacks of asthma were not improved by his marriage but got worse as the marriage became unhappy. He had noticed that the attacks were often precipitated by a quarrel with his wife or by disagreements with the workers at his job. He admitted no conflicts with his two sons (aged twelve and nine) but said they were not getting on well at school.

He had apparently a good social life with men; he joined lodges and enjoyed his work. At times in his life he had gambled. He lost three or four thousand dollars during the crash in 1929. While the market was good, he said he had very little asthma, but when the market crashed he got sick and went to the hospital.

During the first few hours of his analysis this rather inarticulate man found talking freely about personal matters very difficult; also, severe asthmatic wheezing made him uncomfortable. In the sixth hour he experienced much relief when, finally voicing freely his resentments against his wife, he complained that she was fat, sloppy, and quarrelsome and neglected the two children and himself.

In the ninth hour the analyst expressed interest in dreams. At the beginning of the tenth hour the patient reported the following dreams, the first in the analysis. He introduced the first with the remark that he had had a dream: "That's what you want," he added. The dream was dreamed New Year's Eve and reported January 2, as follows:

Dream 10a.—Dream of school days. In weekend I was going home. We always walked unless someone picked us up. I walked alone until I got to bridge. A girl was there leaning on bridge, watching boats. I stopped and pinched her on back, and then we walked on home. Getting dusk. Mother met her and thanked me and asked me in and gave me a glass of milk.

Dream 10b.—Last night kind of embarrassing. I was in railroad station with a lot of people. Wife and me. We were separated, she in one end and I in other. Old friends around. They came and asked me why I married her. I dodged her too.

Dream 10c.—Something toward morning about doctors and ladies. I was taking some kind of treatment. Doctors taking culture. Lady comes along and says now we've hit spot.

Associations.—The patient insisted that the woman in the last dream was not like the analyst but like a servant girl. The bridge was one on which he used to play. It shook when the wagons went over it. "Lots of fun there. Road leading home. It was level. There were trees around and on both sides fields and gardens; nice scenery." The girl lived along the road. No, the patient was not interested in her. He was seldom in her company, only met her going and coming from school. He used to meet girls on the bridge. The mother in the dream was elderly, pleasant. Her son came along with her to meet the girl. The old lady took him to the basement for a cold glass of milk. It was good milk with cream in it, refreshing in summer. The mother . . . had gray hair and was stooped like a farmer's wife. Yes, exactly like the patient's mother. The boy hung around behind his mother and said nothing. A boy of about twelve. The patient was fourteen or sixteen when he went on this road, the boy was younger. Yes, his next younger brother was two years younger. The patient had a sister who died at about ten of scarlet fever. . . . "We all liked her." The girl in the dream was older and taller than this sister.

In association to the railroad station, the patient remembered that the railroad was close to the lake front. He could see the lake (an obvious reference to the analyst's home, where she saw the patient). . . . The patient and his wife were there. The wife was not well-dressed: she was sloppy. The patient was sidestepping her. One lady asked why the patient married her. She said she was sorry the patient had married her. The dream was embarrassing.

At this point the analyst interpreted the dream as the fulfilment of a wish that she sympathize with his desire to leave his wife. The patient replied that he had not liked his wife at first but was talked into marrying her. He boarded with her sister and so became associated with the family. Her mother said she would not mind if the patient married her daughter. He was tired of eating around. Her sister was a good housekeeper and cook, and he figured she was like a home girl. The analyst remarked that the patient married her for a home, that he wanted someone to take care of him like a mother.

In the next hour he confessed that he never put any value on dreams and then complained that he could not stand loud talking or sleep with any kind of noise. He spent the rest of the hour protesting against his wife's loud talking and against the idea of "wives and mothers" talking about sex.

In the twelfth hour, three days later, he brought the following dream:

Dream 12.—Can't remember it. About father and mother. Seems mother doing blacksmith work. She had hot iron and was hammering.

When the analyst reminded him that his father was a blacksmith, he added a few details:

Father was also in the dream but not so clear as mother; he was standing on side of shop, kind of dark. Plainly see my mother. She had hot iron and working at it, flattening it out, and bending it, doing clean work, good job too.

In association he stated that his mother had never done any blacksmith work, although she might have come to the door of the shop.

Corresponding to the patient's inarticulate character, he was quickly through with his associations; so the analyst tried to help him out. She suggested that perhaps she seemed like a woman doing a man's job.

The patient did not reply to the analyst's comment but continued to dwell admiringly on the details of the mother's work in his memory of the dream:

Father standing on side. Mother took iron out of fire, performing the work on it. Long piece of heavy iron.

The iron resembled iron used on the locomotive to pull out clinkers. His mother was shaping it. There was a hook on the end of it.

The analyst remarked that if she was bending the patient like iron, he must be afraid. He agreed that he really was afraid of the analysis. He did not know what it was all about and felt helpless because he was in the dark.

In the next hour, three days later, the patient reported that he had vomited and had had a stomach-ache the day before, after drinking three glasses of beer and winning twenty dollars at poker. He also had lumbago on his left side. The rest of the hour was spent discussing his bad conscience when he won at poker and his need to give at least some of the money back.

In the fourteenth hour, four days later, he complained of a stiff neck. ... He continued: the last time he was here he had a pain in his back; the next day he had a stiff knee and could hardly walk. ... Then he reported a dream:

Dream 14.—My younger boy had awful large snake—tame. He played with it. I was scared . . . snake would sneak into pillow case. Snake had V-face, and flat and pointed, run around eyes, on face a smile or laugh. Snake awful fat.

The patient's associations to this dream were repeatedly interrupted by complaints about the pain in his neck, which filled most of the hour. His younger son, Vincent, was playing with the snake. He looked contented and was not scared but liked it. The patient noticed the snake sneak into the pillowcase. The child walked over and pulled it out. The patient laughed when asked to associate to the snake's going into the pillowcase. He didn't like snakes, got sick. There were a lot of snakes where he worked. They were harmless, but he didn't like them. The other men caught them and put them in his coat pocket. Had he been aware of their doing this, he would never have worn the coat.

He commented that the snake was very big and reminded him of his fat wife. The analyst suggested that the reference was to his wife's pregnancy with the patient's younger child and that his stiff neck was a reaction to his jealousy of his wife's caring for the baby.

Immediately after the snake dream (14), the patient missed two appointments because of illness. In the fifteenth hour he complained that the cold weather was aggravating his wheezing, choking him up. The analyst remarked that a child left out in the cold by the mother can get love by being sick. The patient then told of an argument he had had with a man at work about the federal bonus. The patient was for it. The other man called him "foreign-born." The two nearly came to blows. The patient started wheezing while telling this and recalled that the argument also started up his asthma at the time. The analyst pointed out that the argument was with a brother over their claims on the mother-land. The patient admitted that he had a deep fear of arguments. The best he could do was to walk away and leave.

The next (16) hour he complained that he had been wheezing more than usual. He could not stand loud talking and yelling. The radio had been on full blast. At home the children had been jumping and running about. They had no mercy on anything. The patient said he was very sensitive to noises, especially loud talking and shouting. At home he and his brothers and sisters were allowed to make a noise only if the father wasn't home. . . .

On the other hand, the patient said, when he fell asleep, it was hard to wake him. Recently, when his wife went to the neighbor's, she told him to leave the door open for her; but the older boy snapped the lock. When she came back, she had to pound on the doors and windows for half an hour, but the patient did not wake up until she piled up boxes and tried to crawl through the window. Then he was scared. The analyst called attention to the inconsistency between his sleeping so deeply and his inability to stand the slightest noise when awake and suggested that this may have had something to do with his curiosity, with his listening to the parents while trying to sleep in childhood. The patient said he didn't listen to them. Immediately afterward he was disturbed by the noise of the analyst's baby crying. At home he was annoyed by his wife's shouting at the children. The analyst connected this with the patient's feeling that his wife should not talk about sex and remarked that the patient perhaps felt that it was not right to have sexual feelings toward certain women. At the end of the hour the patient objected to an early appointment on the following day, as he wished to sleep longer.

In the seventeenth hour he brought the following dream:

Dream 17.—At 95th Street. I was walking at 95th and Cottage. Street blocked and all kinds of building material, bricks and timber around. Little shack like real estate office. I walked in. Man and his wife [the man was a friend with whom the patient once dabbled in real estate] and some more [another man]. They were embarrassed when I came in, asked me where I wanted to go. I said to 95th and Prairie Avenue. He said the way was blocked because they were putting up a lot of houses, I could go over to 101st Street and back. While I was there people came in. Mostly cheap politicians, one in particular making fun of me with his eyes, all gathered there in this little office. All at once I found myself naked, stripped of all clothes except for long cotton underwear. I was running down street until I came to empty auto, car, where there were some clothes and a blanket. Policeman came, he led the car like a horse across the street and said, "Here's a good place for you to dress," and he left me.

In association the patient recalled that this real estate man had owed him $400.00 for the preceding nine years. He had since become politically influential but refused to pay it. When the analyst referred to the patient's being stripped, the patient replied, "If I stay longer I won't have underwear. Some ladies, his wife and daughter and more women coming in office." Ninety-fifth and Cottage Grove reminded him of nothing in particular. At Ninety-fifth and Prairie there was only an empty lot and a few shacks with "niggers." The policeman was one he often saw directing traffic. . . . He was very kind, always had a smile. The analyst suggested that she was the policeman. The patient replied that the dream meant that if he stuck longer with that man (i.e., the real estate man) it might cost him more. The man used to be very friendly. He told the patient once that he thought more of him than of his brothers. That was false anyhow. The patient questioned, then agreed to, the analyst's suggestion that the man might represent his (next younger) brother who was a faster "go-getter" than the patient. He agreed to the analyst's interpretation of envy of this brother. The brother married a widow. They had just been talking about it at home. The brother got ahead of the patient all the time. There was a lot of jealousy and hatred. In answer to the analyst's question, he said, Yes, he (the brother) was the favorite of the father, but the mother never showed it. She cared for all of them.

Following the dream (17) of being stripped, the patient missed an appointment on account of tightness in the bronchial tubes. This also kept him home from work two days. In the next hour he reported two dreams:

Dream 18a.—The neighbor and I were going to row boat on big river. He's old fellow who lives near us. He's sick, has ulcers and heart trouble. We were going in row boat but couldn't decide. He wanted to go and asked me to. It was getting dark and I didn't want to. Big river like one where I met girl in dream on bridge. Again like lake front on Michigan Avenue with lights in buildings.

Dream 18b.—I was in a clinic, supposed to be very sick. Lot of people and nurses. One nurse told me to sit down on couch like this one. Building old and dark and shabby. Inside furniture poor, small room. Just like I saw you there, not sure. I was supposed to be very sick.

In answer to the analyst's question, he said that the building was like an old rundown hospital. There were a lot of poor people there, like clinics. It wasn't this building (the Institute). It was like Cook County Hospital. The nurse told him he would be taken care of next. He couldn't remember what ailed him. The nurse reminded him of no one in particular. Maybe she was like the analyst. It was not clear. The first dream was clear. The patient could see the water, the boat, the man urging him to go with him. He wanted to go quite a distance, but the patient wouldn't go because it was getting dark. The man was an old friend who used to work in the railroad yards on the air brakes . . . he lived on the same street. . . . He had been sick for five years. (The patient was now coughing badly.) What had he better do about it? The analyst commented that the patient and the man were in the same boat; they were both sick. The patient replied that he dreamed of being sick often and of being taken care of . . . but he hated hospitals, got out as soon as he could.

The man (in the rowing dream) was near his father's age. The patient had often rowed boats at home and in the park here. He got a great kick out of it; at home he did it near this bridge. . . . If he had a dime he would rent a boat. He guessed that was why he didn't want to go, because the man wanted the patient to paddle upstream. The patient didn't think he would be much help, and he didn't want to go. The man wanted the patient to make a long trip, and, of course, the patient would have to paddle because the man was sick, so he said it was getting dark. When the analyst pointed out the contrast between the masculine effort that the patient was being asked to make in the first dream and his passive need to be taken care of in the second dream, the patient interpreted this as a reproach that he was lazy. The analyst replied, No, that it was on account of the patient's fear of his father. "So it is safer to stay where we were than to make an effort," the patient replied. . . . Later, the analyst suggested that the boat trip was like leaving home. This started the patient on an account of the time he did leave home and came to America after a quarrel with his father, because the father, who had left the patient in charge of the blacksmith shop, insisted that the patient work there late nights and objected to the patient's going out with the "bunch" and meeting girls in the evening. Two months before leaving, the patient had gotten drunk, was sitting on the bridge, had had to be carried home, and the next morning the father had licked him right in bed so that he couldn't move.

The next hour (eight days later) he reported the following dreams:

Dream 19a.—I was walking on street. Lot of people digging up surface of street. I got to corner. There was a girl who was like child at first, had big milk can full of water. She was standing at fireplug and asked me to help carry can home. She turned into grown woman. I carried one side, carried it to her home. She thanked me and offered me a kiss. I kissed and embraced her. Then I woke up.

Dream 19b.—A big truck—like moving or milk truck. Someone had been working on brakes and put on same brakes as we use on freight car [air brakes]. Man doing it wasn't doing it right. I was only watching, but someone criticized me that work was wrong, connections wrong. Of course, I saw the mistakes, but I had nothing to do with it. They were raising hell with me.

The woman at first reminded him of no one in particular. First she was a child, then turned out to be a grown lady. Yes, she was somewhat like the analyst, but stouter, because when the patient held her he had his arms full. Her bosom was big, he could feel her breathing, her warm lips. The can was an ordinary milk container, held at least five gallons or better, made out of aluminum. At the fireplug there were a lot of people on the street, but the patient got hold of one handle and she the other, and while they were in embrace her mother called her and they broke loose and the patient went away. Funny, there were lots of young ladies and mothers! The analyst suggested that the five gallons was an allusion to the five younger children in the patient's family and pointed out that the need for a mother always got in the way of the patient's sexual interest in a girl. The patient then immediately began to wonder if his boy was home yet from the hospital. The analyst continued her interpretation, pointing out the same conflict in the patient's relation to the analyst, between the need for a mother and sexual attraction. . . .

When the analyst pointed out that the criticisms of the patient in the second dream might come from his conscience, the patient protested that he had nothing to do with it. . . . He compared the triple-valve air brake to a heart which equalizes the pressure. The man in the dream was putting the valve on all wrong. Instead of putting the pipes underneath, he was putting them on the roof of the truck. The patient was much amused at the analyst's suggestion that he had trouble with his own "air machinery" and then recalled that he had a pain around the heart while he was eating the night before, which frightened him, as he thought he was getting heart trouble. The truck was large, like a small boxcar. The patient didn't see the engine or the power. All he saw was the body. It was light gray, trimmed with pure white, like a milk truck. When the analyst suggested that the milk truck represented the mother, the patient replied that he saw no milk in it but the place was near a milk dairy half a block away. . . . He wondered if the man could have been his father. The analyst suggested that he saw something going on between his father and his mother which caused trouble in his breathing and in his heart. The patient thought this might be right. The father never abused the mother physically but used to use hard words, and the patient felt awful fear.

In the hour (20) following the fireplug dream (19a) the patient was ashamed and immediately developed asthma when the analyst walked in and caught him looking at a book in her home. He told of having asthma all afternoon while hurrying to get to the hour.

In the next hour (21) he discussed his desire to go to Hot Springs in order to get away from his asthma. He also complained of rheumatism in his arm. At the beginning of the next hour (22) he protested that the analyst didn't want him to talk to her about sex, and the hour was taken up with a discussion of his fear of sex and with an account of a sexual affair and of the patient's fear of the girl's father. He developed asthma at the end of the hour.

In the twenty-fourth hour he complained that he didn't know what to say. As a child he was told not to talk nonsense. He suggested that the analyst should use a sledge hammer on him, then gave expression to remorse that he had probably hurt his children by forbidding them to talk as his father forbade him to talk. After protesting vigorously that he couldn't stand the noise of the radio when they turned it on, he began to wheeze at the end of the hour.

Then in the twenty-fifth hour he reported the following dream:

Dream 25.—Boxcar, in a room or building, like in office where we work. Door open in boxcar. Switchman called my attention to it. We both walked over and opened door further. Full of all kinds of merchandise, all unpacked. I pulled out pad of paper, kind of cheap, so I threw it back. Then picked up lot of pencils all No. 1. Then took any pad, said I might need it later. Policeman or watchman came in and asked if door was closed. I said no and closed it—felt guilty about taking this pad and pencils. All I remember.

As the patient woke up from this dream, he was wheezing hard. He had to use adrenalin.

His associations were as follows: In his work the patient often had to inspect boxcars. When the door of a boxcar was open, the switchman wanted a man to go with him as a witness that nothing was taken. When asked to inspect a car, they often teased by saying, "Bring it into the office." The analyst inquired if the paper and pencils resembled the paper and pencils that the analyst used to take notes. . . . The patient said "No," that the pencils were like those that the railroad furnished. "Maybe I wanted to write a letter," he added, "maybe I do, to father or brothers. . . . I only think about writing home but don't do it. Didn't see father or brother in dream, only the two men I work with, one a switchman, the other a watchman. Here I was stealing, felt guilty, felt he would think I took those articles."

Interpretation Based on Case History and First Nine Interviews.—When we read the patient's first account of his life-history, it is evident that he was very much afraid of his father but clung to his mother for protection. The intensity of his fear is illustrated by the fact that he ran away after being kicked by a horse rather than betray the fact by crying that he had been in the blacksmith shop contrary to his father's orders.

In view of his close relationship to his mother, his difficulty in getting along with his next younger brother may well have been based on rivalry for the mother's love. In the light of this tentative interpretation, it is perhaps significant that his marital unhappiness began at the time of his wife's pregnancy and that his asthma attacks also became more severe at this time.

In the first hours of his analysis he finds it difficult to talk freely about personal matters; as a possible explanation we recall that his father did not allow the children to talk in his presence except when spoken to. Yet, if this explanation is correct, why did his fear of his father affect him so much when his analyst was a woman?

Preliminary Interpretation of the First Three Dreams.—A clue for understanding the first dream (10*a*), which we shall call the "bridge dream," is the remark with which he introduces it: "That's what you want." He evidently is referring to the analyst's expressed interest in dreams in the preceding hour. This suggests that the analyst's comment served as the dream stimulus by awakening in the patient a desire to please her. He is bringing the dream to her as a present. The text of the dream tends to confirm this interpretation, for the dream ends with his receiving thanks and a glass of cool, refreshing milk from a mother-figure. Thus he dreams of pleasing a mother, and the next day he brings the dream as a present to please the analyst.

The next two dreams fit well into the context of a desire for the analyst's approval and affection. In the preceding hours the patient had been complaining about his wife. The railroad station dream (10*b*), which is reported next, pictures an older woman sympathizing with his desire to avoid his wife. Evidently, as the analyst points out, the patient would like to receive the same kind of sympathy from her. His embarrassment in this dream is easily understandable in this context of desire for love and approval from the analyst, for it implies that he wishes to turn to the analyst for the affection he cannot get from his wife and that he is ashamed of it. The last dream (10*c*) reported in this hour tries to make this wish less objectionable by giving it a professional setting, consistent with his professional relation to the analyst as his physician. The dream pictures him in a clinic or, at any rate, receiving treatment. The "lady" in the dream gives him the sympathy that he craves from the analyst by reassuring him that the treatment has "hit the spot."

Other details of this clinic dream (10*c*) and of the preceding railroad station dream (10*b*) round out this interpretation. It is probable that in the last dream (10*c*) medical treatment has been substituted for analysis as an expression of the patient's embarrassment and fear in the analytic situation. His wishes for affection from the analyst are too personal, and he is vaguely afraid of the consequences. He would prefer even a painful treatment, because its dangers are much less mysterious. He also seeks safety in numbers. Instead of his being alone with the analyst, there are "old friends around" or "doctors and ladies." The substitution of a railroad station for the analyst's home suggests even more pointedly a fear of the analytic situation, a desire to go away.

The Influence of Past Conflicts.—This interpretation brings the three dreams into understandable relation with the patient's behavior in the preceding therapeutic sessions and accounts for many details of the last two dreams, but it offers us no adequate explanation why in the bridge dream (10*a*) he is walking home from school with a girl. This dream evidently does not deal directly with the present situation but transports us back into the patient's adolescence. The connecting link is the patient's desire to win the analyst's approval. His wish to please her by bringing her a dream has evidently called to mind how in his boyhood he used to win affection and appreciation from mothers by being protective and chivalrous toward their daughters. Yet there is more than one way of pleasing a mother. Why is just this kind of memory reactivated instead of one of winning a mother's appreciation in some other way?

At the time when these dreams were first reported, our knowledge of the patient's history was very meager. When our data are meager, it is a good principle of interpretation to attempt to exploit to the full the common-sense implications of what we do know. Although our guesses from meager data may not always prove correct, at least we can arrive at hypotheses in this way that can later be tested against more adequate information.

In this instance we wish to know what has reactivated a memory of winning a mother's appreciation by walking home with her daughter in the dusk. Let us examine this question in the light of our common-sense knowledge. Why in our culture does a mother thank a young man for accompanying her daughter home in the dark? The implicit assumption is that the girl is in some danger of sexual attack and has been protected by the young man. The hint that some erotic impulse is bringing this memory to the surface now is confirmed by the fact that the dream starts with the patient's pinching the girl playfully. Hidden behind the dream detail of the mother's thanks, we may now suspect a latent conflict between his erotic impulses and his need for a mother's love. Evidently, he realizes that the mother would not approve of his sexual impulses toward her daughter.

If this is the conflict hidden behind the adolescent memory on which this dream text is based, then we can guess what is bringing this old conflict to the surface now. In the light of the two succeeding dreams, we must suspect that the patient, experiencing some erotic stimulation from being alone with a woman analyst, is attempting to protect himself against his erotic desire, first by substituting a younger woman for the analyst and then by promptly escorting the girl home to win the thanks of the mother. This suggestion is confirmed by his denial of interest in the girl. It also explains why he repudiates any connection between the "lady" in the last dream and the analyst, and depreciates the "lady" as "like a servant girl."

The reader may object that we are basing a fundamental and far-reaching interpretation on scanty evidence. We admitted in advance that we would do this, and we promised to examine our hypothesis critically. Our interpretation does give a clear and consistent picture of this patient's initial reaction to the analysis, and this picture does account satisfactorily for most of the details of these three dreams. His conflict in relation to the analyst is now quite understandable. Yet his behavior is not what we would ordinarily expect from a man who is consulting a woman professionally, even though he should find himself beginning to be attracted to her sexually. Ordinarily, we do not expect a man to be so afraid of offending a woman by his sexual interest in her or to be so much in need of her reassurance. We do not expect him to dream of his relation to her in terms of an adolescent memory of winning a mother's approval by bringing her daughter safely home to her.

Thus our interpretation of these first few dreams gives us a picture of a man who is unusually timid in relation to women, who does not entertain sexual impulses toward them but still thinks of himself as an adolescent boy trying to please a mother. If our interpretation is correct, we must assume that this patient is still involved in a conflict in relation to women which dates back at least as far as his adolescent years and that fear of offending his mother must have played a very important part in inhibiting his sexual impulses.

These conclusions are based on what this patient was able to tell us in the first ten hours of analysis. If this were all the evidence, we ought to be very tentative about accepting these conclusions and should wait to see whether they are confirmed by what the patient tells us later. Fortunately, we are not limited to the evidence that was available at the time that these dreams were reported. Since we have the record of the whole case history at our disposal, we can check our conclusions against the patient's later anamnestic data at once, instead of waiting until they gradually emerge in the course of the therapy.

From our more complete report of the patient's life-history[2] we learn that, except with prostitutes, this patient has never been able to talk and behave freely with women. He has always been shy in making sexual overtures to girls of his own class, and girls sometimes even reproached him for not behaving like a man.

In this patient's history, fear of the girl's father and of his own father played a conspicuous role in inhibiting his sexual urges. Because he is being analyzed by a woman and no man has yet appeared to challenge him, such fears of the father have not yet emerged in the first ten hours of his treatment; but incidents reported later show that his mother, too, played a part in inhibiting his sexual impulses. Once she rebuked him sharply for making sexual advances to a young married

2. See Appendix to Vol. I.

woman who was visiting in the home. At another time he was very much afraid that she would learn of his sexual affair with a maid. These incidents are probably significant not only in themselves but also as indicators of the nature of this patient's relationship to his mother.

The memory of his affair with the maid also makes clearer the meaning of his depreciating the "lady" in the clinic dream (10c) as "like a servant girl"; and in the light of these memories the bridge dream (10a) is evidently a reassurance. He starts with the playful erotic gesture of pinching the girl in the back, but on second thought chooses to keep on good terms with the mother by escorting the young lady safely home.

Interpretation of the Anvil Dream.—We turn our attention now to the next few hours in this patient's analysis.

In the hour (11) after this report of the three dreams, we find a disguised confirmation of our interpretation; for the patient confesses, in answer to the analyst's question, that he never puts any value on dreams, then complains that he can neither stand loud talking nor sleep with any kind of noise; and, finally, he spends the rest of the hour protesting against his wife's loud talking and against the idea of "wives and mothers" talking about sex. The patient is consciously referring to his wife when he says this, but the fact that he brings it up immediately after talking about dream interpretation suggests that unconsciously he may be feeling the same way about the analyst's interpretations.

Yet, if he resented what he felt to be sexual implications in the analyst's interpretation, the next dream indicates that he was also much impressed with it. The "anvil dream" in the twelfth hour expresses the patient's admiration for a woman's ability to do a man's job well. As the analyst's comment indicates, the patient had probably been disappointed at being assigned to a woman analyst; but he was evidently so fascinated by the analyst's interpretation of his dreams of a few days before that he was beginning to feel that she could do as good a job as a man. The clinic dream (10c) gives confirmation of this suggestion. In discussing this dream, we were not sure why the patient introduced "doctors and ladies" in place of his analyst and why he then depreciated the lady. Now we realize that he was already wishing for a man as his "doctor," instead of a woman. This is consistent with, or rather complementary to, the motive that we have already discussed for his depreciation of his female analyst. If his analyst were a man, he would not be exposed to the heterosexual temptation that so frightens him.

The theme of sexual temptation and his reaction to it occur in the anvil dream (12) also. As the analyst's comment indicates, if the

mother's beating an iron bar on the anvil represents the patient's treatment, he must be thinking of himself as the bar that is beaten and bent.
Indeed, the dream of being beaten on the anvil seems to be a prophecy
of the severe muscular and arthritic pains that follow in the next few
days. But why is he in such need of punishment? Apparently, he is intensely chagrined by the sexual interest that the analyst unconsciously
awakens in him. Hence the analyst's job, he feels, is to hammer him into
shape, just as his father used to bend iron bars on the anvil.

At this point, we notice, the patient's fear of the father, which was
so clear in his account of his life-history, is for the first time emerging
as part of his reaction to the therapeutic situation, Actually, in his
young manhood, we learn later in the analysis, his choleric father had
beaten him twice for his sexual episodes. Yet, in contrast to what we
might have expected, his admiration of the mother's skill at the anvil
shows that the basic motive in this dream (12) is not fear of his father
but longing for a father, desire for a male physician to play a father's
role. This dream is activated not so much by fear of punishment as by
a need for punishment, by a need for a father to beat him into shape.

How can we account for this need for punishment? Some acquaint-
ance with the reactions of children in the nursery makes this need quite
intelligible. In the dreams of the tenth hour it was fear of offending the
mother that inhibited the patient's sexual impulses. In the nursery, fear
of estrangement from the parents is often greater than fear of punishment. Paradoxically, as Freud (1916) points out, punishment may even
be welcomed as a means of reconciliation with the parents. In the anvil
dream (12), not only does the dreamer reassure himself that the analyst can do a good job even though she is a woman, but the father,
too, is in the background—probably referring to the fact that it was a
male physician in the asthma clinic who referred him to his analyst.
Evidently, it increases his sense of security still further to know that
there is a father-figure in the background.

An Important Guiding Principle in Interpretation.—In the preceding
discussion we have several times illustrated a rule of interpretation
that we have not yet explicitly formulated. This rule is first to ask ourselves what is the motivating pressure revealed by what a patient is
saying, before we attempt to interpret the intellectual or pictorial content of what he has said. When interpreting a dream, we ask ourselves
first how the dreamer is reacting to the dream that he is reporting,
then what is the predominant emotional pressure or dynamic trend in
the manifest content of the dream itself. As a first test for the correctness of a dream interpretation, we require that it account adequately
for these dynamic pressures in the patient's attitude toward the dream
and in the dream text itself. Only after we have considered carefully
the implications of these dynamic pressures is it safe to interpret the

details of the dream's intellectual content or the less dynamic aspects of its pictorial content.

In accordance with this rule, in the bridge dream (10a) we started with the patient's expressed desire to please the analyst by bringing her a dream; then we were impressed by the fact that in the dream text, too, he was activated by a desire to please a mother. In the railroad station dream (10b) we noted the patient's need to be reassured that the analyst did not disapprove of his desire to avoid his wife. In the clinic dream (10c) his concern about the medical and professional nature of his relationship to the analyst was our starting point. In the anvil dream (12) his insistent emphasis on the mother's skill in beating an iron bar on the anvil was our clue to his need to assure himself that his female analyst was capable of what he felt to be a man's job.

Interpretation of the Snake Dream.—Since such a guiding principle is particularly important when our data are meager, we have formulated this rule of interpretation explicitly before discussing the snake dream (14). The patient was so preoccupied with his muscle and joint pains when he reported the snake dream that he was able to bring only scanty associations.

His preoccupation with his pains is obviously the predominant dynamic pressure in this hour. Whatever the cause of these pains, it is a striking fact that they correspond closely to a materialization of the fantasy of being beaten that underlies the anvil dream (12).

Yet the dynamic trend in the text of the snake dream (14) is in striking contrast to this preoccupation with his pain. Both dream text and associations keep reiterating that the little boy in the dream is in no danger. The snake is tame. The little boy is not afraid. He is contented, plays with the snake, and likes it. The snake even has a smile on its face. Evidently this dream is taking a great deal of trouble to reassure the dreamer against some underlying anxiety; and to a very slight degree such anxiety does emerge in the patient's account. He tells us in the dream text that he was "scared" that the snake would sneak into the pillowcase, and in the associations he admits that he doesn't like snakes, even though they are harmless; that he would never have worn his coat if he had realized that the men at work were putting snakes in it.

But what does he fear? The associative data are too scanty to answer this question with any certainty.[3] If we take into account the sexual conflict underlying the preceding dreams, we might suspect that he is now struggling with fears arising out of his sexual impulses and that the snake is a symbol of sexuality. If this interpretation is

---

3. I am deliberately avoiding interpretations based on universal symbols, until we have discussed (in Vol. II, Sec. III) how such interpretations should be checked. Uncritical use of such symbol interpretation can lead to very untrustworthy conclusions.

correct, then the little boy represents the patient. Yet this interpretation does not explain why the little boy in the dream text should be the patient's younger son.

Another possibility is that the patient is really afraid for his child. If so, what danger threatens this child? The most obvious possibility is that some hostile wish of the dreamer threatens the child. But why should he be hostile to his younger son? We have already learned that he very much craves the love of a mother, and we have suspected that his quarreling so much with his next younger brother may have been instigated by rivalry for the mother's love. Perhaps he is hostile to his own younger son for the same reason; or, perhaps at this moment, to the analyst's child, whom the patient encounters occasionally in the house. Perhaps he resents this child, too, because it comes between him and his need for a mother's love. If so, in the dream he projects this wish: it is not he but the snake that might hurt the child. In any case, the dream seems successful in reassuring him that the child has nothing to fear.

More Light on the Earlier Dreams.—If this interpretation of hostility to a child is correct, why have we not found evidence of such a wish in the earlier dreams? With this question in mind, we now inquire into the significance of a detail in the bridge dream (10a) to which we have paid little attention. In this dream the girl's mother was accompanied by her son, a boy of about the age of the patient's next younger brother.

Our interpretation has not yet explained why this boy is in the dream; but hostility to a brother-figure fits well into the context of the bridge dream to explain the presence of a boy about the age of the patient's next younger brother.

We have interpreted the bridge dream as a reassurance against the fear of losing the mother's love. The presence of a brother-figure in the dream now suggests that his fear of losing his mother's love arose not only because of his sexual interest in girls but also because he resented his brothers and sisters. Indeed, his pinching the girl in the dream may have been an erotized expression of a hostile impulse, as well as a playful erotic gesture. That the sister to whom the dream alludes died in the patient's late adolescence tends to confirm this formulation. We get further confirmation from the fact that the patient's next younger brother is the one with whom the patient always quarreled: later in the analysis we learn that, until this brother was born, the patient slept with his mother and that this brother displaced him from her bed. We also learn that the patient once pushed this brother's baby carriage down a hill and that he once lost him in a hay field.

Other memories, reported later in this patient's analysis, help us to round out our interpretations still further.

In childhood the patient was sickly and so found his way back to his mother's care and attention. Otherwise, his brother might have displaced him to a still greater extent. Only when he was ill was he again taken into the mother's bed. In the clinic dream (10c) he employs the same device for finding his way back to the parents' care and attention. In the dream of the railroad station, on the other hand, he is fleeing from the temptation situation. Later in the analysis we learn that such a tendency to flee from temptation situations is characteristic of him. On two occasions, for example, he became attached to a motherly married landlady, and with one of these landladies he had a sexual relationship. In each case he developed asthma when he learned that the woman was pregnant, then became dissatisfied and moved away. Yet in the railroad station dream (10b) we note that he takes care to assure himself beforehand that there is another mother to whom he can flee.

Summary of the Psychological Situation.—Summing up our impressions from these five dreams, we find a consistent, though still somewhat sketchy, picture of the patient's psychological situation in the early hours of the analysis. Frightened at being alone with a woman analyst, he reacts to the situation as a sexual temptation. Yet he wishes to be loved by the analyst as by a mother, and he resents her child as a rival. Intensely chagrined by these (unconscious) wishes, he tries to protect himself from them by stressing the fact that he is in a professional situation, that the analyst is a "good clean" workman rather than a woman who wants to tempt him sexually. Even so, he feels that a man analyst, who would not be a sexual temptation and who would give him the beating that he deserves, might be better.

The Dawning of a New Insight.—We recall that the snake dream (14) was motivated by hostility to a child who threatened to come between the patient and his need for a mother's love. In accordance with the analyst's comment in the fifteenth hour, we recognize a certain parallel between this rivalry for a mother's love and the patient's argument with a "brother-workman" over their claims on the "mother-country." The patient's intolerance of the children's noise, reported in the sixteenth hour, together with the fact that it is so difficult to rouse him from sleep, suggests a need to escape from his conflict by withdrawing indiscriminately in sleep.

In his associations, there is nothing to suggest that the following dreams have been stimulated by events outside the therapeutic situation; but they are readily understandable as a series of reactions to what is occurring in the analytic sessions.

In the kindly policeman dream (17) we recognize a reaction both to the interpretation of his rivalry with the brother in the fifteenth hour and to the guarded interpretation in the sixteenth hour, hinting at the patient's sexual interest in the analyst. Although these interpretations were made cautiously, the patient reacted energetically to them. In the dream (17) he pictures himself as being shown up, stripped of his clothes. Evidently, the interpretations have "hit home." The dream is equivalent to an admission that they are correct.

When we follow the chronological sequence of the dream text (17), we find that the dreamer is at first able to repress this sense of being shown up: he fights back. Instead of being shown up himself, he embarrasses the real estate man and his family by coming upon them unawares. In his associations he uncovers the dishonesty of this brother-figure. Instead of accepting the analyst's interpretation of his rivalry with the brother for the mother, he complains of being cheated by a man who claimed to love him as a brother. Yet in the next dream incident this defense has failed. He must picture himself exposed, stripped of his defenses (clothes).

The dream ends with a kind of acceptance of this process. As in the anvil dream (12), he returns to admiration and confidence in the analyst's skill. He pictures the analyst as a kindly policeman who can "lead an auto like a horse." We interpret this as an expression of confidence that the analyst knows how to handle his unconscious urges. Although she shows him up, she will not unnecessarily humiliate him. After he has been stripped, he will again be given clothes.

Thus this dream (17) gives evidence of a beginning change in the patient's attitude toward the analysis. In the anvil dream (12) he was looking upon the analysis as a punitive kind of training: he was to be beaten into shape. In the kindly policeman dream (17), for the first time, there is a beginning recognition of the role of insight in the therapeutic process: Being stripped of his clothes is a pictorial representation of his feeling that he has been shown up by the analyst's interpretations, that his rationalizations and defenses have been "stripped" off and seen through.

It is true that he cannot yet grasp or accept the notion of understanding his own hidden motivations. His concept of the analysis is still one of being treated punitively. The atmosphere at first is like that of a detective story: since the analyst is trying to show him up, he will fight back. Yet, after he has been "stripped," he recognizes dimly the therapeutic purpose of this process of being shown up; he is able to reassure himself that the analyst's motive is therapeutic rather than hostile. She may be a policeman representing his conscience, but she provides a place for him to put on his clothes again before she leaves him.

Response to the Analyst's Encouragement.—Our clue for understanding the rowing dream (18a) is the dream that immediately follows it. In this second clinic dream (18b) the patient is again in a

clinic and "very sick." This suggests that the sick old man in the
rowing dream (18a) represents the patient himself. The kindly policeman dream (17) ended with an implied recognition of the analyst's
(policeman's) therapeutic purpose in showing him up. Now, in the
rowing dream (18a) the patient himself is being invited to play a more
active role in the therapeutic process, characterized as rowing a sick
old man upstream. Yet he is reluctant to undertake this task; and in the
next dream (18b) he resigns himself frankly to the role of a sick old
man waiting for treatment in a clinic.

A striking feature of this patient's behavior is his quick reaction
to a slight hint of encouragement from the analyst. In the bridge
dream (10a) the analyst's expressing interest in dreams was sufficient
to reawaken adolescent hopes of winning a mother's approval. Similarly, the analyst's interpretation of the patient's conflict about masculine effort has been taken as a hint and probably served as stimulus to
"play the man" by erotic advances toward the young girl in the fireplug dream (19a). These advances go further than he had dared in the
bridge dream (10a). Yet his boldness is short-lived; he promptly gives
the girl up when her mother calls; and in the brake dream (19b) he has
been putting on the brakes very energetically—he is accused of putting
on a milk truck brakes such as are used on a freight car.

Re-emergence of the Old Fear.—In the next dream—the pencil-
stealing dream (25)—the patient at first is again reacting to his sense
of the analyst's encouragement; yet now he feels this encouragement
as a temptation to do something forbidden, to steal something. The
dream text pictures the temptation as occurring not in the analyst's
office but in the freight yards where he works, and as coming not from
the analyst but from another man. As motive for this substitution we
again recognize the patient's discomfort at being alone with a woman
to whom he feels sexually attracted and his sense that he would be
more comfortable with the men on the job. Repeated references in
dream text (25) and associations indicate his need to substitute the
more acceptable job situation. Yet in the end this substitution fails to
protect him from his old fear of offending a mother by his forbidden
sexual wishes; for the role of the watchman, who next appears, is that
of a forbidding parent, and in his acute embarrassment the dreamer
wakes up with an attack of asthmatic wheezing.

BIBLIOGRAPHY

Bibliography

ABRAHAM, K. 1923. "Contributions to the Theory of the Anal Character," *Internat. J. Psychoanal.*, IV, 400–418.

ALEXANDER, F. 1925. "Dreams in Pairs and Series," *Internat. J. Psychoanal.*, VI, 446–52.

——. 1935. "The Logic of Emotions and Its Dynamic Background," *ibid.*, XVI, 399–413.

FERENCZI, S. 1924. *Thalassa: A Theory of Genitality.* Albany, N.Y.: Psychoanalytic Quarterly, Inc., 1938.

FRENCH, T. M. 1936. "A Clinical Study of Learning in the Course of a Psychoanalytic Treatment," *Psychoanalyt. Quart.*, V, 148–94.

——. 1945. "The Integration of Social Behavior," *ibid.*, XIV, 149–68.

FRENCH, T. M.; ALEXANDER, F.; *et al.* 1941. *Psychogenic Factors in Bronchial Asthma.* ("Psychosomatic Medicine Monographs," Vol. I, No. 4; Vol. II, Nos. 1 and 2.) Washington, D.C.: National Research Council.

FREUD, S. 1900. *The Interpretation of Dreams.* New York: Macmillan Co., 1933.

——. 1905a. *Three Contributions to the Theory of Sex.* New York: Nervous and Mental Disease Publishing Co., 1930.

——. 1905b. "Fragment of an Analysis of a Case of Hysteria." In: *Collected Papers*, III, 13. 3d ed. London: Hogarth Press, 1946.

——. 1908b. "Character and Anal Erotism." In: *Collected Papers*, II, 45. 4th ed. London: Hogarth Press, 1946.

——. 1914b. "Further Recommendations in the Technique of Psychoanalysis: Recollection, Repetition, and Working Through." In: *Collected Papers*, II, 366. 4th ed. London: Hogarth Press, 1946.

——. 1916b. "On the Transformation of Instincts, with Special Reference to Anal Erotism." In: *Collected Papers*, II, 164. 4th ed. London: Hogarth Press, 1946.

——. 1918. "From the History of an Infantile Neurosis." In: *Collected Papers*, III, 473. 3d ed. London: Hogarth Press, 1946.

——. 1919. " 'A Child Is Being Beaten.' " In: *Collected Papers*, II, 172. 4th ed. London: Hogarth Press, 1946.

——. 1923. *The Ego and the Id.* 4th ed. London: Hogarth Press, 1947.

JONES, E. 1919. "Anal-erotic Character Traits." In: *Papers on Psychoanalysis*, p. 413. 5th ed. Baltimore: Williams & Wilkins Co., 1948.

KÖHLER, W. 1931. *The Mentality of Apes.* 2d ed. New York: Harcourt, Brace & Co.

Lewin, K. 1935. *A Dynamic Theory of Personality.* New York: McGraw-Hill Book Co., Inc.

Mead, G. F. 1934. *Mind, Self, and Society.* Chicago: University of Chicago Press.

Rank, O. 1912. "Die Symbolschichtung im Wecktraum und ihre Wiederkehr im mythischen Denken," *Jahrb. f. psychoanalyt. u. psychopath. Forsch.,* IV, 51–115.

Reik, T. 1924. "Psycho-analysis of the Unconscious Sense of Guilt," *Internat. J. Psychoanal.,* V, 439–50.

Silberer, H. 1911*a.* "Symbolik des Erwachens und Schwellensymbolik überhaupt," *Jahrb. f. psychoanalyt. u. psychopath. Forsch.,* III, 621–60.

———. 1911*b.* "Über die Symbolbildung," *ibid.,* pp. 661–723.

———. 1912. "Zur Symbolbildung," *ibid.,* IV, 607–83.

Tolman, E. C. 1948. "Cognitive Maps in Rats and Men," *Psychol. Rev.,* LV, 189–208.

INDEXES

Author Index

Subject Index

Active mastery of drowning fears, 224–28
Aggression turned back against self; see Reversal of aggression
Anal erotism and holding onto possessions, 135, 259, 305–7
Anal interpretation of pregnancy, 135–39

Case report and interpretation, 31–49, 72–74, 82–84, 90–101, 104, 125–34, 136–39
Cognitive field, 5–7, 163–68, 191–204
  and integrative field, 5 (n. 3), 6 (n. 6)
  interpersonal, 163–68, 191–204
  syntactical, 7 (n. 8)
Cognitive map (Tolman), 5
Cognitive structure, 1–28, 161–68, 191–204
  of behavior, 4–8
  of dreams, 3–4, 8–28, 179–80
    and primary process, 10–11, 13–15, 19–23, 179–80
    reconstruction of, 9, 26–28
  of interpersonal relationships, 161–68, 191–204
  and pattern of motivation, 5 (n. 5)
Cognitive structures
  common to groups of dreams, 213–15, 287–89, 328–29
    road-map analogy, 213–15, 288–89
  of different dreams of same person as all parts of a single intercommunicating system, 287–89, 328–29
    road-map analogy, 288–89
  relationship between, 9, 213–15, 287–89, 328–29
Condensation, 180–86
  in chains of association (primary process), 180, 181
  in reorganizations of integrative pattern, 182–86

of dynamically equivalent patterns, 182–83
  at periphery of field of interest, 185–86
  resulting from continuity of pattern, 182–85
Constellations of fantasy patterns common to groups of dreams, 213–15, 287–89, 328–29
  choice points and alternative reactions in, 214–15
  road-map analogy, 214–15, 288–89
Continuity of pattern, 120–24, 181–85, 213–14, 287
  in dream sequences, 120–24, 213–14, 287
  in pattern of dream organization, 181–85

Dependence, integrative mechanism of, 194–95
Dream cycles, 299–304, 308–12
  tonic motor absorption in, 308–12
  effect of timing on, 309–12
  transition from water to grasping-hand symbolism in, 300–304
    an effect of increasing pressure, 301–4
Dreams
  analysis of symbolism of, 28, 65–107, 111–24, 133–35
  cognitive structure of, 3–4, 8–28
  effects of fluctuating integrative span, 180, 192–99
  effects of inadequate integrative span, 180, 187–90
    alternation of conflicting motivations resulting from, 187–90
  historical analysis of, 75–77
  historical background of, 19–25, 28, 75–77, 106–7, 213–15
    analogy to cataloguing system, 23–25, 213

360

Index of Dreams

364